The
GUMBO POT
Poems

A Savory Recipe for Life, Community & Gumbo Through Poetry

Alyce Smith Cooper

Jaime V. Jones   &   Judy Sundayo

Published by

The Golden Brown Fairy Godmother

San Diego, California

Published by:
The Golden Brown Fairy Godmother
San Diego, California

Copyright © 2015 by Judy Sundayo, Alyce Smith Cooper
& Jaime V. Jones

Cover Artist: James Gayles

ISBN   978-1-5007-9362-3

First Printing, September 2015
Printed by Createspace

Dedication

With great appreciation and respect, we dedicate this book to the late *Dr. Maya Angelou*. A poem in honor of Dr. Angelou may be found in the Savory Poems section of this book.

––––––––

We also seek to honor all the poets, writers, musicians, singers, actors, artists and cooks who create masterpieces with their words, art, music, drama, food and friendships. By virtue of their talents, we are reminded of how flavorful this life can be, and of how much we all need to be nourished.

Acknowledgements

We would like to acknowledge the many people who have contributed to this wonderful book. These include our friends, family and colleagues who encouraged the completion of this joy-filled project, many of whom are represented on the pages that follow in various and sundry photographs.

We appreciate the consultation provided by Professor Thekima Mayasa and Professor Starla Lewis in kindly editing several of the works included herein. We are grateful for the thoughtful assistance of Professor Chris Sullivan in his review of several of the poems we have herein included. The input of Dr. Rochelle Bastien and Mr. Michael Turner in terms of their kind examination of portions of our book has been tremendously valuable. Being natives of Louisiana, their assessment was greatly appreciated.

We also extend thanks to Chef Darren Phillips for his assistance and to Mr. Leon O. Allen for his fine photographs, which were perfect for illustrating a number of our poems as well as for his assistance in all respects of the books production and marketing. We appreciate the award-winning artist, James Gayles, for his extraordinary artistic portrayal of Ms. Angelou for this book's cover, as well as Allison Kelly Paschal-Hunter, from whose private collection this painting was graciously offered for our use.

We are especially obliged to the family of Ms. Maya Angelou and to Harpo Productions for the use of the photo of Ms. Angelou, which accompanies her poem in the Savory section.

Additionally, we are grateful to all those individuals who have given us permission to include photos and references to their work as valuable resources to the San Diego community.

Finally, but not least importantly, we give thanks to the Creator, without whom we would not have the life, health, good sense or Grace to have brought this book to completion.

The Menu

The Menu, *(continued)*

The Menu, *(continued)*

The Menu, *(continued)*

The Menu, *(continued)*

The Menu, *(continued)*

The Menu, *(continued)*

14

The Menu, *(continued)*

The Foreword by GBFG

Welcome to the juiciest book of poetry you have ever experienced! It is filled with empowering poetry and Gumbo recipes. The poetry is forward thinking and intended to excite and empower! The recipes for GUMBO are filled with savory, soul-full secrets, and are sure to resonate poetic as you serve this delectable dish to friends and family!

The poems in this book are really about reclaimed lives and the friendships that serve to validate and encourage us to grow beyond our tough times. With the help of my two co-authors, Jamie and Judy, I have reclaimed the magic of friendship that all good fairy godmothers must have to be at our best! In doing so, the three of us have stirred love, respect and quite a lot of laughter into the GUMBO pot of this great enterprise.

Throughout the writing of this book, we've reminded each other of the importance of seasoning our lives with prayer, vision and the fruits of the Spirit. It is only then that we can cook with the Refining Fire of Spirit. The results? Spirit-filled meals and life experiences that are much more digestible!

We come to into this life like we arrive at the dinner table, with a hope that we will be loved, nourished and fulfilled. And, somewhere along the way, we were promised as much. Well, the promise is real. There is a plan for us to be loved, for us to prosper and for us to nurture each other so that at some point before we are done cooking in this great kitchen of our lives, we might each of us emerge with a full belly, a kind heart and a great story to tell.

This book represents our love for life and for each other fostered by our CREATOR and shared with you. We invite you into its pages to dine and be encouraged by the love of GOD, which has produced THE GUMBO POT POEMS. *Bon Appetite!*

~The Golden Brown Fairy Godmother

(GBFG)

An Introduction

If there were a national culinary dish in the United States, it would have to be GUMBO, a wonderful blending of various flavors from a number of different ethnic/cultural traditions. Although there may be disagreement concerning the origin of GUMBO as well as the optimum way to prepare the dish, there seems to be a general consensus that the GUMBO as we know it today, had its development in the state of Louisiana, located in the south central portion of the United States. Also, there is general agreement that GUMBO, in all its many and varied forms, is absolutely DELICIOUS! We capitalize the word GUMBO throughout the book to keep its big flavor and multiplicity of origins uppermost in the minds of readers.

This book serves to share a bit about GUMBO's history and a few recipes to prepare this delectable dish. Another purpose is to honor our friends, family, colleagues and community members by showcasing their names, photos, organizations and what they do or have done to make a difference in their community. Although the limitation of space prohibits us from honoring everyone who is deserving of such an honor, we hope those individuals will understand, and perhaps we can talk about an expanded version for the next book! We hope all readers will find that the poems and the resources we have included will serve as a recipe of empowerment for all communities, particularly African American communities. Just as there are many ingredients in the recipe for GUMBO, there are many individuals, agencies and community based organizations that are part of a successful community. And what's more, it's important for those of us who live in these communities to deduce ways to acknowledge each other and celebrate our successes. Whether readers are members of the San Diego community or not, we hope all readers will be able to "taste" the flavor of some useful information among the many resources we have sprinkled in and among our poems.

The main purpose of this book is to share words of wit and wisdom though poetry. The late Dr. Maya Angelou is our standard-bearer in this regard. She was so masterful in her use of words and in her sharing of herself. Her sense of social responsibility, cultural pride and human awareness come across strongly in her writings and we are particularly graced to honor Dr. Angelou by dedicating this book to her memory. We also selected Maya Angelou for this honor because she was someone who appreciated good cooking and the fellowship that ensues when folks sit down and share a meal together. She understood the transformative power of words as well as good food. We have included in our reference section some of our favorite books by Maya Angelou, which we hope readers will take the time to read and enjoy.

In deference to GUMBO, as well as to the culinary art of blending flavors, we have divided this book into sections, each representative of a different flavor. In so doing, we anticipate readers will come to appreciate how the six traditional culinary flavors (i.e., *salty, bitter, spicy, sweet, sour and savory*) as well as the wonderful seasonings, which accentuate these flavors, serve as parallels to the diversity of our everyday life experiences.

The Salty Poems primarily incorporate those poems we have associated with sensuality, sexuality and the impulsive activities of youth. These are the poems that speak of the time when we were young, hormone-driven and perhaps felt somewhat invincible.

The Bitter Poems include those poems representing lessons that startle us in life. These include the rude-awakenings or wake-up-calls. In concert with African cosmology, it is believed that our ancestors often communicate with us by virtue of these experiences. Therefore several poems in this section reference the ancestors or historical information from classical African civilizations as well as historical information from the period of the mass enslavement of African people. So, *the Bitter Poems* are not only those that wake us and shake us to attention, but are also representative of those facets of our experience that strengthen us for what will inevitably come later. So, they might also be called, the startle, wake up and strengthen poems. They serve a foundational purpose in our lives, much like the foundation of a house, or the roux for GUMBO. These writings also acknowledge those individuals who have taught us invaluable lessons or have reminded us that at some point the recklessness of youth will lose its allure and we must learn to think of more than just ourselves. In *The Bitter Poems* we must awaken from youth to see that there are serious issues in life and consequences, sometimes dire, for NOT paying attention to those issues.

The Spicy Poems are those primarily that honor nature, including food, animals, the many facets of the earth, the universe and everything in the natural order as these things spice up or accentuate our lives. These poems also speak to those things that are manmade, including our talents in art, music, literature, theatre and other areas of human endeavor as these things make our lives richer. Although in many ways, we have rivaled the beauty of the natural world with our talents, nature predominates hands down. Is there anyone or anything more talented or more prolific than the Creator?

The Sweet Poems are those we have associated with idealized love, marriage, family, babies, children, and those emotions associated with them. These poems also include those individuals who through the passage of time or emotional connection have become honorary family members. And even though this book is primarily for adults, there are a few poems in this section that may be enjoyed by children. Since as adults, we are the caretakers of our children, we leave this to the reader to ascertain what may or may not be shared with children or teens.

The Sour Poems are those we have associated with death, dying, fear, loss and the other emotions that might accompany these states. Death is one of the most universal experiences we share. The grief that follows is also universal, although as humans living in different cultural contexts, we may grieve differently, or at least exhibit our grief in different ways. Related to death and grief, is loss and fear. For loss is not only relegated to the loss of a loved one through death, but includes the loss of a first love, the loss of a husband or wife through divorce, the loss of a teenager who has run away from home, or the loss of a family member to the ravages of drugs or a life of crime. These are all reflective of loss in one way or another. Related to loss is fear. We might fear for a loved one's life because of the choices he or she is making or we might be plagued by our own personal fears. *The Sour Poems* explore the dimensions of fear, loss and grief. These poems have been written with respect for those emotions and in utter and heartfelt sympathy for those who are faced with loss of any kind.

The Savory Poems are like the wisdom poems as they help us to make sense of all of life's experiences. These poems speak especially to friendship, traits of character, personal beliefs, philosophy, religion in the philosophical sense, humor, and those lessons we tend to learn later in life as seasoned travelers. They also include the actions we have decided to take in response to our life experiences or our ancestral history in order to move the whole community in a positive direction. Individuals, past and present, that have helped to advance wisdom and positive action in the community are acknowledged. This section is also replete with poems, which advise or instruct, as wisdom gifts from the authors.

Finally, **The Poems Spiritually Seasoned** are those we have associated with spiritual experience, spiritual lessons, the love of God, and all the blessings that accrue to our spirit as a result. These poems are presented here with the belief that there are different paths to spiritual awareness. Although much of the writing in this book comes from a Christian perspective, our intention is to champion the love, hope, faith and charity that *ensue* from spiritual experience, i.e. *the fruits of the spirit*, rather than a particular religion or category of beliefs that often lay claim to our experiences if we dare call them divine.

Each of the poetry sections in ends with a palate-cleansing poem. We hope readers will approach the reading of this book as he or she would approach a meal, savoring each morsel and looking forward to tasting anew the flavors of each subsequent course. To refresh those cognitive taste buds we present the palate cleansing poems to prepare the reader for the next poetic serving.

All of the flavors represented here work together in GUMBO to make it a delight for the senses, just as all of our life experiences, lessons, hopes and dreams work together to give meaning to life as well-lived. As we become more seasoned with age, we often become connoisseurs of life, better able to savor our blessings and digest the most seemingly indigestible occurrences, once they are aptly cooked together with friendship, prayer and the Holy Spirit!

The poems contained in this book were written for an adult audience, both those who like to cook and those who are not particularly inspired in that direction. To give greater interest to the different ingredients in GUMBO, the authors have shared instructions related to each of the main ingredients at the beginning of each of the poetry sections associated with one of the respective flavors mentioned above. Instructions for preparing rice, a usual complement to GUMBO, are also included at the beginning of the Sour Section. For those cooks, who wish to cut to the chase, complete GUMBO recipes in their entirety are provided at the back of the book.

Much of the language, context and perspectives used in this book are drawn from the African American experience. We believe the rich international, national and mostly local (San Diego) history noted throughout the book will add quite a bit of flavor, which we hope readers will find delicious! At any rate, the authors are confident that every reader will find *something* in the African or African American cultural nuances and/or historical references that will blend in with his or her tastes.

Additionally, we have added photos of family, friends, colleagues and community members to give visual interest to our words. Readers may ponder what if any relationship might exist between a poem and a photo. Some photos and their captions may chronicle historical information considered by some to be provocative, graphic or disturbing. For others the photos and captions will be eye opening and occasion new insights.

We also include a discussion section and a resource section, referencing books and websites, at the end of the book to encourage critical thinking, research and dialogue about the ideas conveyed through the poetry, the photographs and the photo captions. We hope the poems will inspire and encourage the next generations of writers and poets who will continue to tell our stories. We believe there is an aspect of social responsibility in writing, which is important for those artists of both the spoken and the written word. The discussion section includes questions which we hope will be starting points for open ended dialogue on many salient social issues, but we also hope readers will develop his or her own unique questions and formulate personal opinions about what is read.

Since the authors are residents of San Diego, California, most of the photographs are of friends and family from this region or of local heroes and sheroes who have been involved in community contributions, activities and events. However, the issues raised in the poems are ones, which we believe transcend a specific region. In the discussion section we encourage readers, especially students, to compare and contrast the information learned about San Diego with their own communities, regardless of where those communities are located.

This is especially critical, as the book has been written from the experience of three African American women who live in San Diego. Therefore, most of the resources included are those which we ourselves have found to be of personal value as well as those we feel would be of historic value to all readers, especially those who are interested in the history of the African American experience or in advocating for equity and social justice.

Regardless of community of origin, readers are encouraged to review their *own* experiences of the topics covered, including, youth, sensuality, hard lessons learned, nature, talents, family, children, death, grief, loss, character, wisdom, philosophy and religion. Regardless of ethnicity or cultural background, we hope all readers will be persuaded to give critical thought to how they might relate to or oppose the issues raised in the poems. Some topics might be seen as universal, e.g. grief and loss, whereas others, e.g. the feelings evoked when reading about the "N" word, might be different for the African American reader.

Reading a book is only part of the obligation of a reader. Discussing what one has read with family, friends and colleagues encourages cross-cultural awareness and unity. Having courageous conversations on difficult topics fosters cultural competency and ultimately cultural proficiency, a worthy life-long endeavor. Like GUMBO, this book is a culinary delight, which it is hoped will bring everyone to the same table to discuss and digest different opinions in an atmosphere of mutual respect.

It is for this reason we invite readers to savor our poems while cooking up a pot of GUMBO. Some may enjoy inviting friends over to share in the fun! While some chop vegetables, others might be reading, laughing and philosophizing, while a scrumptious pot of forever memories is simmering on the stove. We hope you will savor our poetry. Just make sure that at the end of all your cooking, laughing, and sharing, you don't forget to sit down and enjoy a bowl of GUMBO!

- The Authors

A Taste of GUMBO's History

The Bantu people of Africa refer to the vegetable okra as *"ki ngombo."* Both the Umbundu Bantu word *"ochinggombo"* and the Tshiluba Bantu word *"chinggombo"* incorporate the sound of "ngombo" meaning okra. Most consider okra to be a staple ingredient in GUMBO, which adds to the thickening as well as to the flavor. This fact and the similarity of the Bantu word for okra to the word GUMBO, lead many to believe that the word GUMBO originated with Africans. Many Africans were brought to American shores enslaved, while others came as free and educated, i.e. *"gens de coleur libres" (free people of color).* As many Louisiana inhabitants were descended from Africans, cultural habits, including culinary skills persisted in the Americas, having been passed down for generations. The West African use of okra, rice and hot peppers in their cooking continued in the Americas. In fact, there is an African culinary dish made of okra and rice, which is commonly prepared in many West African nations even today. The fact that GUMBO often includes okra as a staple and is traditionally served with rice gives credence to the belief that the culinary dish of GUMBO has African roots and the word GUMBO originated as a derivative of the Bantu *"ki ngombo."*

The Choctaws, a Native American Indian nation indigenous to the south and eastern part of the United States *(Alabama, Florida, Louisiana, Mississippi - and later Oklahoma),* referred to dried and ground sassafras leaves as "kombo" and used this ground powder to thicken soups and add a distinctive spicy flavor to stews. The Choctaw people had lived in Louisiana and the neighboring areas for many centuries. In fact, Choctaw oral traditions speak of their having hunted giant animals, which had roamed the ancient Americas. Modern archeological evidence lends support to these stories, meaning the Choctaw civilization may actually be thousands of years old. The Choctaw Indians' contribution to GUMBO via the ground sassafras leaves, now called filé (FEE-lay) powder, is quite clear and legendary. What is fascinating is the linguistic similarity of the African Bantu word *"ki ngombo"* and the Native American Choctaw word *"kombo"* especially since both words in each language refer to substances, which have the effect of thickening a stew. It brings to mind the theory presented by Professor Ivan Van Sertima who wrote the book, *They Came Before Columbus*, where he writes about ancient Africans having travelled to the Americas in antiquity. They left much evidence throughout the land. Linguistic similarities of this type may lend credence to this theory. At any rate, filé is one of the key Choctaw contributions to GUMBO. Perhaps just as importantly, they also added their use of local fish, game and shellfish to the dish.

It seems evident then, that the African and the Choctaw together form the right and left handles of the GUMBO pot, each contributing name and key substances to the dish. Both peoples also shared much in common. Although there were some free Africans in the Americas who had never known enslavement, most of the Africans had been dispossessed of their freedom, their land and much of their heritage. The Choctaws, like most Native American Indians lost much of the same and on their own soil. In addition to the backbreaking field labor, Africans did most of the cooking in the south during the period of their enslavement, and afterward for that matter, not only for their own families, but also for the families of the wealthy whom they served. Their use of okra, rice and peppers became key ingredients in GUMBO. The Choctaw, being indigenous to the land, were prolific agriculturalists, growing corn, beans and other vegetables. Additionally, they were seasoned hunters, gatherers and fisherman. They mostly cooked for their own communities, but became expert traders with all whom set foot on their shores. Their use of ground sassafras (filé), fish, game, and shellfish also became key ingredients in GUMBO. Both nations made significant contributions to this wonderful culinary dish.

There were additional contributions to GUMBO, for example, from the French. Louisiana was actually named for French King Louis XIV, who ruled France in the mid- 17th century. The French governed the area for almost a hundred years. The most impactful influence of the French in Louisiana began when the city of New Orleans was founded in 1718. And French influence to the culture of the region has been significant. Distinctive cultural gifts of the French include the French language, influencing both Creole and Cajun dialects, and of course, French cooking. Probably the signature contribution of the French to GUMBO is the *"roux,"* made from flour and fat to add flavor to and thicken the dish. The word roux in French originates from the Latin *"russet"* which means *"brownish."* As flour is cooked in fat, the mixture turns brown, therefore the name, roux.

The French also contributed to GUMBO via Creole cuisine. Many people have heard the word, *"Creole"* especially in reference to Louisiana, but who are the Creoles? The term *"Creole"* can be found rooted in the Spanish *"Criollo"* which refers to *"a person native to a certain place,"* and in the Portuguese, *"Crioulo"* meaning *"someone who is brought up in your home."* Both words originate from *"criar"* which means *"to bred"* or "to raise," rooted in the Latin "creare" which most people will recognize as the origin of the word "create." The word was originally used to distinguish between those born on European soil and those individuals born in the territories they had colonized. Those born in the territories were often of mixed ethnic and cultural heritage.

Therefore, the word Creole has come to be used to refer to mixed-race peoples, especially those of European and African descent. During colonial expansion the French, Spanish and Portuguese, intermixed with enslaved and vanquished peoples in conquered territories. In the case of our example here, the conquered people included Africans as well as Native Americans. This inter-mingling and/or intermarriage resulted in a distinct cultural group known as Creoles. And, as previously mentioned, the term was also used to differentiate those who were actually born in the conquered territories (Creoles) from those who were born in Europe. Similarly, *Louisiana* Creoles represent a people born in Louisiana of blended cultural descent, notably French, African, and Spanish, but also may include other Europeans,

Native Americans and individuals from the Caribbean *(especially Haitian)* as well. Louisiana Creoles speak a language, originated primarily from French, but which includes blended words and phrases from different languages, and is also quite distinguishable from the parent language. In reference to GUMBO, Creole cooks are more likely to use butter in making a roux that is a little lighter in color and usually prefer a "red" *(tomato-based)* GUMBO of a consistency that is more like a soup than a stew.

The French also contributed to GUMBO via Cajun cuisine. The word *"Cajun"* is an abbreviated colloquialism of the word *"Acadian"* i.e., those people who were exiled by the British from French speaking Acadia, which included the countries of Nova Scotia, Prince Edward Island and New Brunswick off the east coast of Canada in the mid- 18th century. The Acadians resettled in Louisiana and some of them intermarried with Louisiana Creoles and other ethnic groups. Already speaking a different dialect from regular Canadian French, the Acadians once resettled in Louisiana and having intermarried with different ethnic groups in Louisiana, further differentiated their language and culture to form distinctive linguistic and cultural patterns referred to as Cajun. In terms of the culinary habits of the *Acadian-Creoles* i.e., "Cajuns", Cajun cooks are more likely to use oil in making their roux, prefer a darker "brown" GUMBO *(sans tomatoes, i.e. without tomatoes)* and usually make a thicker stew for their GUMBO than do Creoles.

Although some people use the terms Creole and Cajun interchangeably, and the peoples do share some common history, they are in fact, different culturally. Creoles tend to lean toward French/African/Caribbean music *(like Zydeco)* and participate in a multiplicity of religions. Most Cajuns are Catholic and lean toward folk music much of which incorporates elements of jazz or blues. In terms of cooking, Creole cooking has maintained cultural influences from each of the African, Native American, French, Spanish and Caribbean as more distinctive and in-tact. Therefore, the vegetables used by the Africans, local game used by the Native Americans, sauces common to the French, spices used by the Spanish and seafood by the Caribbean peoples all seem to hold their own in Creole cuisine, although one ingredient may predominate over the other depending on the specific dish. In GUMBO, each contribution seems to hold its own. In Cajun cooking, there seems to be a significant reliance on spices. So, the use of bell pepper, celery and onion *(fondly referred to as the "holy trinity")* is traditionally found in most Cajun cooking. Similarly, the use of cayenne pepper, thyme, pepper and paprika are common. The holy trinity is quite commonly used in the preparation of GUMBO in both Creole and Cajun cooking, although in Creole dishes, one might more commonly find tomatoes and garlic added to the dish. We must note, however, that as time passes, there is a lessoning of the division between the two cultures, both in terms of music, cooking and other traditions. So though traditionally, you might find more chicken and sausage in Cajun GUMBO, and more shrimp and crab in Creole GUMBO, today it is not uncommon to find all of the above in GUMBO irrespective of whether it is Creole or Cajun. Like GUMBO itself, there has been a blending of ingredients and traditions that is now claimed by all.

Additional contributions to GUMBO, include tomatoes *(Italian--especially Sicilian)*, spices *(Spanish, who like the French, also ruled Louisiana at one time)*, sausage and potato salad *(German)*. Yes, it is not uncommon to serve potato salad as a side dish to GUMBO! Although, we do not include a recipe for potato salad in this book, we welcome the reader to experiment with this often-acclaimed compliment to the dish. Other European immigrants, notably the Portuguese, British, Irish, Dutch and Croatian are also included in the ethnic/cultural milieu of Louisiana, each with some albeit small contribution to Louisiana cuisine. Although having less of an impact on the origin of GUMBO, it bears mentioning that later immigrations of Filipinos, Latinos and Asians have added to the cultural variations of much of the modern-day Louisiana cuisine in many areas.

Perhaps the city of New Orleans in Louisiana should be given greatest credit for the origin of GUMBO. It's true that the name New Orleans has become synonymous with both Creole and Cajun cuisine, but there are variations of magnificent GUMBO dishes from all over the state of Louisiana. Interestingly enough, in the north, Louisiana cooking may be a bit more typically "southern." You might find a greater reliance on pork, sausage, chicken and wild game in the GUMBO. In the south and in New Orleans, the cooking may take on more of the elements of typical Creole or Cajun cuisine, incorporating more spices and a greater reliance on fish and shellfish in the GUMBO due to the proximity to the coast. GUMBO is a dish, which reflects not only regional and seasonal variations of what is available for the pot, but for the poor people of Louisiana, the ingredients served over rice tended to fill the belly. And remember, rice was plentiful, being Louisiana's number one cash crop! Despite its humble origins, chefs from Europe and local home grown Creole and Cajun chefs honed GUMGO recipes to the point where in 1972 the United States Senate had GUMBO added to options on the Congressional menu in honor of Senator Allen Ellender, a native of Louisiana, after his death. So from humble beginnings to the halls of Congress, GUMBO has made an impact as a beloved American dish.

Over centuries, many culinary skills were shared between the people of Louisiana. What ended up in the GUMBO pot reflects many nations. The GUMBO table is where all nations come together to heal the wounds of racism, enslavement, grief, anger and loss, to celebrate family, community and good food! Hurrah for GUMBO! And now for the next course, enjoy our poems sprinkled with a love for all the flavors of the palate!

The Libation

In the African tradition . . . it is customary to pour out upon the ground (or into a receptacle) a few drops of an alcoholic beverage *(or water if that is all that is available)* out of respect for the ancestors, before beginning an important event or gathering. For African Americans, especially, this ritual has become a fitting and respectable reminder of the sacrifices of those who have gone before us, the significance of those who will come after us, as well as the gratitude and honor we gladly affirm to the Creator who provides the necessary oversight, grace, guidance and protection over all our human endeavors.

Libation Poem

We pour libation for our ancestors
Enslaved but never beaten
We pour to honor our elders
And the bitterness they've eaten

We do this to teach our children
For our future is in their hands
May blessings accrue to the unborn
And this earth on which they'll stand

As we pour, we thank the Creator
And ask that our words and deeds
Reflect Truth, Justice and Righteousness
Which today, we plant as seeds

-Judy Sundayo

Fourth Course

Poems Peppered with GUMBO

Part 1 SALTY
Meat, Poultry & Stock

Part 2 BITTER
Roux

Part 3 SPICY
Filé or Okra?

Part 4 SWEET
Holy Trinity

Part 5 SOUR
Rice

Part 6 SAVORY
Seafood

Part 7 SPIRITUAL SEASONINGS
Herbs & Spices

Part 1 – SALTY

Meat, Poultry & Stock

Cook the meat or the poultry
Then set aside
Remove all the bones, the gristle; the hide
What's left is a stock full of flavor and flare
To make sure there's quite enough GUMBO
To share!
~Judy Sundayo

There are several different types of meat and/or poultry, which are commonly used in the preparation of GUMBO. These usually include, but are not limited to, chicken, turkey, duck, rabbit and sausage. In reality, Louisianans used whatever fresh game they could bring to the table. For some Cajun families, this might include venison and squirrel on some occasions and on others, maybe even armadillo. There are some folks who declare that if you use poultry, no sausage is allowed! Then, there are others who could never imagine Gumbo without both! It's all a matter of personal taste!

[Regarding seafood, see a separate section later on in this book. Since shellfish does not take long to cook, we have placed the instructions later on in the order of production for GUMBO!]

GUMBO RECIPE Step 1:

Meat, Poultry & Stock
(For Chicken & Sausage GUMBO)

What You Need
>   10" stainless steel or cast iron frying pan
>   10-12 quart stainless steel pot with lid or
>   Heavy cast iron pot (like a Dutch oven)

What You Gotta Get *(This recipe should feed a family of 6 for a day or two!)*
>   6 pounds of chicken thighs
>   5 pounds of sausage
>   6- 8 quarts of spring water

What You Do with What You Got
- **For chicken**, wash thoroughly
- Store in refrigerator separately, until use
- Place pre-washed chicken thighs into pot, with bones and skin intact, and boil
- When chicken is tender, remove from broth and refrigerate
- Once chicken has cooled, remove skin and bones
- Cut chicken into bite-sized pieces
- Store in refrigerator until ready to use
- Cool the broth (chicken stock)
- Remove congealed fat and set fat aside
- Chicken stock can be refrigerated for later use or Kept out for active GUMBO preparation

- **For sausage**, wash thoroughly
- Cut sausage into ¼ to ½ inch slices

- Place sausage slices into pre-heated, medium hot frying pan
- Fat will be rendered from sausage
- Remove rendered sausage from pan and add to chicken stock
- Set frying pan with fat aside for making roux later

What You Bet Not Tell Nobody

- Many cooks believe that the longer you cook your stock the more flavor is pulled from the bones of the chicken, so you might find many people will cook their stock for two hours or more. In this case, you will want to make sure you strain your stock to ensure you have strained out all the bones from the stock before using it for GUMBO.
- You can also make stock out of seafood. If you are adding shrimp to your GUMBO, after you have de-shelled the shrimp, you can cook the shrimp shells in water to make a wonderful shrimp stock. Just filter the stock when ready.
- You can do the same thing with crabs. Just put the crab legs into your water (along with your shrimp shells if you like) and cook down for a wonderful seafood stock!
- You can use canned or packaged stock if you don't have time to make your stock from scratch, but homemade stock is always best!
- Some chefs swear by using several beef bouillon cubes to make a beef stock for GUMBO. It's all a matter of taste!
- You can also use canned or pre-packaged chicken *broth* in place of chicken stock!
- You can freeze stock for several months and it will still be great.
- If you brown your (cooked) chicken in some oil prior to adding it to the GUMBO pot, you will add a little crust to the meat and a lot of flavor to your GUMBO.

- When choosing your sausage for GUMBO, most cooks prefer an Andouille sausage. This is a Louisianan smoked pork sausage. Although you can use any sausage, GUMBO enthusiasts say a smoked sausage, like Andouille, is absolutely the best!
- Another good choice for sausage is Chorizo!
- Any smoked meat gives the GUMBO a terrific flavor!
- After you slice your sausage, instead of cooking it on the stove, you can also lay the slices out flat on a baking sheet and cook them in the oven on medium high heat. You can turn the slices over once before they are done. When ready, add the individual sausage rounds (without the fat) to your GUMBO!
- If you are using any other meat, like turkey, rabbit, etc., these will also make a flavorful stock. Just substitute the meat of your choice for the chicken! But a word to the wise, regardless of the other type of meat or poultry you might use, sausage is a wonderful complement for any GUMBO recipe!
- A word about the consistency of your GUMBO: although your stock will most likely be pretty watery, after you add the roux (next Step) as well as your meats, vegetables, and seasonings, the consistency of your GUMBO should be much thicker. When ready to serve, your GUMBO should have a consistency somewhere between a soup and a stew! Yum!
- If you want to use the absolute best stainless steel cookware there is, check out *Saladmaster* cookware. They use 316Ti Titanium Stainless Steel for the interior of their cookware. This is the purest raw material there is for cookware and it protects the quality and purity of the food you cook in it, thereby allowing the best flavor possible. This also insures you aren't getting any metal byproducts in your food. It is a little more expensive, but it has a lifetime guarantee! See *healthsystemsforlife.com*.

Introduction to the Salty Poems

The salty flavor in Gumbo is delightfully represented by a mouth-watering stock made of meat or poultry. In this book, we associate the taste of salt with sex, seduction and youthful abandon. The poems in this section have to do with experiences acquired during those times in our lives when we were influenced more by fantasy than by reality, more by our hormones than by common sense and more by our passions than by reason.

In preparing Gumbo, the meat or poultry is simmered in a pot to allow the salty flavor of the meat to pervade the water for a flavorful stock. In cooking the sausage, the salt in the sausage is part of what is rendered off in the fat as the sausage is cooked in the frying pan. In both cases, there is a salty exchange, using heat as a conduit. For many of us, especially in our youth, passion is a conduit for the exchange of playful and sensually-charged emotions. Like the salty flavor in GUMBO, these experiences in our lives add a flavor to our existence that can hardly be beat. Please enjoy our "Salty" poems as you simmer your meat or poultry to make the stock for your Gumbo!

*Judy Sundayo's aunt, **Ruth (Smith) Ray** (on left)*
*And her sister, Judy's mother, **Thomasia (Smith) Moore**,*
Washington, D.C., circa 1950's

Salty

Salty saunters in with flavor
times three
Exuding a seductive quality
Pushing us forward to stimulate
Receive, rejoice and regenerate
Salty is. . .
Sexy,
Sweaty and hot
Add a little or a lot
Without it, life would clearly be bland
Still a parade,
But no marching band!
So, let's blow the trumpet and beat the drum
Got salt?
Then, honey, give me some!

~Judy Sundayo

Sexy Sally

Sexy Sally made her living
Flaunting what she had
As time went on, with hardened years,
Her charms began to sag

When Sexy Sally laid her pride
at last upon the shelf
She searched within that she might find
new visions for herself

Slowly then, she shed her shoes
trekking up the mountain
Teary-eyed, she sang the blues
while wading in a fountain

With toes she fished a penny out
for thoughts of love's requiem
"Just enough," she heard God shout,
"Down payment for your dream!"

~Judy Sundayo

*Quilt by **Janet Harris**, from the Collection of
Judy Sundayo, La Jolla, California*

Alyce Smith Cooper, Registered Nurse,
San Diego, California

You Want to Love Me

In my youth, I didn't know - -
Allowed myself to be misused
Now I know there is a law of use
This here for this here; that there for that there
Misuse breeds a cloud
On the soul of the user and the use-e
So, no more misuse
If you want to love me, you must take time to know me
And let me know you
We must like each other to love each other
Pray with the same understanding
You want to love me? Can you handle it?

~Alyce Smith Cooper

Hot to Trot

Oh, she's hot to trot

God gave her a lot

But I hope she don't go to town

With a dress that tight

They'll sure be a fight

Lawd, simmer the young girl down!

~Judy Sundayo

Sista'-Ku: Meat and Taytahs

My meat and taytahs man
He be de salt a de earth
I savor de flavor

~Judy Sundayo

Philoso-Ku: Fire

Fire,
Absorbs inflammables
Spreads like passion
From heart to heart!

~Judy Sundayo

Jaime V. Jones, San Diego, California

Celebrate

Want to be balanced let's work to educate
Shout it, say how much you appreciate
Every flower, favor, breath and step you take
Every chance you get celebrate

Change your attitude from good to great
Change your life change your state
Change your destiny change your fate
Every chance you get celebrate

Change your style change your weight
Change your mind change your faith
Change your words change your mistakes
Every chance you get celebrate

Change your car change your license plate
Change your dessert piece of cake?
Change your age change your date
Every chance you get celebrate

~Jaime V. Jones

51

My Jeans

I got into 'em today. . . my jeans
No cause for celebration, you say?
Oh, yes it is!
It has been two years,
Since I could squeeze these hips into 'em
For me it is cause for celebration
The weight came off. . .
Because I no longer needed it to hide
No longer must I hide my true self
From myself
A great sigh of relief. . . Whew!!!
But not too deep. . .
The jeans are tight yet!
~Alyce Smith Cooper

Alyce Smith Cooper on the Potomac River, Washington, D.C.

Judy Sundayo, Miami Beach, Florida, circa 1970's

Enter Sobriety

Panting breath of a lusty day,
awakening sensory cues,
hot and breathless years of living,
with youth to pay the dues

Just a taste is never one;
just one snort is two,
just two totes, and a decades gone,
for clouds of lies hide true

Enter a bad decision or three;
come cops with cuffs at the curb;
arrested opportunities,
that misfortunes may freedom disturb

Enter fear on the faces of family
and questions with answers that fade
When experiences are lost in memory,
it's time to end the charade

Enter sobriety and it seems to suck;
to be present, to be clear and to feel?
No alcohol to take the edge off?
No pot to smokescreen what's real?

(continued)

Enter Sobriety *(continued)*

And then one-day serenity appears,
in a new and magical fashion,
to enjoy the sights and sounds of life,
and to live with incredible passion

Enter forgiveness and gratitude,
as new eyes adjust to the light;
what follows is clarity and a touch of class,
portending a future that's bright

~Judy Sundayo

*Judy Sundayo with her fiancé, **Al Washington**, Solana Beach,*
California, circa 2011

Alyce Smith Cooper, San Diego, California

Peculiar Spark

I thought it was love
My eyes were a-sparkle
My lips tingled with unspoken joy
My heart opened to receive

I thought it was love
You're special he had said
I've always loved you
My heart leaped

Out flowed glowing words
Everything had a rainbow aura
Pulled out the gumbo pot
Began stirring in ingredients

(continued)

Peculiar Spark *(continued)*

A flippant smile; A flirty wink
Skirt a little tighter; Blouse cut a little lower
Toes polished bright red

When questioned he said
I'm not chasing romance
But I value you as friend
Gumbo pot is on now

Love like gumbo comes differently
I'm still riding with the peculiar spark
Now, calling it creativity

~Alyce Smith Cooper

Alyce Smith Cooper, San Diego, California

*Judy Sundayo with fiancé **Al Washington**, at Harry's Restaurant, La Jolla, California 2004*

A Wink and a Smile

Sunny side up
Let's breakfast in style
I sure like my eggs
With a wink and a smile!

I sure like my toast
With lots of jam
Warm and sweet just like I am
I like my apples baked
So turn up the heat
Just like your breakfast kisses
Hot and sweet!

Sunny side up
As we breakfast in style
I sure like my eggs
With a wink and a smile!

~Judy Sundayo

A Sexy Male Moment

Girl, have you ever watched your man shave?

Fabulously foaming fresh

Nothing else quite the sexy same

The water, the mirror, his reflection relaxed

Without tension or rage

The look in his eye no matter his age

Focused intently as he enters the final stage

The look that commands,

Tonight I'm getting laid

Then the final stroke of the blade

Wow, sexy man, I love to watch you shave!

~Jaime V. Jones

*Judy Sundayo's maternal uncle, **Covert Smith***
Photo taken, Washington, D.C., circa 1950's

Jaime V. Jones, Los Angeles, California

I Know How You Make Me Feel

Eyes wide, brown, moist and steady
My brown body your eyes make ready
Scanning slowly every strand of hair, face and body
Clothing, jewelry, the faint fragrance of jasmine
The scent of loves toddy

Gentle, yet passionate, quick and sweet
Your brown eyes turn up the human heat
Words, voice strong, soft and deep
Leave me pulsating,
Vibrating at a hundred heart beats
Leave me pulsating,

(continued)

I Know How You Make Me Feel *(continued)*

Vibrating at a hundred heart beats
Come here, come now, you are worth a repeat
Leave me breathless,
Pulsating at a hundred heart beats
Leave me dizzy,
Sizzling at a hundred heart beats
Come with me, close the door
Arms, heart, lips open waiting for more

The admiration, love, laughter and tears
Mellow memories
Whisper lusty words in our ears
Desiring, needing, wanting you,
All of you near
Holding, touching, kissing you
All through the years
Difficult to express now here come the tears

Trembling lips wait and anticipate
Leave pulsating, vibrating
At a hundred heart beats
Leave pulsating, vibrating
At a hundred heart beats

The first kiss, which is never too late
Loving you in my mind and heart has been great
I know how you make me feel
And, I can't wait!
I can't wait!

~Jaime V. Jones

60

Jaime V. Jones, San Diego, California

Try Me Tonight

I've been watching you all night!
You're beautiful, wonderful, magnificent,
A truly inspiring sight and if I am right
I am not quite your type
My recommendation: Try Me Tonight!

I've got this lusty, lusty notion
To rush you out to the beach
And wash you in the ocean
Take you home and rub you down
With hot oil and lotion
Lay you down wet on my bed
Of decadence and devotion
Whispering wild wonderful words

(continued)

Try Me Tonight *(continued)*

Sure to go to your head

While I make sure you are ever so faintly

Fruitfully fed

And then, make mad, mad, passionate love

To you all night, Is that right?

In the morning I'll wake you

With the smell of fresh homemade cinnamon rolls,

One or two?

A big fluffy light omelet, maple sausage,

Fresh strawberries too!

Chilled champagne or maybe some hot herbal tea

So now, tell me baby

What is it going to be?

Are you leaving with me?

~Jaime V. Jones

Judy Sundayo with fiancé, Al Washington

Alyce Smith Cooper, San Diego, California

Fanning That Flame

What we got for the gumbo pot?
This man, he done bring a deep affection?
Just stir it in for a sweet confection,
Well, the deep sense of kinship
and warmth of heart
Ain't nothing to throw out the gumbo pot!

It be good when a man done express his feeling
And this gumbo gone do a lot for healing
For your words done brought everything to the top
Now you can see what cooking in that pot!

Got sis's saucy, pie-girl ways,
Got lots of friends be done speak your praise
You be done keep on fanning that flame
To keep that soup hot all the same

Till somebody done bring that super-hot spice
That you been waiting for all your life
Whatever you wanna add
Sure ain't gone to waste,
Lawd knows, longer it simmers
Better it's gone taste!

~Judy Sundayo

Pimp Trilogy

A Pimp Don't Always Ride in a Cadillac

Yeah, a pimp can drive a jeep or a Datsun or a Pinto
Pendin' on his level of thinkin'
Chevy, Oldsmobile . . . any of them rides will do
He can wear hush puppies or Pierre Cardin Kicks
Dress out of Penny's or GQ
'Cause a pimp's a man what hold out on his woman
Makin' her think she don't think
Getting' her to believe she's less than whole
And all the time, he is profitin' from her hurtin'
Naw honey, a pimp don't always ride in a Cadillac!

———

Pimps and Athlete's Feet

I figure a pimp must be somethin' like athlete's feet,
A fungus that eats away at your foundation,
That is until you discover Absorbine, Jr.

———

Pimp is Short for "Pimple"

You know it must be the truth
I always did wonder
Where did that word come from?
Check it out, pimps are full of corruption
And they thrive on living flesh
But I have known of pimples that were busted
Sure, they scare a little. . .
Just enough so you won't forget they were there.

~Alyce Smith Cooper

Beach at La Jolla, California, Photo taken by
Judy Sundayo, circa 2010

In Reverence to Passion Resurrected

Paschal sequence lingering
Gently on the misty air
Sun departing in a whisper
Glistening on their bodies bare

Bodies brown yet silver,
Shining, dripping wet with salty spray
Bodies young and energetic
Beckoning the ocean play

To and fro the pulsing heartbeat
Lifts with every wayward breeze
Chanting, humming lullabies
She drifts around their sinking knees

Deep and dark, despairing, brooding
Mother Nature nods her head
Rowing, sweeping throngs of ocean
Offering up her Paschal dead

(continued)

65

Washing over minute traces
Imprints were their feet had trod
Leaves she gifts and precious creatures
On the sandy breast of God

Cool and calm, serenely singing
Every passing wind a song
Crooning, praising her creator
He alone the whole night long

In the distance firmly haulted
One silhouette against the sky
Stands a single wearied figure
Clinging to a reason why

Patient 'neath a light embracing
Innocence from earth is born
To a figure eastward facing
Comes the resurrected morn

~Judy Sundayo

Cote' de' Azur, Photo by Judy Sundayo
Of the French Riviera, 2008

Alyce Smith Cooper, San Diego, California

Sista'-Ku Trilogy

Profound passion
Heart skips beats
Then lives on

———

Creativity door finally opens
Do not fall in love
With the doorman

———

Gifts repossessed
Goddess garments
Shaken out
Wrinkles pressed
Show Time!

~Alyce Smith Cooper

Palate Cleanser

———

Water

Sweetly slowly sipped thru

Slightly smiling lips

Silver speckled water

Smoothly clears away

Each memory of morsels munched with merriment

Water cleanses coaxes down

The gullet

What has come before

In patient or

Impatient anticipation

Of what

Will next

Deliciously appear

~Alyce Smith Cooper

Mountain stream photo by Maliz Ong
publicdomainpictures.net

Roux

Photo (left) by Max Straeten & (right) by Ronnieb, morguefile.com

To hot butter, oil or fat
Stir in some flour
Keep stirring with patience,
For at least a quarter hour
When your mixture turns a pretty
Peanut butter brown
You'll know that you are throwing down
And if you really
Want to make your dinner guests holler
Keep stirring till you get a deep chocolate color
And the whole room smells like hot buttered toast
Go 'head for yourself! You deserve to boast!
Add peppers and onions, celery and stock
This will keep it from burning or getting too hot!
You should name this mixture before you're through
Don't you dare call it gravy!
The French call it Roux! (Pronounced "ROO")
~Judy Sundayo

The making of roux for some is a scary proposition, because it can burn if you have the heat too high or are not diligent in your stirring. But this is a key ingredient in GUMBO, which adds flavor and thickening. So enjoy the process! You'll be an expert in no time!

GUMBO Recipe Step 2:

Roux

(Flour and Butter, Oil or Fat)

What You Need

    10" stainless steel or cast iron frying pan
    10-12 quart stainless steel pot with lid or
    A large cast iron Dutch oven
    Wire whisk for stirring, or a
    Large wooden spoon for stirring

What You Gotta Get

    2 cups of all-purpose flour
    5 pounds of sausage
    1 stick of butter

What You Do with What You Got

- Wash the sausage thoroughly
- Cut sausage into ½ inch pieces
- Cook in medium hot, pre-heated frying pan
- Fat will be rendered from sausage during cooking process
- Remove the cooked sausage from pan, setting the sausage fat aside for the roux
- Spoon sausage into the chicken broth you have simmering in a stainless steel pot or Dutch oven
- Allow broth with sausage to simmer on low heat for 1 hour while making your roux
- To make roux, heat frying pan with sausage fat to medium high heat
- Stir flour into the frying pan slowly using wire whisk (preferred) or wooden spoon to blend flour thoroughly into the fat, being careful not to splatter the hot oil

70

- Keep wire whisk moving constantly as mixture browns to keep it from burning
- The longer you cook roux, the darker it becomes
- Stir slowly until the roux becomes the color you desire *(Some like roux the color of dark chocolate, while others like it a lighter shade, like the color of peanut butter)*
- You may find your roux is ready when you smell an aroma reminiscent of hot buttered toast!
- When the roux is the color you desire, add one stick of melted butter and stir in well. It's done!

What You Bet Not Tell Nobody

- The amount of flour you use to make your roux is *roughly* equal the amount of butter/oil/fat you will be using. However, since oil is heavier than flour, most experienced cooks like to use a little more flour than oil. So, for every cup (8 oz.) of butter/oil/fat, you may want to add about a cup and three quarters (14 oz.) of flour. Some cooks just double the amount of flour to oil. You must find your own balance of flour to oil based on how thick and flavorful you want your roux!
- Try Bob's Red Mill All Purpose Gluten-free Flour or sorghum flour if you are gluten-sensitive!
- Some cooks brown the flour a bit first in a separate pan before adding it to the hot butter/fat/oil as this seems to add even more flavor to the roux
- Using clarified butter instead of fat holds the flour better *(without separating)*!
- If you decide to use all butter for your roux, instead of oil or a combination of oil and butter, be attentive to stir CONSTANTLY, as butter will burn very easily!
- If you find your roux is burning, or even beginning to smoke, you may want to reduce your heat!
- Although experienced chefs can make their roux more quickly and at higher temperatures, in your first few

71

attempts to make this dish, we recommend cooking your roux at a medium high temperature rather than on high! The roux you save may be your own!

- Using bacon fat instead of sausage fat adds a particularly distinctive flavor to roux, which some people find irresistible!

- When the roux is the color you want, and many believe that the darker roux is the more flavorful and traditional, add the Holy Trinity *(chopped onions, peppers and celery)* as this cools the roux down immediately, preventing it from burning

- After you add the Holy Trinity and are stirring the roux, allow the onions to stick a bit to the bottom of the pan for a minute; we call this the *"barely burnt-basting"* technique, which you will find allows the onions in the Holy Trinity to caramelize, releasing their natural sugars into the mixture; the smell is delicious and this technique will add a scrumptiously sweet flavor to your roux!

- A few chefs swear by preparing their roux in the oven! Just mix the flour with butter, oil or fat as recommended above, place in a Dutch oven and bake in the middle of your oven at 350° until it gets the color you want, anywhere from forty-five minutes to an hour and a half, stirring occasionally

- Some chefs like to add shallots, a cousin to the onion, and often indistinguishable, to their Holy Trinity and then to the roux to give the roux a distinctive flavor

- If you don't have time to make a roux, you may substitute a pre-made roux you can buy in a store, or online. Many people love Zatarain's New Orleans Style GUMBO Base or Tony Chachere's Roux in a pinch!

- Go ahead and allow yourself to burn at least one trial mixture of roux, to lose the fear of doing so; you will find you will not burn it again!

Introduction to the Bitter Poems

The process of making roux can produce a distinctly bitter flavor, depending on how the Roux is made, how dark it gets and whether or not it is burned. For most cooks the slight nutty flavor of the flour as it is browned for roux is slightly bitter but flavorful like the roasted flavor of darkened toast. This slightly bitter taste will not harm the final GUMBO, but will only give it character! However, if the flour burns in the making of roux, the bitterness looms large and takes over. The resulting GUMBO will not recover. *The Lesson* we must learn in life *and* in preparing GUMBO is one of care and patience!

The attention needed in preparing roux is reminiscent of the diligence needed to ensure that we don't ruin a perfectly good relationship, or a perfectly good friendship or a perfectly good job. We all want to make an impact, to leave a good impression and to make a statement, but we are tasked with learning those lessons, which temper our tempestuousness. Some lessons are difficult ones, i.e. bitter ones, but we must learn to make something positive out of the bitter experiences.

Finally, we learn that concentration, patience and diligence pay off. We have just enough of the bitter experiences to say, *'Okay, I get it! I have learned that lesson! I better pay attention!'* Then, we don't burn the roux and the bitterness does not take over and ruin our lives, or our GUMBO! Please enjoy these poems which remind us of important early lessons we learn, the "Wake-up Calls" and the individuals who have served us those "bitter pills" necessary to get our attention.

73

*Judy Sundayo's jegna (teacher/guide) and colleague, **Dr. Asa G. Hilliard, III,** (1933-2007) Psychologist, teacher, historian and expert on Classical African Civilizations; One of the founders of **The Black Child Development Institute;** Photo taken by Judy Sundayo at Sullivan's Island, Charleston, South Carolina, harbor where over 40% of all Africans who were brought to North America, enslaved, first set foot on shore; it is estimated that millions Never made it to shore, but died during the **Middle Passage**; for Info on **Association for the Study of Classical African Civilizations**, go to* www.ascac.squarespace.com

Bitter

The flavor of bitter is

Quite sharp

An acrid pill

On shriveled tongue

A shrill and solitary call to arms

Against an enemy

On the run

Like revenge,

Bitter takes no prisoners

And will never take a fall

It's a full-on assault

And a scathing wake-up call!

~Judy Sundayo

In Harmony

The evening sun sparkling on the water
Is a dance
To a melody of waves
Rolling sand pebbles
Up on the beach
A light shining deep
From within the earth
Warms the ground
Slowly sand and tide mold me
Into one form
One harmony
This imprint
Will never be washed away

~Judy Sundayo

*Judy Sundayo's friend and former professor, **Dr. Harold Greenwald**,
Student of Dr. Theodor Reik and creator of Direct Decision Therapy; author of The
Happy Person; Pen & ink drawing by Richard Wallich, San Diego, California, circa
1980's*

Alyce Smith Cooper, San Diego, California

Bitter Sweet Savory Season

No one I listened to ever told me
I would grieve the loss of the erotic gaze
No one said I'd need to change perfume
Or have some other plan
For attracting loving attention and touch
Maybe they said and I just didn't/couldn't hear
How I would longingly remember
Tight dresses, high heels, uplifted breasts,
Quick recall,
Sparkling eyes and glistening teeth
I thought gracefully aging meant
Having bible study in my home
Having lots of prayer partners
Being content in widowhood

(continued)

Bitter Sweet Savory Season *(continued)*

Yet, I find
There is still fire burning
In my belly
Vital life forces to be tapped
And used faithfully
Else why would they still exist?
Eyes and ears may not be as acute
Hair thinning
Hands occasionally shake
Stairs do not get bounded upward
But I do seem to speak more gracefully
Or not at all
Employ a smile, instead of darting words
The proverbs come to mind
My heart fills with compassion
More easily
Realizing the seasons
Youth must pass through
My eyes fill now with tears of joy
Witness to tenderness
A baby's face
Or hand well formed
I will listen more attentively
To signals of this nostalgic age
I am willing to share with them
Those who can take time to hear
Of bitter sweet savory seasons to come

~Alyce Smith Cooper

Dr. Wade Nobles, world-renowned psychologist, friend, jegna (teacher/guide), Expert on African history, author of several books, including "Seeking the Sakhu" and Judy Sundayo, following his keynote address at the 16th Annual Africa Trade & Business Conference, Mesa College, San Diego, California, 2012; Dr. Nobles is also Founder and Executive Director of the Institute for the Advanced Study of Black Family Life and Culture in Oakland, California
http://www.iasbflc.org/old/nobles.htm

Before Socrates Said It

Before Socrates said it, it had already been said,
"Know Thyself"
And so, *I'm just saying*
Let truth be wed to reason
'Cause everyone needs to know
That the ancient nation of Kemet
Was where everyone had to go
For the best education in antiquity
And the highest regarded in history
Yes, it was found at the Temple of Wa'set
So, for the *Truth*, don't stop at Socrates
Keep going back further yet!

(continued)

Before Socrates Said it *(continued)*

To the cradle of civilization; to Africa along the Nile
And when travelers seeking knowledge arrived there,
They had to stay a while
Forty years was required to obtain the highest teaching
Socrates was there for 15; that means
He was still reaching by the time he left the scene
But not before he noticed
What was carved on the temple wall
"Know Thyself"
So let it be known everywhere, less anyone be forlorn
Africans had been teaching this, a thousand years
Before Socrates was born!

~Judy Sundayo

Dr. Wade Nobles *(left), with Judy Sundayo's cousin,* **Rafiq Bilal** *(seated at center)
author of* **"Egyptian Sacred Science in Islam,"** *historian, activist, Founded "The
Upper Room" the first non-smoking, non-alcoholic club for youth performers in San
Francisco; two of Rafiq's children, oldest daughter, Aziza (back row center), Falilah
(center right), Aziza's son, Trey (right) Falilah's baby, Evelyn (right front), and
Evelyn's father, (upper left) San Francisco, California; circa early 2000's*

Judy Sundayo's jegna (teacher/guide) and sister of another mother,
Dr. Nsenga Warfield Coppock, *first Historian,* **National Association**
of Black Psychologists, author or co-author of a number of books, including,
"Transformations: A Rites of Passage for African American Girls," *Photo 1990's*

Everybody Listen to African Mother

(In honor of the African continent, the birthplace of humanity; the first letter of each word in this poem is the first letter of a country on the African continent.)

Everybody listen to African Mother
Can mankind maintain blindness now?
Can society escape disaster's slow spear?

Study, gather, seek greatness!
Labor in guarding thy birthplace!
Nearer children, come embrace service!

Give respect back to great African nations
Zambia, Zimbabwe . . . massive metaphors
Remember before enslavement

Self-knowledge defines self-love
Self-mastery conquers memory
Can mankind remember wisely?

~Judy Sundayo

81

Courage of the Ancestors

The human sequence comes to pass
In love and art and lore
The voices of a million souls
Have passed this way before
A rush of voices calling from the sea
And years of death and sacrifice for me
In haunting memory pierces from inside
Like cutting waves of cold and bitter tide
And though I stand a living soul and free
Four hundred years of slave songs beckon me
To know the pain and understand the fight
To set my course against the winds of might
And nurture goodness and savor peace
And find by way of knowledge, Love's release
I hear ancestral voices rise in song
Entreating those of us who listen long
To honor those who've gone before
And teach our children to open wide the door
Of love and hope and human quest
That we might enter in and find our rest
Then this day, let us set our sails
To catch the winds of morn'
That we might see in our children's eyes
This courage be reborn
~Judy Sundayo

*The great visionary peacemaker-activist, **President Nelson R. Mandela,** Former President of South Africa; Author, **"Long Walk to Freedom: The Autobiography of Nelson Mandela;"** Photo from his 80th birthday souvenir calendar, South Africa, July 18, 1998, courtesy Dr. Earl Suttle, Atlanta, GA*

*Judy Sundayo's friend and colleague, **Professor Chuck Ambers,** Professor Of Black Studies at San Diego Mesa College; founder and proprietor of **The African Museum Casa Del Rey Moro,** in Old Town, San Diego, showcasing books, paintings, posters, sculpture and other art pieces on over 6,000 years of African world history, with focus on African-Spanish, African-Mexican and African-American heritage; for more info, see: www.africanmuseumsandiego.com*

The N Word is a Dirty Word

The N word is a dirty word
Meant to tear you down from inside
The N word is the *only* word
That can *never* be said with pride

Only ignorance of our history
And the knowledge, *some folks were depraved!*
And their vehemence is no mystery
Against Africans they enslaved

The N Word is a sad word
Don't tell *me* the meanings been flipped!
That's the word even little children were called
While being spat upon and whipped!

The N word's disrespectful
To the lives our ancestors gave
Defending our right to dignity
Let the word fester in its grave!

(continued)

83

The N Word is a Dirty Word *(continued)*

Better think about what you're saying
There's a power in the tongue
And the N word was the last word
Many heard before they were hung
Let the living speak a language
Meant to honor and convey
That we speak for ourselves and name ourselves
Kugichagulia is the way!
If there're no other words you can use to convey
Your thoughts, better ask yourself why
And consider self-hatred's polluted your brain
And hung it out to dry
The N word is a boomerang
That the sender doesn't expect
To return to take aim at his own empty mind
And lack of self-respect
The N word is an insult
No matter how you might dress it up
Better know what you claim a*nd are claiming to be*
If you don't know, l*ook it up!*

~Judy Sundayo

*N Word Legacies: From left, 1) an African, named **Gordon**, enslaved in Louisiana, horribly scarred by slave master's whip, photographed in 1863 after his escape; 2) the horrific lynching of a young African American girl, **Laura Nelson**, OK, 1911; 3) **unidentified African American man** lynched in Georgia, 1960; 4) **Trayvon Martin**, 17 yr. old unarmed African American teen, who was profiled "real suspicious . . .up to no good . . .on drugs or something. . . looks black. . .these assholes they always get away;" said, G. Zimmerman who shot the teen to death in Florida, 2012*

Jaime V. Jones, San Diego County,
San Diego, California

Don't Mess With the Messenger

Don't mess with the messenger I say
I've come to deliver with much love I pay
Please don't stand in my heaven sent way
And don't be deceived by how hard I play

For years I sat quietly watching
And waiting for this day
Growing gradually into genius, brilliance, splendor and
More magnificent every day

(continued)

85

Don't Mess with the Messenger *(continued)*

Now, I stand bold, victorious, and fearlessly clear
Focused, articulately armed and so seriously sincere
Exploding power, blasting the deaf to hear
Raging hot with passion,
Cooled by compassionate tears
Muted yellow- orange danger crouches
Before me in fear
Wondering why- why did it take me all these years?
Don't mess with the messenger,
I'm finally here
It took a decade or two for me to see
That life is for living and death 'sho' ain't free
I know this; I believe this
Finally!

And I am the messenger as you can see
Don't mess with the messenger;
Don't mess with me!
~Jaime V. Jones

Judy Sundayo's granddaughter, Rachel, 2014

86

*Friends of the authors', **Rev. Dr. Asha Mawusi Bell**, prayer warrior with **Mrs. Rosa Parks**, "Mother of the Freedom Movement", her refusal to give up her seat on segregated Montgomery, Alabama bus in 1955, sparked **Montgomery Bus Boycott**, resulting in Supreme Court Upholding lower court's decision: segregation of buses was unconstitutional; Photo, circa 1990's, courtesy Dr. Asha Bell*

Survival Gene

We carry the survival gene
From the very bones that lie between Africa's coast
And America's shore
The gene of resistance, persistence and more. . .
The determination to fight and learn
How to bust back through that DOOR of NO RETURN!
Bigger and stronger! More resolute!
Creative! Contemplative! We don't give a hoot
Who knows!!! As long as that same blood flows in our veins
Our ancestor's courage is what keeps us sane!
Don't you know. . .
We carry the gene that's survived the lie?
And so, we're tenacious, audacious and fly!
We got the genetics of tougher stuff!
And if you think scratching our symbols in stone
On the DEATH CELL floor wasn't enough
We've survived 336 years
Of the most horrific holocaust inflicted by peers!

(continued)

Survival Gene *(continued)*

But through our great faith, intellect, brute strength
And oh, how many grandmother's prayers and tears???
WE'VE SURVIVED!!!
Though sometimes it might feel like we just
Hanging on by a thread
That thread is 10,000 years of sinew
Wrapped 'round the bones of our dead!
Ain't no way that thread is thin!
It's a gilded cord connecting us to where we've been
So, HOLD ON to that thread that ties us to our roots!
HOLD ON! Imhotep did!
HOLD ON! Queen Hatshepsut did!
HOLD ON! Marcus Garvey did!
Harriett Tubman did! Sojourner Truth did!
Mary McCleod Bethune did!
Malcolm X did! Rosa Parks did! Martin Luther King did!!!
Your parents and grandparents did!
Barack Obama *still does!*
Your UMOJA professors will ALWAYS hold on because
YOU ARE WORTHY of all they do!!!
And WE of the survival gene
HAVE SOMETHING OF WORTH TO HOLD ON TO!
TRUTH, JUSTICE and RIGHTEOUSNESS!!!
The Principle of *MAAT!*
FEED that Sankofa Bird! Say What?
Do you really understand how much strength we got?
In our ancestor's will, we've been left a lot. . .
WISDOM, DISCERNMENT, VISION, BREATH,
INTEGRITY, POSITIVITY and a GUILTLESS REST!!!
THAT'S how it is we have come this far!
I AM, my brothers and sisters *BECAUSE WE ARE!!!*
And *YOU ARE THE BEST* of what we've come to be
The *PRIDE* of our struggle through history
So, remember, and *NEVER, EVER GIVE UP* the day!
'Cause survival is imprinted in your *DNA!*

~Judy Sundayo

Judy Sundayo's maternal Grandmother,
Florence Boston Smith, *McLean, Virginia, circa 1940's*

Grandma's Shoes

Grandma's walkin' shoes
Weren't no wise cute!
But they carried her to church
And gave my Uncle the boot!

They walked through all kinds of weather,
And were sturdy and tough,
They would kick you
Where the sun don't shine
If Grandma said, "Enough!"

Never let the wind defeat her
Dressed her mind against the cold
Step by step she walked the many years
And only the years got old!

Sharp as a tack, Grandma put a shine on those shoes
And they carried her all the way through
Discrimination, integration and that
So-called, post-racial era too!

(continued)

89

Grandma's Shoes *(continued)*

Some would look at Grandma and say,
She's a tough old bird
But I knew my Grandma used to cry
When she didn't think we heard

Been on her feet all day
Lot a cookin' Heap a cleanin'
For someone else's family
If you get my meanin'

But Grandma's shoes just kept her on her feet
With loads of optimism
She visited all who were sick and old
Despite her rheumatism

The thing I remember most 'bout Grandma's shoes
Was when she died,
She left them to me in her will
With a note, saying, "Wear with pride!"

~Judy Sundayo

*Judy Sundayo's maternal great, grandmother, **Eliza Harris** and her Daughter, **Florence Boston Smith**, Judy's grandmother, McLean, Virginia, Circa 1960's*

90

*Judy Sundayo's Father, **Dr. Granville N. Moore**, Graduate, Meharry Medical School; practiced medicine for over 50 years in poorest communities of Washington, D.C; Made house-calls well into his seventies and never turned away a patient; Honored on the Washington, D.C. Heritage Trail; Photo taken circa 1960's*

Dr. Moore

Dr. Moore, husband, father, veteran . . . more

A man devoted in heart to God

Physician healing where the poorest trod

He taught me to pray

In his way

He supported me

In work and play

He acted like a preacher, pious and terse

So he could quote you chapter and verse

And if he thought you needed, God's Daily Word

He'd be sure . . .

You'd have it heard!

(continued)

91

Dr. Moore *(continued)*

My father, stern, serious and gruff,
Could laugh at himself
And if that weren't enough
He could tell a story
That would split your side. . .
Or perhaps a Buffalo Soldier escapade
Embodied with pride

I loved my father for who he became
A man honoring God, family, nation and name

~Judy Sundayo

*Judy Sundayo with her father, **Dr. Granville N. Moore**,
Washington, D.C., circa 2001*

*Judy Sundayo's mother, **Thomasia S. Moore**,*
Washington, D.C., circa 1950

Thomasia

Ooh, ooh, could she sing!
If you ever heard Thomasia sing *'Summertime,'*
You could feel the warm, summer breeze caress your cheek
Now, let me tell you 'bout my mother,
She wasn't meek

Had a look, let me tell you, like to cut through steel
But, she sure could throw down
On a scrumptious meal!
Taytahs and salad and chicken fried
Pickles and tickles and kisses on the side!

Thomasia was something!
A beauty like none
But didn't nobody mess with her; she packed a gun!

(continued)

Thomasia *(continued)*

Ooh, and she would tell you 'bout yo'self
If you didn't come correct!
She put the "S" in S-C-A-R-Y
And the "T" in R-E-S-P-E-C-T!

Naw, you didn't tell Thomasia nothin'
She knew her stuff!
She had the best of hearts,
But, was tougher than tough

She made me believe I could do anything
Swim, write, ice skate; get my Ph.D.!
But not without her warning,
"Don't be getting too big for your britches!"
So, she taught me to laugh!
In fact, she kept me in stitches!

At times, she was prim, proper and kind
Of that there is no doubt
But the very next minute, you better watch it!
She just might curse you out!

I loved my mother for her puzzling ways,
She lived her life free-style all her days
She was soft as cotton yet hard as rocks!
My mother was an amazing paradox!
~Judy Sundayo

Three Generations: Judy Sundayo's mother, **Thomasia Moore***,*
Judy's daughter, Aurora and Judy at Family Reunion, Virginia 1999

94

*Jaime V. Jones' sister, **Marilynn R. Jones-Sims**,*
As a child, Coronado, California, circa 1949

Everything Happens for a Reason

Everything happens for a reason
or so they used to say
But this can be hard to remember
especially on those nerve
racking, spine tingly, upsetting, challenging days
When things don't turn out right,
turn out your way
Stop!
Reflect, you are headed for greatness;
short detour, short delay
Everything happens for a reason
God help us we pray

(continued)

95

Everything Happens for a Reason *(continued)*

Everything happens for a reason Ms. O
likes to say
"God, has a bigger dream for you
than you can dream coming one day"
When life's got you all hemmed up
and try as you may
You're no Houdini, afraid?
Yell at fear to get out of the way!

~Jaime V. Jones

*Jaime V. Jones' sister, **Marilyn R. Jones-Sims**,*
as a baby, Coronado, California, Circa 1949

*Alyce Smith Cooper and **Diane Drummer**,*
San Diego, California

Sister Woman

No blood bond here
Except the blood of the people
Running through battered battling loving bodies
No family resemblance
Except for skin, hair, nose, feet
All speak to blackness
The family of multicolored skins
Many faceted personalities
Some flawed; many whole

Roots grow through time, space, water, earth
To the rich verdant mother Africa
Sister woman
Mistress/master of your corner of life
My blessings to you
(continued)

Sister Woman *(continued)*

Continue your research
Your mission, your growth
With each step of your feet
Each spot of ground watered by your tears
Every word of rebuke or touch of tenderness
You make my life more

Then I too, can replenish the streams of life
By touching. . .
Brother man
Sister girl
Brother baby. . . who is born of
Sister woman

~Alyce Smith Cooper

Opalanga D. Pugh, *world-renowned storyteller*
With Alyce Smith Cooper

*The authors' friend, **Dr. JoAnne Cornwell**, Associate Professor, Africana Studies & French, San Diego State University; Founder of **Sisterlocks**, a sassy, contemporary, natural style for the tightly curled hair of African American women; JoAnne is also a successful businesswoman; CEO of the Sisterlocks Company; Executive Trainer and Coordinator of the Internationally renowned Annual Sisterlocks Conference; Photo courtesy of Dr. Cornwell, San Diego, California*
www.sisterlocks.com

The African American Woman's Diary

We watched the sunrise over the Nile
Breathed in the fresh morning air
And bathed in peace
Then, sat a while 'till our children
Awoke from sleep

We stood stiffly on the auction block
Cold and shivering and watched
Our children being sold off
One after another

(continued)

99

The African American Woman's Diary
(continued)

We held on dearly, trying to
Close our ears and hearts to their cries
But, to no avail
A strong man of foul odor pried us apart
We felt a blow; knees buckled
All went dark; that's all we know
There's a hard crust over part of our heart
On account of it

We picked cotton 'till our fingers bled
At night we were raped upon our bed
Never enough clothes to keep us warm
Or food to fill our bellies
We cooked, cleaned, scrubbed, swept and mended
We washed, dried, ironed, folded and befriended
No one

*Friends of the authors' the Honorable **Dr. Shirley Weber**, Assemblywoman, 79th District, California State Assembly; formerly Professor & Africana Studies Dept. Chairperson, San Diego State University; Educator and Advocate for Civil Rights & Community Empowerment; http://asmdc.org/members/a79/*

(continued)

The African American Woman's Diary
(continued)

*Friends of the authors' **Dr. Carolle Jean-Murat**, an Intuitive Healer,*
With years of training and experience as a physician with Board Certifications in
Obstetrics and gynecology; Clinical instructor (15 yrs.) UCSD School of Medicine;
San Diego Book Award for "Staying Healthy: 10 Easy Steps for Women;" USA
*Today's Finalist: Best Memoir for **"Voodoo in My Blood: A Healer's Journey from***
***Surgeon to Shaman;"** Founder of Health Through Communications Foundation*
Providing health care access to the underserved in the U.S., Haiti and the world;
http://www.healththroughcommunications.org/index.html
Founder, Dr. Carolle's Wellness & Retreat Center of San Diego, a place where
Women can find "True Healing" from physical, emotional and spiritual dis-ease
http://www.drcarolle.com/

It wasn't safe and besides
One more loss would tear out our insides
We suckled, changed, tidied and raised
Everybody's children but were kept from our own
Fear and self-loathing
Into the fabric of our lives was sewn
Whip and chain and noose were there to keep us in line

(continued)

The African American Woman's Diary
(continued)

And if we ever even began to think we were somebody
Centuries of racist lies were there to change our mind
Fed the worst of the hog and scraps of garbage
What we could grow or what little we could find
Three centuries of this was done to us
To beat us down and yet we resisted
And we persisted to keep our crown
We drank from the water fountain marked,
"Colored Only"
We stepped off the sidewalk when whites were
Coming, unless we wanted to get pushed off,
Spat upon, and called the N word
Or worse

*Long-time friends of the authors' **Starla Lewis**, Retired Professor,
Black Studies Department, San Diego Mesa College; dynamic motivational
Speaker; educator, life coach, seminar facilitator in the areas of Cultural Diversity,
Life Mastery and Human Potential; Seven-time recipient, Teacher of the Year
Award, Mesa College; 2015 Inductee into the San Diego Women's Hall of Fame;
Author of **"Sunkisses"** a Multicultural, Multilingual Coloring Book, ISBN-13:
9780982243206*

(continued)

The African American Woman's Diary
(continued)

Friends of the authors' **Gennene Wilburn**, *Founder of* **Mpoweru***;*
Life and Business Coach, Public Speaker, Author, Poet, Visual Artist,
San Diego, California
https://www.Mpoweru2.com
Owner and Designer for Ne-Ne's Collectibles Cards & Gifts
https://www.facebook.com/Nenescollectibles

We endured insults and beatings
And as cute as we thought our little bonnets were
We colored women, were also lynched
A sad testament to the hatred and evil
Our heads twisted permanently to one side
As if questioning why?

We sat at lunch counters
Where we were refused service
We stood in lines at courthouses
Where we were refused the right to vote
We marched and picketed and sang
And sat down and prayed for change to come
And before it did come
We were clubbed and hosed down and beaten
And bitten by angry dogs

(continued)

The African American Woman's Diary
(continued)

We buried our children and our husbands
(When we could find what was left of their bodies)
We cursed and cried and died
A thousand deaths before we saw any change come
And slowly, too slowly, hard-won battles
Resulted in some change

Now, we remind ourselves
Of all that happened before
We contrast the overt acts of racism in the past
To the covert slights and micro-aggressions of today
We compare the overt acts of racism in the past
To the blatant acts of murder today
Justified by a badge

Lydia Fort, *Executive Artistic Director* **Mo'olelo Performing Arts Company,**
San Diego California; Directed Theatrical Productions for Women's Project Theatre,
Women Center Stage, Urban Stages, FreeFall Theatre, Classical Theatre of Harlem,
Planet Connections Festivity (where she received the 2013 Best Director and
Greener Planet Awards); for theatre information, see http://moolelo.net/

(continued)

The African American Woman's Diary
(continued)

*Long-time friend of the authors' **Dr. Vickie Butcher**,*
*Co-Founder & Executive Director of **Water for Children Africa**,*
a non-profit dedicated to providing clean water and sanitation
to the poorest of children in African villages many have forgotten
http://www.waterforchildrenafrica.org/

In this day and age
Our children wag their heads at us
Wondering when we'll close that
"Old slavery door"
Well ever since I went through the
"Door of No Return" on African soil
I *refuse* to forget
Three hundred years of backbreaking toil
FOR NO PAY, by the way
But many of our children think,
"After all, racism is in the past, isn't it?"
"Come on, you've really GOT to move on!"
This is what the young think and say
And it's true, there has been progress
In freedom to learn; in movement and travel,
In being able to vote, *(most of the time!)*

(continued)

The African American Woman's Diary

(continued)

In where we live and what we drive
It's clear we do more than just pick cotton these days
Maybe our fingers don't bleed as much anymore,
but our hearts do
We might be doctors, lawyers, teachers and judges
Film-makers and musicians; writers and poets
But too many of us, still don't have jobs at all
We might be in the military and in other
Branches of the government
And in corporate boardrooms
But not in the right ratios
Our unemployment is still twice as high
As that of our white counterparts
Our income and education levels are still far behind
In fact, we are three hundred years behind in this race
And they say affirmative action is unfair?
Give me a break!

Dr. Ida Greene, *Inspirational Presenter, Facilitator,*
Love and Relationship Coach, specializing in Marriage & Family
*Therapy; Author of **"Looking for Love in All the Wrong Places"***
Self-Love Coach at Journey to Self-Love Workshops & Retreats
http://www.idagreene.com
http://www.journeytoselflove.com

(continued)

The African American Woman's Diary

(continued)

*Judy Sundayo's friend and colleague, **Dr. Tanis Starck**,*
Assistant Dean for Special Projects, College of Education, San Diego State
University; former Director SDSU Office of Intercultural Relations; former dancer
with Alvin Ailey Dance Troupe; professor, poet, advocate for social justice, and
*Author of, **"And Her Name Was Katrina: Life After the Storm"***
tstarck@mail.sdsu.edu

Everybody knows you adjust a footrace
For the unfair advantage of the uneven track
But in a racist world, that would be called unfair
No matter how many centuries we were victimized
Blacks have seemingly been sentenced permanently
To the outside track
Racism is still alive and we still struggle for sure
Just ask President Obama and the First Family
How much they endure

And we don't want our children to ever forget
We've fought too long and hard
To earn respect

(continued)

The African American Woman's Diary
(continued)

Black women
We're a conglomerate
Of infinite possibilities
Though our past gives us strength
And cause for pause
With God
We're co-creators
Of our own destinies

~Judy Sundayo

*Long-time friend of the authors' **Dr. Dorothy Smith**,*
first African American Woman elected to public office in San Diego, 1981, to the
***San Diego County Schools Board of Education**; Served as President of the Board of*
Education twice; during her tenure, helped establish core curriculum program,
equity in student placement, and a Policy for Gifted and Talented Assessment
*providing all students regardless of race or color access; Awarded **Distinguished***
***School Boards Award** by U.S. Secretary of Education; Continued her distinguished*
career as a Professor for the San Diego Community College District until her
retirement; Wife of Dr. Car L. Smith; Grandmother of Loren Lott

*Judy Sundayo's friend and colleague, **Professor Thekima Mayasa**, Chair of the Black Studies Department, San Diego Mesa College, with **Dr. Runoko Rashidi**, acclaimed historian, author, speaker, activist, and African Studies Scholar; author of many titles, including **"African Star over Asia: The Black Presence in the East"** Photo taken in San Diego, 2014*
www.runokorashidi.com

Orange the New BLACK

Powers and principalities in high places intending to enslave
Broken system no longer justice does it give
No longer intending to correct
But only looking to kill the spirits
Incarcerate the souls and suspend
Creative ascent in to conscious life
Orange the color of prison garb
Intended to replace the black of classic elegance sober achievement
Scholarship or holy attainment
The substance from which creativity Is born
WRONG THEY CHOSE WRONG

(continued)

109

Orange the New Black *(continued)*

Orange is the sacred color of WISDOM KNOWLEDGE
CONSCIOUSNESS ABUNDANT
ORANGE IS THE COLOR OF HOLY FLAME
Coming in to incinerate all unrighteousness to transform
injustice into harmony to turn misguided energy into the
power of peace
How else will the children learn to live lives of dynamic love
which snatches peace out of a fiery furnace and seals the
lion's gaping jaws
Orange is the victory banner the transformation FROM
darkness INTO the MARVELOUS LIGHT.

~Alyce Smith Cooper

Min. Tukufu Kalonji, *long-standing friend of the authors;*
Community Activist, teacher, supporter of African American traditions,
Founder & Kasisi: Kawaida African Ministries; San Diego, California

*The authors' friends, **Denise Giuisti-Bradford (Adande' Imashima Ra**), one of the original elders in the Rites of Passage Program for African American Girls; with her husband, **Duane Bradford (Baye Kichwa**), Founder of the Boyhood to Manhood Program in San Diego, Former, long-standing President of the SD Pan African Association of America and Initiator of the Commemoration of **Nakumbuka Day** (The Day of Remembrance) of **The Maafa,** (The African Holocaust) in the United States, pictured here with their son **Qamar**, at Duane's Graduation from San Diego State University, with his Master of Science Degree in Rehabilitation Counseling*
www.**nakumbuka**.org/history.html
http://www.africanholocaust.net/html_ah/holocaustspecial.htm

I Remember

(To be read each year on Nakumbuka Day)
I remember the days were warm
The sun's caress was home
The sounds of friends and family
Meant no one was ever alone

I remember the day the strangers came
And brutally took us away
The screams and cries
That filled my ears
The blows that made me sway

I remember arriving at a house of stones
A dark and airless place
I recall the pain that racked my bones
The look on a dead child's face

(continued)

111

I remember *(continued)*

I remember the deadly stench
That filled my nostrils as I breathed
The waste, the inhumanity
My hunger all dry-heaved

The oh, too dizzying sadness, the rape of little girls
The months of shivering madness
As our bodies with sickness hurled

I remember the day we were marched to our deaths
Through the door of no return
May the sea be my grave I prayed to the gods
But another hell we would learn

A dark and dank and smelly beast of a ship
Had swallowed us whole
A churning, heaving living death
That shook us wave and roll

For months again our senses lost
My mother's arms I missed
Heaped one upon the other we were
What kind of a captor was this?

Perhaps these strangers were not men at all
But creatures with whip and gun
We writhed in pain and begged for mercy
But of mercy, there was none

I remember the daily ritual
Of tossing the dead overboard
To the thousands of sharks that followed the ship
For their feeding was assured

I think it was the ancestors
Who must have heard our cry
For after an eternity we were blessed to see the sky

(continued)

I remember (continued)

I wanted to shed tears of joy, but alas my flesh was dry
The air was fresh, but my throat was parched
I gasped like one drowning in lye

Our captors did not slow down for us
Though our limbs barely worked and were bare
The heavy chains clanged and cut our flesh
But our captors did not care

In this pitiful condition
We dragged ourselves slowly onto shore
And, finally under merciful rains
Was God's libation poured!

Then fiendish hell, they put us all upon an auction block
And sold us, every man, woman and child
Like so much animal stock

Whipped, beaten, starved and stranded
Our homeland nowhere in sight
Chained, maimed, burned and branded
Still many put up a brave fight

For 336 years, I remember,
We endured unspeakable pain
From sun up to sun down in back-breaking labor
For our so-called master's gain

While our women were traded
And raped and sold, and our children were shipped far away
Men, women & children were worked near death
To survive was our mission each day

Forbidden to learn how to read or to write
Under threat of death we would hide
So we messaged each other with song and drum
I remember, though enslaved, we had pride

(continued)

I Remember *(continued)*

The Emancipation of '62
Said we would soon be free
But the news was kept from us
Because of economic utility

And then in 1863 this freedom
Was *supposed* to start
But it wasn't till Juneteenth in '65
We were finally allowed to depart

They said they'd give to each of us forty acres
And a mule for our pain
But we ain't seen a hair on a mule's ass since
Our captors kept all our gain

Freedom's a curious commodity
Though our chains we cannot see
Do racism, unemployment, poverty and drugs
Still, chain us --- mentally?

The slave trade was a crime of racist greed
12 million died at a minimum
Though apologies are fine, we still need justice to repair the
damage done
And so, I say . . . "Nakumbuka!" ***I remember!***
What else can I do?
I think of all my innocent ancestors
Who never made it through

I remember, "Nakumbuka!"
And I swear, I'll repay this debt
To those ancestors who went through a living hell
"Nakumbuka!"
I'll never forget!

~Judy Sundayo

Alyce Smith Cooper's great, granddaughter,
Lisa Jayda Mungo *with her trophy after All-Star Basketball Game*
At Encanto Recreation Center, standing next to her tall cousin,
Theresa Janea Thomas, *High School Basketball Coach,*
February 2015

Code Switch

Multi lingual, Multi cultural
Doing it all at once, creating as you go
Most of you genius children
Don't even know when and what you are doing
Or how you Impact your world
Your words, your swag are heard, seen, co-opted,
Then sold back to you on the Internet
Before you sleep that night
You are keenly studied by deception

(continued)

Code Switch *(continued)*

Told *you* are the enemy . . . the ones we should fear
When all the manipulators
Are raking in profit from your time in Plantation jails
From the higher interest you pay
From the low Paying jobs you must accept
Because you spent time in the Plantation jails
WAKE UP MY YOUTH
YOU THE MAKERS OF THE CODE, THE CREATORS OF THE SWAG
SWITCH CODE
CHANGE TO THE WINNING SIDE, JOIN THE ARMY OF LIGHT
Turn the dark shadows of doubting, your creativity
Into mounts and founts of Wisdom flowing in your veins
Nothing new under the sun; you have
ALWAYS BEEN VISIONARIES
VIDEO YOUR VISION, PLAY IT ON YOUR MIND SCREEN
Soften your heart to receive from your heart
The wisdom of the elders; turn to the I AM GOD within
CODE SWITCH.

~Alyce Smith Cooper

Alyce Smith Cooper teaching youth, Bennett College,
Greensboro, North Carolina, 2006

Alyce Smith Cooper and her grandson, DeEdward

13 Steps to Survival from Police Encounter

You are in a tight spot police have pulled you over
Use the wisdom given by GOD
WALK IN THE LIGHT

Use your spiritual gifts first:
1) Take a deep breath - pray to GOD FOR PROTECTION
2) Take a deep breath - see yourself in a bubble of light
3) Take a deep breath - know that GOD is with you

4) Be polite be respectful
5) Keep your hands in sight not in your pockets
6) Take a deep breath - banish fear
DO NOT RUN

(continued)

13 Steps to Survival from Police Encounter *(continued)*

7) DO NOT ARGUE - keep your mouth closed
Anything you say can be used against you -
Curb the desire to defend yourself
8) Take a deep breath
Claim the calm!

9) Avoid physical contact with the police –
YOUR GOAL? - GET HOME SAFELY
10) In calmness watch your tone of voice
Your body language facial expressions
11) KEEP YOUR HANDS IN PLANE SIGHT

12) Remember you belong to GOD~
SO LET HIM DO YOUR BATTLES,
Say nothing without legal representation
IT IS YOUR RIGHT!

Take the deep breath of wisdom
13) DO NOT RESIST ARREST!
Take a deep breath

Conquer your fears!
Stay alive - you are ALIVE!
Give GOD SOME PRAISE!
Live on to give your testimony as to
How you got over!

~Alyce Smith Cooper

Alyce Smith Cooper's grandchildren
And great granddaughter

Lessons

Life ain't nothing but a school
Every year a grade, every experience a lesson
Like we don't get our full body growth till 25 or 26
Our spirit hits its peak at just about 40
(Plus or minus five pendin')
Death is graduation
Between the beginning and the end are lessons
Which one are you working on in this
Correspondence Course – called Life?
Is it the one about thinking the world
Owes you something 'cause you got a gift?
The test for moving on is when you realize
You must work, and work hard. . .
To have the privilege to use your gifts
Oh yes, there are many lessons
Just ask me and I'll tell you more. . .

~Alyce Smith Cooper

119

Insidious

Insidious knows
But won't say a word

Oh, sorry, what?
You haven't heard?

This whole matter is undercover
Like a lover
With a secret he won't reveal
So sneaky and plotting
You don't know what's real

Insidious is . . .
Irritating!

I *would* throw a fit!

If for all my objections
The glove didn't fit!

~*Judy Sundayo*

Judy Sundayo, with that "Who told you, you could take
that picture of me doing laundry?" look, La Jolla California, 1996

Alyce Smith Cooper, San Diego, California

Gold Ankh on Purple Silk

A RED "S" on a skin tight T-shirt
Could never tell the accurate tale
Of the superior power
The average Sister carries in her breast
In her heart fueled by incredible intellect
not to mention Mother Wit
From the Sister balancing food stamps section 8
children's homework vaccination schedules
Did she get the Father's day card?
Does she have stockings for church?
did she make the PTA committee calls?
is the phone bill paid?

(continued)

Gold Ankh on Purple Silk *(continued*

Are the baby's shoes too small?
To the Sister living in the WHITE HOUSE
making choices and decisions for her family
and decisions that affect families all over the world
for generations

Will they eat foods to help them grow strong
will they read literature to polish their intellects can they live
in safety not fearing abuse
or being sold into bondage?
From one spectrum's end to the other
the SISTER's deserve
A Royal Cloak of PURPLE SILK
on which a GOLDEN ANKH is emblazoned
to trail in the wind in the wake of the power
they each exhibit daily

As they tend to their portion of the garden
care for the souls in their baskets
watch for the bargains of the day
A RED "S" stands for Super
The GOLD ANKH on PURLPE SILK stands for
SUPERIOR MOTHER FANTASTIC WOMAN!
We shall celebrate her/us
and be celebrated.

~Alyce Smith Cooper

Renowned cross-cultural educator, facilitator and presenter,
Dennard Clendenin, *Judy Sundayo's brother by another mother,*
Re-enacting a Buffalo Soldier, San Diego, California
http://www.apbspeakers.com/speaker/dennard-clendenin

That Much Stronger
(Statement at the closing of an event)

We've been blessed with words of wisdom
Peace and love will guide our steps
We've been reminded of the Presence
That blesses us with every breath

And we know it's about family
From the unborn to the babies
From our sons strivings to be men
And our daughters to be ladies

From our uncles and our aunties
To our greats and our grans
From our mothers and our fathers
We are all of one great clan

Thus, our ancestors, we've honored
That our days on earth be longer,
For we know what hasn't killed us yet
Has made us that much stronger!

~Judy Sundayo

Palate Cleanser

Rev. Alyce Smith Cooper, San Diego, California

Lemon Sorbet

Piquant puckering lips
Pausing to pursue the entrance
Of the next course
Sour sweet smooth cold
Savory savored spicy
Sauce from the pasta
Just reached my hips

~Alyce Smith Cooper

File' or Okra?

Photo by Peonia, morguefile.com

Don't let another second pass
Grab some leaves of Sassafras
Hang them, dry them; grind them up
In a bowl or in a cup
Spicy it will be today, this thickener they call filé*
Or maybe you are from the south
Where okra is what tempts your mouth
This veggie is also very nice, oh, which to choose?
Oh what the price? Filé and okra both thicken the plot
This is GUMB, baby, throw 'em both in the pot!
~Judy Sundayo

Although roux thickens GUMBO, many cooks will still add filé *or* okra to the pot, because they both make the dish more flavorful. Of the three thickeners, roux, filé and okra, most cooks almost always use two in their GUMBO. It is almost a given for *all* GUMBO recipes to include roux. Most will also add okra *(especially when it is in season)* but some will use filé instead of okra. Some chefs frown on using all three. However, this is GUMBO; who says you can't have it all? But be prepared! If you use roux, okra *and* filé, your GUMBO will be very thick! If you like it that way, we say, "Go for it!"

*(Usually pronounced "fee-LAY," however in some parts of Louisiana, don't be surprised if you hear it called "FIGH-yay")

125

GUMBO Recipe Step 3:

Filé or Okra?
(That is the question!)

What You Need
- Sassafras Leaves (to make filé from scratch!)
- Coffee Grinder
- Large Stainless Steel Pot with lid or
- Large cast iron skillet

What You Gotta Get
- 10 leaves from a Sassafras tree (to make from scratch) or
- 1 Bottle of Zatarain's Finely Ground GUMBO Filé
- 4 - 6 cups of sliced okra (*sliced in rounds*)
- 3 Tablespoons of oil
- 1 onion
- Salt, pepper, cayenne pepper

What You Do with What You Got
- Obtain approximately 10 leaves from the Sassafras tree and bind together with string or rubber bands
- Hang the Sassafras leaf bundle in a dry area inside your house; you don't want too much light to hit the leaves
- Let the leaves dry for at least one week
- Put the leaves in the coffee grinder and grind the leaves until you obtain a find green powder; this is filé powder!
- You should store the filé in an airtight container preferably glass.
- Keep in a cool, dark place until you are ready to add the filé to your GUMBO just before serving.

- Add the filé ONLY after the GUMBO is ready to be served. DO NOT COOK THE FILÉ! If you do your GUMBO will become unpleasantly stringy OR—If you are using OKRA- - -

- Place sliced okra in a covered stainless steel pot
- Add 3 Tablespoons of oil
- Cook down on medium heat
- Chop 1 onion (fine) and add to the okra
- Stir
- Cook until the okra is de-slimed (or as some call it, de-roped), about 10-15 minutes
- Add salt, pepper and cayenne pepper
- Set aside
- Add okra to the GUMBO pot when you are about 20-30 minutes away from serving. Some chefs like to add the de-slimed okra just after the other vegetables (*see Holy Trinity*) are added to the roux. This is completely acceptable as it will give the okra more time to get acquainted with the other veggies and spices!
- Others add okra to GUMBO simultaneously with the seafood, about 10-15 minutes before serving. As long as the okra has been pre-cooked and de-slimed, it's really your call. Those who add the okra later notice that the okra holds its green color a little better for presentation in the final dish.

What You Bet Not Tell Nobody

- Instead of adding filé to the actual GUMBO pot, savvy cooks add the filé powder directly to the individual bowls of GUMBO when it is about to be served. In this way, cooks are assured that the filé will NOT COOK in the GUMBO pot that day or the next if it is re-heated for leftovers!

- You can usually find filé powder in stores that cater to gourmet cooks or you can order it online
- Zatarain's Pure Ground GUMBO Filé Seasoning is well regarded by most GUMBO enthusiasts! So, is Tony Chachere's Creole GUMBO Filé!
- The reason your filé powder may have the aroma of root beer is because root beer, like filé is made from the Sassafras tree!
- Just before cooking (whether sautéing or boiling) your okra, try soaking it in a mixture made from 1 cup of vinegar *(either apple cider vinegar or white distilled vinegar)* and 1 quart of water for 1 hour. Then drain and dry completely by patting down with a paper towel. The acidity will help de-slime the okra more effectively.
- Just before cooking the okra, add 1 teaspoon of lemon juice or lime juice to the okra. This will also help de-slime the okra more effectively.
- Alternatively, you may sauté your sliced okra on high heat, stirring constantly for about 20 minutes. This will also cut down on the sliminess.
- Some chefs boil their sliced okra on high heat for several minutes to de-slim and prepare to add it to the GUMBO pot. Experiment and then you decide!
- When purchasing your okra, choose the smaller, okra pods, which are firm, yet tender to the touch. Then, cut the stem off just above the ridge. This will also decrease the likelihood of sliminess.
- When slicing the okra, slice in wider rather narrower rounds. This will also cut down on the sliminess.
- Don't add salt to the okra while you are cooking it. Wait until it is cooked or added to the GUMBO pot before seasoning. This will help preventing it from wilting.

Introduction to the Spicy Poems

The dried, ground leaves of the Sassafras tree wonderfully represent the spicy flavor in Gumbo! The Sassafras tree is native to North America and North American Indians often used its leaves. They dried and ground the Sassafras leaves into a fine powder, known as *filé* powder for use in cooking. It was a particularly tasty addition to soups or stews. This is how filé powder came to be an ingredient in the Louisiana culinary dish of GUMBO. Filé has the effect of thickening GUMBO while affording it a wonderful, spicy flavor.

The other wonderful ingredient in GUMBO, which adds thickening, is the vegetable, okra. Okra was a staple vegetable of inhabitants of nations on the West Coast of Africa. Over three hundred years of enslavement did not deter Africans in the Americas from cooking their beloved okra. Although okra itself is not a spicy foodstuff, it has the wonderful capacity to absorb all the spices in which it is cooked.

The poems in this section have to do with facets of our natural world, which add spice to our lives. These include, but are not limited to food, animals, produce, our health, the moon, the stars and the seasons. *The Spicy* also has to do with our reflection on these things and what we ourselves create to "spice" up our lives. This includes music, art, dance, literature, construction and politics. As filé and okra give substance to GUMBO, so the earth and our talents give substance e to our existence. Think about what *thickens the plot of your existence*. Then, enjoy the poems in this section that exude that special spice!

Judy Sundayo at The Koala Sanctuary,
Brisbane, Australia, circa 1990's

Spicy

Lawd, you knows
You done seasoned dis here pot!
Of all dere is ta git, I done got a lot!
De rich herb o' health
You done added a good po'tion
Fo' ta keep deeze po' ole bones in motion
I seed ya stirred in some a dat red hot peppa'
So, on de dance flo' look out!
I gone be de high steppa'
Den, had ta calm me down a bit
Wid some a dat settle-down spice
Ta make me kinda cord'l n nice
My man he say, "Baby, you sho' is sweet!"
Das nothin' but yo' blessings Lawd
Dat done flava'd dis heah meat
Come hard times, come pain or come misery
De flava' o' dis gumbo done took a hole o' me
Till I *know* I ain't no wise
Gone be no fretta'
'Cause dis life you done give me, Lawd,
Jus' couldn't be betta!
~Judy Sundayo

131

Of Morality

Me took it to be vigilance
That manifest me ways. . .
Me thought it was a gilded path
Morality had lain
In treading it with diligence
Alas, me took a fall!
Surprised to find those precious stones
Were not of gold at all!

~Judy Sundayo

Philoso - Ku: Daytime

Daytime
Never comes
Unless it's time
Its time, Daytime!

~Judy Sundayo

Philoso - Ku: Moon

Moon,
A dove's breast
Holding Life!

~Judy Sundayo

Judy Sundayo, California, circa 1990's

Jaime V. Jones, in production mode, California

Welcome To San Diego

San Diego sunshine; silver streaks
Loudly laughing liquid gold; platinum peeks
Rainbow colored smiles; God speaks
Clouds sprinkling and spreading love beyond reach
Welcome to San Diego,
from her oceans to her creeks
Sunrise sneaks in oranges and yellow
All during the week
San Diego, where love, joy, peace
and people meet
Sun light warm, inviting us down to the beach
Rainbows of people, walk, work,
and sing in the streets
Welcome to San Diego;
the weather can't be beat!

(continued)

Welcome To San Diego *(continued)*

Star-studded, spangled sunsets, oh my,
Want a treat?
Evening fireworks and hot popcorn free;
better find a seat

Beneath San Diego's blue velvet star lit skies, Yeah sweet!
Sunsets fabulous, magnificent,
The absolute best, I repeat
Welcome to San Diego's renowned resorts
And retreats
San Diego sunshine, get up! Got to get a peek!
Sunrise up early, headed for the beach
Sunset, love, joy and peace;
Come dance in the streets!
Beautiful people from EVERYWHERE,
Food, festivities unique
Welcome to San Diego,
Sit and stay a while, my sweet!

~Jaime V. Jones

Judy Sundayo's son, Hasar, La Jolla, California

*Long-time friend of the authors' **Rev. George Walker Smith,***
First African American to hold public office in San Diego, when elected to San
Diego County School Board, 1963; Served 4 terms until 1979 (7 times serving as
president); During his tenure initiated change in Board Elections to a districting
process to give greater representation to Black and Latino residents; helped bring
into operation Magnet Programs toward equal opportunities for all students;
increased inclusion in employment by hiring over 800 African American & Latino
teachers; Former member of White House Conference on Children & Youth, the
White House Committee on Education & the Arts; Co-founded the Coalition for
*Equality which provided forums to address discrimination; Pastor of **Christ United***
***Presbyterian Church,** 1956 until retirement in 2000; Founder of **The Catfish Club,** a*
place where concerned citizens meet weekly to lunch together while discussing
matters of social and political import
http://www.catfishclub.net/

The Catfish Club

It happens in the presence of food
and good company
Elders proliferate
as the relatively young lean in
hungry to learn
Everyone savors the appetizing vibes
(continued)

The Catfish Club *(continued)*

Conversations compete with the main course,
fried catfish and just as crusty social issues
Corn on the cob coming in just ahead
of the hot topic of schools
Who needs buttering up?
What are the rules to make this work?

Potato salad and politics
Just a little more pepper please!
Who's running for what?

Big wigs, humble, speaking in whispers
Little wigs, speaking without restraint
Who's working where?
The soulful sharing over soup
Who's in charge of what?

Neighborly networking over greens and cornbread
How are we going to make this happen?
Many a commitment
Made over the peach cobbler

The good Reverend George Walker Smith
A staple
Keeping it all together
From grace to grits to grateful friends

How does a community work together?
One bite at a time
at The Catfish Club
Hands down,
the best Catch of the Day!

~Judy Sundayo

136

Judy Sundayo's grandchildren, Rachel and Alex with
*Paternal grandfather, **John Chedester**, London, Kentucky, 2013*

Kitchen Etiquette for Life

Wash everything! That's first things first!
You've got to be as clean as a nurse!
Then, get prepared and choose your tools
God did *not* make a kitchen for fools!

Set out your bowl and sharpen your knife!
'Cause you're gonna be doing some cookin'
In this life!

Better know what you're making
Lay out the best plans
Collect your ingredients
Then your pots and your pans!

Begin with purpose; one step at a time
Life's not *just* about eating; but how best to dine!
When your preparation's done, bring on the heat
Then, braise, boil, simmer, or sauté the meat

Prepare your veggies, some raw in a salad
Then steam the rest and season to palate!
Preheat the oven with the timer set
It's safety first, so don't forget!

(continued)

137

Kitchen Etiquette for Life *(continued)*

It's the same in life! First purify!
Cleanse your heart and mind,
So you'll know why
God put you in this kitchen in the first place
It certainly wasn't to scorch his Grace
Or moan and complain or stir up strife
But to cook up a deliciously righteous life!

Our friends are helpmates,
So, select the best
They'll help you clean up
The worst kitchen mess!

You need a recipe?
The Good Book has a lot!
You have a dream? Just throw it in the pot!
But don't forget to stir in clarity
And before you're done,
Add love, hope and charity!

For love is the comfort food that heals
Hope sprinkles joy on all our meals!
Then long before your charity starts showing
Decide what you'll need to get where you're going!

What pan will you need to simmer your sanity?
What pot will be big enough to boil your vanity?
What kind of experiences will you bake in your oven?
And what's in a mate-cake, *besides* good lovin?

Live and cook simply is my suggestion!
For arrogance brings the worst indigestion!
Then season each serving with lots of laughter!
And enjoy this meal of life happily ever after!

~Judy Sundayo

Judy Sundayo with dear friends, **Dr. Philip Raphael,** *past president of the San Diego Association of Black Psychologists, Judy's sister of another mother,* **Carolyn Graham** *(right) and co-author,* **Jaime Jones,** *San Diego, California, 2012*

Gumbo Be Like De Life

Gumbo be like de life chile
Every'ting in deah
Cooked in tagedda'
Spicy, sour, bitta', sweet. .
Salty, sav'ry, sacred eats!
Bes ting . . .?
You neva gotta ax
Where de' meat?
It all up in deah
Mo den enuf
Wid all kines a udda stuff
Mixed in tagedda'
So now, chile,
Das it 'bout de Gumbo
An' ain't no need ta fret
'cause ya ain't learned nuttin'
If it ain't bin et
So now dat I said it
You done bin tole
So bes' sit right down heah
An' hav ya'self a bowl!

~Judy Sundayo

Lady Lettuce

Frilly, dainty, of her is spoken,
Romaine, Red Leaf, Iceberg, Endive,
Lady Lettuce convenes all her friends
Roberta Radish, Shirley Celery, Cora Carrot,
Polly Parsley, Pricilla Peppers, Tommy Tomato
And Ollie Onion
Invites them to come and bathe in the kitchen sink
Offers them a towel to dry off
Convinces them to let her introduce them
To her salad bowl.
"Don't be afraid" she says
"Jump right in!"
After a spicy splash of lemon juice,
Balsamic vinegar, a slather of olive oil,
You will find us a colorful array
Of healthy mouthfuls
Lady Lettuce opens the door to
Agnes Almond's knock
She enters into the health-producing rainbow of
crinkly, crunchy good to you,
Good for you, salad world
All the friends get to love you at the same time
Don't forget the blessing!

~Alyce Smith Cooper

Alyce Smith Cooper, storytelling session, San Diego, California

Ancestral Conversations on Canvas

Wisdom told with visual grace
Represented by every single trace of truth
To stimulate the memory
Of our ancestral history

Colors rich; dark detail
Every stitch of cloth warms
Each carpenter's nail penetrates
Solemnity holds her head up high to tell the story
Unfolding pride in frames of glory

(continued)

Ancestral Conversations on Canvas *(continued)*

From oppression to freedom to victory
Heralding our heroes and sheroes we see
The canvas come alive

Now they walk among us
In our homes and in our schools
And in books
Giving us the courage, the conviction
And the looks as we hear them say

We KNOW you!
We died for you!
We love you!
Don't ever forget!

~Judy Sundayo

*Judy Sundayo's friend, **Dr. Fern P. Nelson**, a Dermatologist caring for our veterans at the Veterans Administration (VA) San Diego Healthcare System; Founding member of the **Southern California African American Museum of Fine Art**, bringing internationally known ethnic artists to southern California. "Through exploring art, you explore the world." Photo taken in NY, NY 2013*
www.facebook.com/sdaamfa

Judy Sundayo's great, great grandmother **Eliza Harris** *(son), was captured escaping from slavery in Maryland as a girl, with sister, Ophelia; Eliza got away by biting the hand of her would-be captor & spitting out blood as she ran; she never saw her sister Ophelia again; photo taken in Virginia, circa 1800's*

Love Letter to the Earth

Dear Mama Deep Spirit,
You been a holding me in your memory a long time
I 'preciate it; I done learned a lot from you
How to be patient and loving
Even with those what don't deserve it
How to suffer . . . not saying nothing
And how to speak my mind when the time is right
You taught me that I is as beautiful as anything else
What got your spirit and your name an I 'preciate that too
Sometimes when I smell something real nice
Like a flower or the salt in the ocean
I remembers how powerful you is
And how much you done give me
And I just want to weep I's so grateful
Those times, I just go and hug my grandbaby
And I feels I's just about as close to you as I can get
Anyway, Mama, you been around a long time
I's just a child in your eyes
But I sure do love you and I been asking the good Lord
To bless you and all your children, Love, Liza

~Judy Sundayo

143

Grill Master

Strong hands glisten with marinade
Press, press pressing
Black/tan sesame seeds to
Encrust the Ahi
Perfect temperature 3.5 minutes on each side
Grill Master lovingly taps lifts turns Ahi
Tends the Zucchini
More love shaken down pressed together
Over flowing
Deftly placed salad greens into awesome
Four cornered Bowls
Invitation to participate given to a friend
Wasabi Cream Fresh
Citrus Vinaigrette fresh cut basil
Petite Fruit Tart
Tea
Punctuated with music
Whisked with laughter
Masterful Grill Master
Has made his mark

~Alyce Smith Cooper

Alyce Smith Cooper, San Diego California

*Friend of the authors' **Manuelita Brown**, award-winning sculptor; San Diego County resident; former educator, Manuelita uses her art to tell stories; best Recognized for her 8 life-sized dolphins "Almas de Mar" permanent fixtures at the Westfield Shopping Center, University Towne Center (UTC) in San Diego, her Bronze bust of Thurgood Marshall at Marshall College on campus at the University of California, San Diego (UCSD), and her bronze sculpture of Triton at UCSD; this photo shows her standing with her sculpture of Sojourner Truth, at Thurgood Marshall College, UCSD; unveiled in January 2015; Photo by Mary Arana www.manuelitabrown.com or http://tsahaistudio.blogspot.com/*

Spirit Speak

Spirit speak
Come alive
Unburden yourself of centuries past
Speak of who you are
At last
Show yourself in every detail
Bronze and beautiful
Yearning to be real
It is we who shall witness
Your essence congeal

(continued)

145

Spirit Speak *(continued)*

May history make room for you
Resurrecting memories from earth
Reminding us, less we forget
Of the importance of your presence past
From the long ago times

Spirit Speak
And without a word
Tell us your story
In sentences of solid stone
Let it not go unnoticed
And neither go un-said for
You *may* have transitioned, but
Your story's not dead

Spirit Speak
Your legend precedes you
And on firm ground sets the foundation
For your new life of smooth countenance
Reflecting the light of our understanding
Spirit Speak
And as you come into your christening
All those who would learn of your truth
Will be listening

~*Judy Sundayo*

Manuelita Brown's sculpture of Matthew Henson
On exhibit at the James E. Lewis Art Museum, Baltimore, Maryland

Jaime V. Jones' mother, **Evelyn Jones** *and sister,*
Marilyn R. Jones-Sims, *San Diego, California*

San Diego Season Silvery Spells

Summer suddenly silently swallows spring
Summer smiles signaling seasonal spells
For marrying things
Stretching, squeezing summer stirs up,
Silver wedding bells rings
Forging fall golden red fiery leaves
Indian summer sings
Air brushed shiny and crisp fall air , chilled just a bit
Sweaters and boots on everybody's list
Sunsets early, evening's emotional summer
And falls final kiss
Long lusty nights fireplaces; fired up and lit
Stars bright full moon matching lovers lips
Stroking, snuggling, sweater wearing humans sit
Fall chasing winter may that never quit

(continued)

San Diego Season Silvery Spells *(continued)*

Fall and winter ice skating recycling
Thoughts of innocents
Fall following wonderful winter, gosh no regrets
Winter showing up, showing out
A foggy masculine mist
Screaming-shoveling snow; who can forget?
Shouting, snowboarding, sleighing and skiing
Who can resist?
Merry Christmas, Happy Holiday
All winter long; I'm loving this!
Winter reminds, rewinds and replays
The moon's final fling
Windows of winter snow melting
Into spring's stormy streams
Silly snow man grins-smiles
And snow angels, winter brings
Winter gives up the dream
Of ever marrying spring
Spring single, sassy, showing off
Wonderful wide wings
Soft silver sterling strong,
Spring speaks without sting

Sprinkles short savory songs, love spiritually sing
Succulent spring showers
Like pearls on a string
Pink and white blossoms skipping
Into summer swiftly swings
Soaring, searching, sipping
Strawberry shakes and things
Strapless sundresses, some diamonds and ice cream?
Sexy, silky, strutting sandal wearing
San Diego summer soulfully sings

~Jaime V. Jones

Alyce Smith Cooper with granddaughter, **Diona**
And great granddaughter, **Lisa Jada,** Bethel A.M.E. Church
San Diego, California, Palm Sunday, 2014

Cruzin to Santana Beat

Freedom from fears
Spun in the darkened anxiety cavern in our chest
Turn on your lights
Powered by the geothermal heart-beats
Of Mother Earth
The purposes of our lives ever unfolding
As we listen to the whispering voices
Of cool gemstones
Mined from the heart and waterways
Of MOTHER EARTH
The majestic musings of FATHER TIME
Breeze by wind burned earlobes

(continued)

149

Cruzin to Santana Beat *(continued)*

Reminding us of mortal existence
Wake up People! Wake up!
Time is changing the faces of everything
Reach in to grab the real stuff
Stuff your memories of truth faith
Your experiences of GOD
Into the infinite estuary
Leading to deep seas
Take your generational photos
On your catamaran of consciousness
Join into the Mambo Rock
Cruzin' with Santana

~Alyce Smith Cooper

*Alyce Smith Cooper with prayer flag in church with **Tey Sa Thiosanne**
West African Dance and Drum Troupe, "Keepers of the Tradition"
A San Diego based non-profit organization providing performances &
Programs in African music and dance;
Bernard "Yiriba" Thomas, Founder, Co-Director & Lead Drummer;
Aminisha Cunningham, Co-Director, Choreographer & Lead Dancer;*
http://teyesathiosanne.org/Teye%20Sa%20Thiosanne.html

*Judy Sundayo's brothers of other mothers, **Dan Baehr** (left) who lives in San Diego, California and **Michael Turner** (right) who lives with wife, Susie and son in Valley Center, California, Photo by Judy Sundayo, Mission Bay in San Diego, 2012*

These My Brothers Be

Black from the good earth, rich in hue, my brother
Ripe from the bright sun, warm in heart, his seed
Where he walk, I be ground kissing his feet
Where he rest, I be moon caressing his temple
Where he play, I be wind molding his laughing cheeks
Where he die, I be earth taking him into me

(continued)

These My Brothers Be *(continued)*

Black from the good earth , our roots reach down
To grasp a heritage of growing freedom
Ripe from the bright sun, our seed of Truth reaches up
To blossom full into heaven's infinity

My brother? Be a seed of love
What leaves the depths of earth behind
To grow into a flower of Truth and rise above
The thorns of mind

My brother? Be a seed of love what take the strength
Of burning sun inside itself to make it grow
And blossom into Love as One
These seeds of Love in Grace abide
Though planted far from me, it matters not the soil,
I know that these, my brothers be

Grown from the good earth, rich in Love, my brother
Ripe, from the brightest Sun, warm in Truth, his seed

When he call, I be glowing Light
What light his way
When he come, I be taste of sweetest nature
Invite him stay
When he listen, I be sound of thousand streams
Rushing to the sea
When he answer, I be ocean of endless Love
Drawing him into me

~Judy Sundayo

Jaime V. Jones and friends, *Aline King* and *Wendy Matulich,*
Christ United Church, San Diego, California, 2012

California Human Gumbo

Splashes of next door multimillionaires
Dashes of California ideas fill the air
Dances of athletic stars in all their glory
Traces of Hollywood and all its stories
Schools and study in Sacramento
Shopping at Rodeo
Splashes of California street people hungry faint
Dashes of slim, healthy, binging overweight
Dances of purple pain and pleasure,
Rarely seems to wait
Parades of California politicians
Parked at the gates
Glances of the San Diego theatre,
Concerts, CD's and tapes

(continued)

California Human Gumbo *(continued)*

Chance of much money California stands to make
Splashes of roses Marilyn Monroe
Dashes of California poppies row after row
California children cheerfully put on a show
Adoring adults applaud then before you know
Dances of California Sequoias big and tall
Traces of available avalanches
of abundance for all
Glances of spiritual skiers wall to wall
Chances for California comfortable life style calls
It is a California Human Gumbo after all!
~Jaime V. Jones

Jaime V. Jones and Judy Sundayo, La Jolla, California

Judy Sundayo with daughter by another mother,
Heaven Leigh Johnson, *La Jolla, California, 2009*

Peacocks

Peacocks, peacocks, in the great parade
Spreading feathers. . .
Stretching necks. . .
Strutting down the glade

Oh, day don't baulk
Just let them walk,
Before their beauty fades!
~Judy Sundayo

Sista' Ku: Roots and Leaves

Roots and leaves
To cure
Dried and ground as a healing lure
A prayer
From bitter potions pour
~Judy Sundayo

Sista' Ku: Bell Peppers

Bell peppers are sweet
And the flavor scintillates
Like a slice of youth
~Judy Sundayo

155

The Picture I Owe

Woman sitting
Leaning forward into the rest of her life
Roses blooming, varied hues of pink and red
Form the backdrop
As my mind snapshots this view
Refusing to be still for man or camera
She moves in deliberate fashion
To create just the right mirrored image
On her personal reality
To set in motion just the right dreams
For the balance of her tomorrows
Woman sitting yet somehow moving forward
Into the rest of her life
I know this woman
She has stepped down from a painting
On the wall of my heart
She is an African woman full of joy
And purposefulness
She is an artist and a poetess
And she has painted a new picture
On the canvas of all that I know

~Judy Sundayo

*Judy Sundayo's paternal aunt, **Esther L. Moore**, cousin, **Betty Ann Freeman**, aunt,*
***Ruth Clifford**, & aunt **Naomi Lancaster**, Peace Baptist Church, Washington, D.C.,*
founded by Judy's Grandfather, Rev. Nathan Moore, at Founders event where
Judy's father, Dr. Granville N. Moore gave keynote address, circa 1960's

*Judy Sundayo's brother of another mother, **Richard Oleksiak** and Dear friend, **Kali Rodriguez**, Long Beach, California, circa 1990's*

Coffee and Danish

The cafe stood against the red-orange sky
Like a sentinel guarding the last great treasure
On earth
It was here, at sunrise
I knew I would find my brother
In a coffee shop, smiling and sipping
A steaming hot brew
"What is the meaning of a Danish dessert?" I asked
"It's a delicious delight, like life," he said,
"Sweet, delectable and fattening!"
"And, coffee?" I queried.
"Something startling, like death!" he replied.
"Hot, pungent and bitter! The eternal paradox,
The unity of opposites,
A startling and sugarcoated symmetry
Masquerading as a great breakfast!"

(continued)

Coffee and Danish *(continued)*

I chuckled warily
As I watched my brother down the last of his so-called
Life, washing it down with what he had so casually referred to
As a hot, pungent demise
Seeing my uneasiness,
He sat me down on a barstool
And spun me around
"Little sister," he said, "Life is both sweet and bitter
It's ice-cream cones and the bitter herbs
Which cure the stomachaches they cause
It's the sweet, cooing babies
And their great, great grandmothers
Who don't have the strength to pick them up anymore
The unity of opposites
One extreme helps define and give meaning to the other!
It's all about balance
And you and I are in balance, too, little sister!"
"How so?" I asked.
"All of us half-crazed, coffee-drinking, Danish-eating,
philosophizing fanatics like me, give all of you
Sweet, caring, psychologist types something to do
Otherwise, you would have no purpose in questioning every
existential cup and crumb of life!"
The morning sun had begun streaking in through
The coffee shop windows now, warming the counter
"You having breakfast?" my brother asked
"Sure, since we are in balance, I will have
Gluten-free toast to equalize your Danish and
Wheat grass juice to balance your coffee!"
My brother smiled, "And then again," he suggested
"There are different types of fanatics!"
And he was off again!

~Judy Sundayo

158

*Judy Sundayo, her honorary niece, **Nandi Atashe Simon, Starla Lewis,** **Alyce Smith Cooper,** and **Makeda Dread** (far right), former owner of the Prophet Vegetarian Restaurant; current Executive Director, **Worldbeat Cultural Center,** dedicated to promoting, presenting & preserving African and indigenous cultures through music, art, dance, education and technology; San Diego http://www.worldbeatcenter.org/*

The Prophet

There be a prophet who sat himself down
'mid flowers that grew in the middle of town
'mid gardens and branches that sheltered his head
'mid beggars who shared what they could of their bread

there be a prophet of highest renown
who flowed with what be going down
who took the worst and shared the best
who found in love his only quest

who laughed and cried and tried to teach
who filled with hope all those in reach
There be a prophet what known as a place
Where truth be the blossom that peak out its face

(continued)

159

The Prophet *(continued)*

Where Grace is the shelter of all who are fed
And beggars still share what they can of their bread
There be a prophet what be on the case
What love be trying to replace
So one can rest they tired soul
And think to find that inner goal
A place for the weary of heart to seek
The pure, the innocent, and meek.

~Judy Sundayo

*Authors' friend, **Makeda Dread** being presented with a*
Community Service Award by Judy Sundayo, circa 1990's;
In 2013, Makeda Dread was inducted into the
San Diego Women's Museum Hall of Fame

The WorldBeat Center, San Diego, California;
http://www.worldbeatcenter.org/

One World

One world, one world, get on the beat
Come on down to the our own WorldBeat
Where all nations gather for lessons in peace,
Let love be the answer
Let music release any fear that you're feeling
For now you're at home
Where your presence is healing
And you're never alone
You can draw, paint, garden or act in a play
Come on down, learn your history today
The Worldbeat Center is the community's place
No matter your age, your gender or race
It's a place where all are welcome to sit, talk and eat
Come on down to our own WorldBeat
Where health and wellbeing are number one
Come on down and have some fun
The building is spectacular in colors painted round
In Balboa Park at the center of town
One world, one world, get on the beat
At the Worldbeat Center
Where we always meet!

~Judy Sundayo

161

Rhythm & Drum

Drum Call
Power pounding through the heart
Drum Call motion moving
Now, let's start to remember
Why we've come together in the first place
To speak the truth and tell our story
To dance the dance of our people's glory
Drum Call; power pounding
Drum Call; rhythm resounding
In our spirits loudly
Can't you feel the power in your soul?
That's our memory returning
At each drum roll
Hear the drummers challenge
See the dancers respond
Power pounding our spirit song
Drum Call; rhythm and drum
Now can the Spirits of our Ancestors come
~Judy Sundayo

*__Teye Sa Thiosaanne African Drum and Dance Company__, under the direction of
Founder/Lead Drummer __Yiriba B, Thomas__ (center) and Lead Dancer/Group Dance
Choreographer, __Aminisha Cunningham__ (right); this group whose name means
__"Keepers of the Tradition"__ Has been providing the San Diego community with
African Cultural expression through music, song and dance since 1988;*
*http://www.actaonline.org/content/teye-sa-thiosanne-african-drum-dance-
company*

162

*Friends of the authors, **Calvin Manson**, who founded*
***Ira Aldridge Repertory Players**, 1973, a group of talented actors, artists, and*
Musicians, dedicated to creating and producing theatrical works reflecting
*African American life, with wife, **Minola Clark Manson**; For more about the*
***Ira Aldridge Players**, see http://iarpplayers.org/;*
***Common Ground Theatre**, go to http://cgtsd.org/;*
***Black Ensemble Theatre** see, http://sdbetheatre.homestead.com/;*
***Community Actors Theatre**, http://www.communityactorstheatre.com/;*
***Mo' olelo Performing Arts Company**, go to http://moolelo.net/*

We Got Talent

We got talent; we got grace
We got what it takes to fill this place
Writers and artists and musicians abound
To put on a show that will surely astound
Feel the music and stay in step
Enjoy the performance of the *Ira Aldridge Rep*
And if you intend to stay around
Don't miss the next show at *Common Ground*
Another theatre company with a soulful show
Is the *Black Ensemble* for those in the know
Community Actors, the Moxie and *Mo'olelo*
Are other venues
On your 'got-to-see that show' menu
We got talent; we got grace
Now all we need is you, to fill this place
~Judy Sundayo

Sista'- Ku: Tamayta Haytas

Tamayta haytas

Miss de' saucy side a life

Dat sweet and sour soup

~Judy Sundayo

After Dinner Rhyme

Coffee, tea or melody can soothe us when we dine

Aroma, taste or rhythm all comfort in their time

So serve me, sweet,

A pungent, neat and syncopated rhyme!

~Judy Sundayo

*Authors' friend, **Rev. Dr. Asha Mawusi Bell** with **Iyanla Vanzant**,*
Legendary author, speaker, T.V. personality and empowerment guide,
*For more information about her numerous books, audios and her **"Forgiveness"***
kit, see http://iyanlavanzant.com/ ; Photo taken in San Diego, California, circa
1990's;Photo courtesy of Rev. Dr. Asha Mawusi Bell

*Poet, painter, advocate for social justice, **Jihmye Collins** (1940-2011);*
*Founder and CEO of **The African American Writers & Artists, Inc.***
San Diego, California; For more information, go to
http://www.aawasd.org/About-Us.html

Once Upon a Time

Once upon a time
There was a writer
Extremely fine and much mightier
Than most
He would speak in sacred sentences
And all who listened
Were transformed
From meek, mindless, mealy-mouthed
Minions
To profoundly powerful, provocative and
Prodigious Masters
Of their own fate

If you haven't heard him, it's not too late
You can listen, and hear and read
What he wrote
But I want to caution you
You better take note

(continued)

Once Upon a Time *(continued)*

Your life as you know it
Will cease to exist
Awakened, you will find your life to consist
Of love and challenge and confrontation
Service and hard work and emancipation
From all that would hold you back from freedom

Yes, reading is a revolutionary act
That will entice you
To happily ever after!

~Judy Sundayo

Dr. Annjennette McFarlin, *(1935-2013), Author, Educator, Professor,*
And Chair of the Speech Department at Grossmont College; Author of
"Black Congressional Reconstruction Orators and Their Orations"
*Founder of **The Black Storytellers of San Diego, Inc.**; for more info, see*
http://www.bssdinc.org/our-story.html

*Judy Sundayo's cousin, **Linda Woodson** and her husband **Sam Carcione**;
Linda's graduation, with her MSW, Howard University, Washington, D.C., 1998*

Thanksgiving Dinner

Please pass the turkey
And then the honeyed ham
Don't forget the collard greens,
The dinner rolls and yams

Please pass the green beans,
Then the mac and cheese
I love those mashed potatoes,
With gravy if you please!

Please pass the cobs of corn,
The cranberry sauce and dressing
And then before we eat,
Let's bow our heads and ask the blessing

Dear Lord, bless this family
As we gather here today
Bless the hands that prepared the food
And our children as they play

(continued)

Thanksgiving Dinner *(continued)*

And bless this food we're about to devour
And as it fills us head to feet
We pray all the children of the world
Will have enough to eat

And Lord, don't forget to bless the dessert
Got pound cake and sweet tater pie
And if we add a scoop of ice cream
Bless that too, oh Lord on high!

This Thanksgiving dinner is truly fine
Yes, totally scrumptious and sweet
We're grateful for this blessing,
Lord, we thank you!
Now, let's eat!

~Judy Sundayo

*Judy Sundayo with childhood sister-friend, **Paula Lewis**, (right)
Maryland, 1989*

168

*Judy Sundayo's colleague, **Art Boyd**, (far left) Professor, San Diego Mesa College, with the ever-popular local group, **The Choice Entertainers**, Best known locally for their smooth and mellow doo wop on the King Stahlman Bail Bond television commercial*
https://www.facebook.com/TheChoiceEntertainers

My Niece Likes

My niece likes her young men
Like she likes her ice-cream
Chocolate, chocolate, strawberry, vanilla ice
Mixed, smooth, sweet, very nice

My niece likes her young men
Like she likes her ice-cream
Nutty, jean wearing slim and trim
Oh yeah, she is into him~

In a bowl or on a cone
Drinking root beer or maybe alone
My niece likes her young men
Like she likes her ice-cream
Tall, swirled, mostly hard, a little melted soft
He has got to like to listen and talk

(continued)

My Niece Likes *(continued)*

About comic con, aliens, spirituality, Dr. Spock
Better be in shape for long, long walks
Gotta like my niece, gotta like her a lot
My niece likes her young men
Like she likes her ice-cream
T-shirt wearing, fast food eating, petting cats
He better like playing and everyday a new act
Never grow up and never grow old
For my niece this is an important fact
My niece likes her young men
See my niece likes eating ice-cream everyday
Then, like a lot of us, she likes
Eating her ice-cream with music and friends
Any young man interested in my niece
Come trick or treat
Come packing candy, ice-cream, fast food, dolls,
Better be sweet!
Be talking spirituality, aliens, music, Sci-Fi,
What beautiful eyes has my niece
Look like and dance like Michael Jackson
Sweep her off her feet
My niece likes her ice-cream
Like she likes her young men
I will say it again,
My niece likes her young men
Like she likes her ice cream
Prepare you money to spend!

~Jaime V. Jones

170

*Judy Sundayo's great, great aunt **Helen Boston**, an Algonquian
Indian of one the tribes of Chief Wahunsonacock (Chief Powhatan),
The father of Pocahontas; Photo taken circa late 19th century, McClean, Virginia;
Over 90% of the 12,000 Indians under Chief Wahunsonacock's rule were
annihilated by war & disease within 60 years of English arrival in early 17th century*

Corn Mother Goddess

(In honor of and respect for our earth mother and her guardians)

You know Corn Mother Goddess?
Me too!
Be done born from hur woom
Seen her dancin'
Husk skirt twirlin' wide at time of full moon
What she say?
Be abundant like she, giv'n all what da' children need
Bring'em up ta be fulla courage, fulla laughter,
Peace and luv to sprout like seed
Corn Mother Goddess be a big booty woman
And got breasts dat done nourished da hole wurl
We be done born from hur
Das why we twirl!
Corn Mother Goddess, she say,
Da earth is heah for you!
I done prepared da table!
Got corn, tamaytas
(continued)

171

Corn Mother Goddess *(continued)*
All kines a greens
An herbs ta' keep yaself able
Move! Corn Mother say!
Dance dat dance
And shake dat hip!
You be done shif da hole wurl
Jus' like dat!
From yo' sho' nuf god-like powa'
Da hole wurl gone flip!
Den ya'll gone see Corn Mama
Face ta' face!
You da powa from hur woom
Be done transform dis place!
Corn Mother Goddess be ancient an wise
Be honess like da earth! She say,
Don't tell no lies!
Be kine ta one 'notha
An wen you meet somebody new
Look deep in they eyes
Till ya can see da luv
Dat bine us tagetha'
Den ya heart will be light
As da eagle featha'
An when sumpin start a bringin
Dat stress at yoe doe'
Jus' say, "No thanks, don't need no moe!"
Rememba', Corn Mother Goddess be royal
Like moon-reflected light!
But, huh, I seen hur Bollywood dancin' las night
She jus' wink at me an say,
"Baby, always rememba' at da end a da day
Wen all yoe work an fuss is done,
Jus' giv thanks! Den have some fun!"

~Judy Sundayo

172

*Alyce Smith Cooper and grandchildren, **Dajuan,***
***Dashon, Diona, DeEdward, James** (De End!),*
San Diego, California

Rainbow Children of Indigo Hue

Children of the cosmos
All colors of the spectrum
Rainbow children of indigo blue
We await with such eagerness your arrival
The galaxy has been your playground
You hum celestial tunes
Bright rays emanate when you smile
Happy are we
You chose us as your family
We awaited your arrival
Praying for wisdom
To guide your soul's journey

(continued)

Rainbow Children of Indigo Hue *(continued)*

*Alyce Smith Cooper's great granddaughter, **Lisa Jayda**
Holding her new baby sister, **Lyric Adriana***

Our dreams are to present to you
A world peacefully harmonized
Filled with joy
Our dreams. . . and prayers
For you to realize
Rainbow children of Indigo hue
We await
The power of your sweetness
~Alyce Smith Cooper

*Alyce Smith Cooper's great, granddaughter, **Lisa Jada**
At her piano lesson with Ms. **Bobbie Hearns**, 2014*

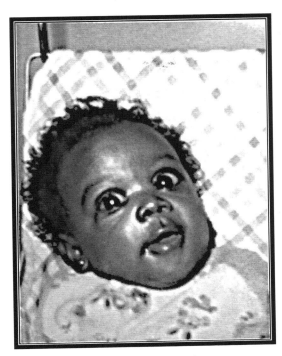

*Jaime V. Jones' niece, **Lucinda Jones,***
as a baby, San Diego, California

Mango Juice Everywhere

Whenever I am eating ripe juicy, mangoes
I love to share
With the walls, floors, table
even the chair
Mango juice all over my lips, nose, fingers
even in my hair
Eating plump red and yellow mangoes
juice everywhere

~Jaime V. Jones

*Photograph by **Leon O. Allen***

Moon

(For Kali, in honor of the divine we are sometimes blessed to see reflected in our friends)

Oh, moon, your face aglow
In all this darkness stands,
Suspended in such serenity
Like Kali's eye it lets me see
That same Light
The sun has given her, Moon
That one true Light
Shown so bright
For how else Moon, could I see tonight?
Ebony folds
Embrace your countenance round
Like Kali's hair it reaches down
Until it meets the earth
Then reaches up again
Covering the whole of Heaven
Becoming highlight
To the beauty of that celestial glow
Like Kali's smile it lets me know
That same Grace
The Lord has given her, Moon
That one true Grace
Born in trust
For how else, Moon,
Could I love so much?

~Judy Sundayo

176

*Judy Sundayo (at right, 2ⁿᵈ row) with brothers, **Leon** (upper left),*
***Granville** (lower left) and **Kelvin** (center partial headshot) & friends,*
Rock Creek Park, Washington, D.C., circa 1958

Feedie

Back in the days when there were farms
We had a chick was full a charms
When little, her feathers were just like down
She used to follow us around

We named her Feedie; she sure was cute!
Used to get herself caught in the feeding chute
Years passed and one day we were out to play
And overheard our Papa say,

"Now, Liza, tain't no need to fret!
Dat chicken weren't meant to be no pet!
You know we got to feed doze chillen!
Prepare de pot! I'll do da killen!"

(continued)

Feedie *(continued)*

If it weren't so sad, be kinda funny
Watching Pa chase Feedie 'round da coup
But later, we felt sentimental
Staring down at Feedie soup!

Pa thanked da Lawd for we was blessed
And t'was a fine meal; I had to confess
And then I commenced to realize
How one life helps another life to live

Like Feedie done for us
So wasn't no need to make a fuss
'Cause on account a Pa's suggestion
Feedie *still lived*, in our digestion

Now, that I know what it's all about
I thank da Lawd for lookin' out!

~Judy Sundayo

*Judy Sundayo's maternal great, grandmother, **Eliza** and
Her husband, **Wm. Harvey Boston II**,
Virginia, circa early 1900's*

178

Judy Sundayo feeding a baby rhinoceros at the
San Diego Wild Animal Park, 2010

Pets are Precious

Pets are parrots
Pets are cats
Pets are doggies on their mats

Pets are lizards
Pets are fish
Pets are turtles in a dish

Pets are hamsters
Pets are guineas
Pets are horses, making whinnies

Pets are chickens
Pets are goats
Pets are lambs in winter coats

(continued)

Pets are Precious *(continued)*

Pets are spiders
Pets are snakes
Pets are ferrets eating cakes

Pets are rabbits
Pets are frogs
Pets are ponies jumping logs

Pets are monkeys
Pets are mice
Pets are pigs behaving nice

Pets are precious
Pets are kind
Pets are family
Just like mine!

~Judy Sundayo

Judy Sundayo, horseback riding in Virginia, circa 1970's

*Judy Sundayo with childhood sister-friend, **Michelle Henderson**,*
Photo taken at the Great Pyramid at Giza, Egypt, 2010

Ant

Ever wonder what it would have been like
To have been born an ant
And to have been happy to transport a small crumb
From one destination to another, daily
And wonder at the marvels of the huge grass blades
And the boldering sand grains
And sometimes huddle down deep
In the dark, damp earthiness
And tremble at the sounds of the
Thundering cricket noises!
But, I was born myself
Many years ago

(continued)

Ant *(continued)*

I awoke from a dream to look on my life now
A thing apart
I am a woman, tall and straight
And happy doing woman things
Taking awe at the splendorous mountains
And the ever-stretching sea-waves
And sometimes retreating
To the inner quiet of my mind
To wonder at the mystery of it all
And knowledge found there says,
There is something in everything
That makes big things seem bigger
And great things seem immense
That keeps the sky from ending
And a man from his beginning
There is something that is childlike in all life
And is mother even to itself
Its capacity for love and knowledge
Is boundless and complete
It reasons why I am a woman
And not an ant
And moves us both to do our thing
~Judy Sundayo

*Judy Sundayo's friend, **Kali Rodriguez,***
***Hacienda Todos Los Santos** in Baja California Sur*
http://www.tshacienda.com/

*Judy Sundayo's brother-friend, **Anthony***
Photo taken in California

Genesis of Sunrise

Anthony is the storm of magical beginnings

Abundant energy in the air

Thunder-strong movements

Re-sound in the aftermath

Of the lightning's appearing

Quick flashes of dreamtime visions

That nurture the soul

Illumination here and there

Like stormy surprises and mellowing rain

(continued)

Genesis of Sunrise *(continued)*

Anthony is the mountain against which the sky

At twilight sets its splendorous blue rock

Solid on firm foundation

Always reaching toward the heavens

Anthony is the teacher,

Learner, brother, friend

Exuding power like the storm

And magnificence like the mountain

Emanating a resoluteness of spirit

That flashes ideas like lightning

And beacons of hope like the dawn

That reaches toward tomorrow

As the genesis of sunrise

~Judy Sundayo

*Friend of the authors, **Dr. Fern Nelson,**
Dermatologist, Veterans Hospital, La Jolla, California*

Alyce Smith Cooper as a child, with her mother,
Anita Lorraine Smith, *Riverside, California, circa 1940*

Name That Tune

Scared. . . don't know what to expect
Been doubting self so long
Never knew who I was
Now, mirror has a new face
When I look into it
Isn't thin or young
Is brown sugar pretty
Smart, sexy, strong
An artist Par Excellent
Hey!
That's the name of this tune!

~Alyce Smith Cooper

Ongoing Prophecy

Sumpins 'bout to turn
Sumpins 'bout to break
Sumpins goin' on
Sumpins gonna shake
Dunno what it is
Frankly, don't care
I know we all gone git our share
Deys laws
Deys rivers
Deys streams
Deys po' men's dreams
Who knows where dey gonna end up?
Aint't yall seen de weatha turnin 'round?
Rich an po' alike gone drown
An no one will know whats become of a town
Sumpins 'bout to turn
Sumpins 'bout to break
Sumpins turnin 'round like a hungry snake!
Quick, get inside; don't make a mistake!

~Judy Sundayo

Photo by Judy Sundayo. La Jolla, California

*Judy Sundayo's maternal grandmother, **Florence Smith**, (left)*
*Her mother, Judy's great grandmother, **Eliza Harris Boston**, (center)*
*Judy's aunt **Helen Dawson** (far right) and Judy's cousin, **Sandra**, (front)*
Aunt Helen's eldest daughter; Four Generations

Bloodrunner

Bloodrunner spirit
Haunting eyes
Half-draped; half-closed
In blood-red skies
Listen to what our father's say
Trade pain in past
For joy today
You know the road
Then follow quickly
Or else remain
Encased in sickly
Memories
Let go
Healing abounds
In all you hear and see and speak
Bloodrunner mission
Not for the meek!

~Judy Sundayo

187

Family Spirit

Behold the spirit of this family
A blend of destinies complex
Black man, White man, Red man mix
Mysteries affirm the sacred fix
Best strive against those who seek
To dominate the earth, the meek
Spirit brings balance with what is needed
Know yourself, that peace be heeded
Spirit reminds, there's a temple in man
Crawl before you walk; sit before you stand
Remember to read the book of you!
And savor this knowledge in all that you do
Words of the ancestors close in our ears
Guiding us toward righteousness
Overcoming fears!
Family spirit hovering to give us protection
And keep us all moving in the right direction!

~Judy Sundayo

*Judy Sundayo's cousin, Mr. **Rafiq Bilal,** brilliant writer, researcher, artist, Co-author of Egyptian Sacred Science in Islam & Christianity; Founder of **The Upper Room**, the first non-alcoholic, non-tobacco club in the Bay Area; San Francisco, California, circa 1990's*

*Al Washington, **Judy Sundayo**, Judy's two nieces, **Deitra Moore** and **Pia Hill** and Judy's daughter, **Aurora Chedester**, San Diego Wild Animal Park, 2009*

Come Summer

Her icy breath complains no more
Her chills have gone away
The softness of her quiet tears
Have washed the clouds away

Her warm voice whispers through the trees
She's quiet through the night
At dawn, she breaks a sunny smile
All day remaining bright

Proud tosses of her tresses green
As if she now is free
From branch to branch the birds proclaim
Her grand recovery

The color of her painted face
Reveals her ecstasy
Playfully she beckons you
As if she'll never let you be

(continued)

Come Summer *(continued)*

She showers you with sunshine
As she grins from ear to ear
And frolics and just carries on
As if her end were nowhere near

But all too soon her voice grows hoarse
She turns a color pale
Her hands and feet grow very cold
And likewise she gets frail

Her splendors fall dead to the ground
Gone now is all her wealth
She covers up in beds of snow
Until she is her same old self

~Judy Sundayo

*Judy Sundayo's son, **Hasar** and good friend, **Fardowsa**,*
an aspiring attorney; photo taken in La Jolla, California, 2015

Judy Sundayo's cousin, **Mohammed Soriano Bilal**, CEO and Founder of **SIMBLR, Inc.**, Mobile Entertainment Company; Executive Director of **The African American Art & Culture Complex**, San Francisco, California; Graduate of U.C. Berkeley; Also, completed MA in Diversity & MBA in Design Strategy; Conscious Hip-Hop Musician; Poet; Singer and Songwriter; Former performer and co-proprietor along with his Father, **Rafiq Bilal**, of The Upper Room, the first Tobacco and Alcohol free club in San Francisco; Former Cast Member on MTV's The Real World: San Francisco; Internationally renowned Motivational Speaker with over 450 Presentations, Workshops and Trainings to his credit on many topics, including Diversity, AIDS, HIV Prevention, Drug & Alcohol Abuse; Resides with wife & children in San Francisco; for more information, go to http://www.aaacc.org/index.html

Telling Our Stories

The poet speaks it with a word
An artist paints and the story's transferred
From heart to heart
A singer releases a soulful song
With lyrics conveying a lifetime of pain and celebration
Resonating in bone-deep narrations
An author writes and we can see passion on page after page
Giving voice to history, imagination and
All of our persistent possibilities
In nail-biting intrigue
And then there comes the point in each of our lives
When we finally reach our final few chapters
After decades of decisions that leave us wanting more
(continued)

Telling Our Stories *(continued)*

It is then we begin to write a new story
And this one includes service and cooperation
And more songs, and even more poems
And we laugh and teach and tell each other's stories
And we watch our children's dreams become manifest
Between the lines of life, making apparent their
Vision and talent and tenacity, and so I say. . .
Write your stories; share your verse
Let your brilliance shine throughout this universe!
And never stop writing! Your words need to be read
Never stop speaking; the truth must be said!
Keep on painting and sculpting in stone
We need the images that you alone can create
On your canvass and your pedestal stands our fate
So, keep on singing in conscious verse; Represent!
The people who were first on the planet
And keep on learning; your life's in reach
Keep on organizing; and each one teach another
Never ever doubt yourself or succumb to worries
For we're trusting YOU to tell *our* stories!
~Judy Sundayo

*Friend of the authors' **Dajahn Blevins**, Community Organizer; Engineer for Positive
Change; Founder of **Kuumba Fest**, a 3-Day Festival that's San Diego's longest
running & premier celebration of African-American Expression, Culture & Heritage,
with African Art, Drama, Workshops, Community Leadership Awards, an African
Marketplace & Health Fair; For more info, see http://www.kuumbafest.com/*

Jaime V. Jones as a young girl, San Diego, California

My Creativity

My creativity, it has absolutely no consideration
Whether I am busy cooking
Or in deep fried meditation
My creativity knows no boundaries;
While being decadently demanding
Stop and write down everything
With unique understanding
All that my creativity tells me
And write it now clearly

My creativity it is a constant companion
Wherever I go
My creativity comes along
And continuously lets me know

(continued)

193

My Creativity *(continued)*

That I am a God's vehicle
For what must be even though
I am not sure what today,
Life will at me throw
My creativity is so amazing see
Though I can't hear its voice , it speaks to me
Filling me up like some hot air balloon colorful pretty
Then releasing me against the blue, black sky
Of the country or city
Write down all that comes into view,
Write it now, be quick, be witty
My creativity shows me no mercy, no pity
Thanks to my creativity
I am able to deliver the quantity
While my God delightfully
Delivers the quality

~Jaime V. Jones

*Judy Sundayo's long-time friend, **Francita Love**,
Licensed Professional Counselor, Atlanta, Georgia*

*Judy Sundayo with long-time, friend **Starla Lewis** (on left)*
Retired Professor, Black Studies Department, San Diego Mesa College;
Nationally renowned speaker, motivator, poet & jegna (teacher/guide);
*Author of **"Sunkisses"** an empowering book for children about skin color;*
Photo taken by Heaven Leigh Johnson, San Diego, California, 2014

I'll Take Laughter for Dessert

I'll take laughter for dessert, please!
Big bowls of belly laughter
That shake like Jell-O!
Soft, creamy laughter, doubled over on its side
Like a fabulously funny flan that is SOOOOO SWEET!
Enough! Enough! Through tears!
Please, no more!
(But, right before I hit the floor),
I'll take a slice of that SWEET-POTATO LAUGHTER,
Mmm! Mmm!
That's righteous, right-on, DOWN-HOME HUMOR!

(continued)

I'll Take Laughter for Dessert *(continued)*

Did I hear you say, you got that right?
Now go ahead and take a bite!
And see if that don't digest those blues
A heapin' helpin' of laughter feels you better
From your head to your shoes!

Go ahead, I tell you
And you'll soon know why
When you try a slice of that GIGGLE-BERRY PIE!
Or maybe a slice of that DOUBLE-CHOCOLATE TICKLE CAKE
And I'll *LAAAUGH* as I watch your belly shake!

What's so funny? Honey,
Just pay attention!
You got great big GUMDROP GUFFAWS!
HA! HA! HA!!!!
You got purely pleasing PUDDING PUNS!
Ho! Ho! Ho-Ho's!

You got big, old bust-a-gut
BUBBLE-GUM CHUCKLES
That'll tickle your fancy
And loosen your buckles!

What a rollicking good time!
Laughing your belly full!
Topping off the meal with some SHO'NUFF JOY!
The cherry on top of good food, good friends,
And a slaphappy good time!

It's *LAUGHTER*
That makes fine dining fine!
Do I want dessert?
Of course!
I'll take laughter for mine!

~Judy Sundayo

*Judy Sundayo's friend and colleague, **Dr. Nola Butler-Byrd**,*
Past-President of the San Diego Chapter of the Association of Black Psychologists;
A scholar/activist, Professor, Director of the Community-Based Block Program
at San Diego State University, San Diego, California
http://go.sdsu.edu/education/csp/cbb.aspx

Affirmation for Healing

Everything that needs to be known
Is being known
Everything that needs to be strengthened
Is being strengthened
Everything that needs to be healed
Is being healed
That within me that is NOT helpful
Is being diminished
That within me that is good and helpful
Is being multiplied
Health, harmony and healing predominate
I am well in mind, body and spirit!

~Judy Sundayo

197

What's the News?

What's the news?
What's the word?
Who's running for office?
What have you heard?

What's happening 'round town?
Let's read and converse
If it's happening in our community
I want to know first!

We've got to stay informed
It's our obligation
To understand what's going down
Here and 'round the nation!

What's the news?
What's the word?
The community's coming together!
Haven't you heard?

~Judy Sundayo

*Friend of the authors' **TJ Dunnivant**, worked as a photography assistant,*
Hansen Photography; and as a photojournalist,
San Diego Voice & Viewpoint Newspaper,
http://www.sdvoice.info/

Friends of the authors' **Abdur - Rahim Hameed** *founder and President of the National Black Contractors Association and his wife* **Janiece Hampton - Hameed,** *the Executive Director of the Black Contractors Association of San Diego, Inc.; For information about the* **Black Contractor's Association** *in San Diego, see* <u>www.bcasd.org</u>

The Business of Building

The business of building
The business of trade
A time to be proud
A community made
Brick and stone and mortar built
Our cooperation has forever tilt
The hands of time in our favor
It's there for all to see
A structure
A community
A lasting treasure
A fortress of heart
What skill and perseverance it took to start
Business savvy sealed the deal
Hard work has made for visual appeal
The business of building
Starting with the past
Raising up a community
Built to last

~Judy Sundayo

Dandelion

When I grow up I want to be
A bright-full dandelion
And with my long, green skinny stem
Wrap round the friends of mine

~Judy Sundayo

Dr. Judy Sundayo, Dr. Nola Butler Byrd (center), Dr. Rochelle Bastien, (right) and Dr. Philip Raphael (The Original Dr. Phil, seated); all former presidents of the San Diego Chapter of the Association of Black Psychologists and good friends-like-family; Photo taken at the Annual Convention of the Association of Black Psychologists; Los Angeles, California, 2012; www.abpsi.org

Of Friendship

Peacefully enters joy
On wings of light
When a flower speaks
Of Friendship

~Alyce Smith Cooper

*Judy Sundayo's friends, **Vou Athens** with her honey, **Lynn** of La Jolla, California; Vou is an Integrative Therapies Specialist, specializing in Mindfulness, Meditation, Energy Healing and Yoga*

Healing Breath

One breath and then another

And blessings flow as healing by the hour

Heartfelt and freely given

A blessing asked in love . . .

Inhale and catch a glimpse of twilight's crest

To deem the childlike heart as blessed

Exhale one breath, another then

Invoking healing for a friend

Then waiting for the Grace to shower

As breath of babies come to flower

~Judy Sundayo

The Promise of Peace

The horizon stands clear in my mind
Such lines as would separate truth from darkness
Such lines as would be the bridge on which I stand
Which holds my soul above the earth
While lifting it to heaven

The horizon, which separates and connects
Such lines as form the brightness of a rainbow
Such as appears after the storm of mind
After the rain of truth has sunken deep within this earth

The light of the soul refreshes with love
Such are the lines of this horizon across my mind
Quieting the whole region
Such are the lines of the rainbow across this heaven
Promising peace

~Judy Sundayo

Photo of rainbow taken by Judy Sundayo
From her office window, San Diego Mesa College 2014

*Long-time friend of the authors' **Dr. Richard Butcher,** has maintained a family medicine practice in San Diego for over 50 years; Former President, **National Medical Association**; Co-Founder, **Water for Children Africa** with his wife, Dr. Vickie Butcher; This photo was taken with Judy Sundayo in Pyramid Bookstore, a San Diego bookstore that specialized in books by and about African Americans, run by Barbara Brown; circa 1990's*

The Importance of Health

Without health most of one's wealth
Disappears
It's what we almost all have feared
Old age, without the ability to think, speak
And move about
We all want to live, but not without
All our senses and abilities intact
Matter-of-fact
I plan to live to a hundred and five
Like my mother's friend's mother had
It wasn't so bad
(continued)

The Importance of Health *(continued)*

Maybe it took her la little longer to get around
But her mind was just as quick and sound
As ever
Played poker and held her own
No one ever told us that when we were grown
We'd have to think about these things
Our final days
Our finishing position
And what our lives might look like
When we make our transition
We all want to be like that thoroughbred horse
That runs in a derby and finishes the course
In style
Good Health is the horse that will win this race
And champion for us as we age
That Blue Ribbon of grace!

~Judy Sundayo

Friends of the authors' **Solluna M. Moyoah** *is a Master Empathic Holistic Health Practitioner, Herbalist, Minister, Teacher, Personal Insight Counselor, Medical Massage Therapist and Reiki Master; specializing in the diminishing and elimination of pain: physical and mental; professional member of the American Massage Therapy Association;* **Solluna & Company Therapeutic Massage:** *sollunaco@scbglobal.net*

What is an Athlete?

If you could hit it harder
Throw it farther
Hook it; Dunk it
Run it faster
Score more points
Or learn to master
A sequence of moves
That put you on top
That broke records,
Set standards and made the fans roar
You were in!
And in many neighborhoods
Athletes got a pass
"Man, don't mess with him
Make a way! Don't you know? He's NBA!" Or . . .
"Hey, don't put ole homeboy down!
He's NFL, first round!" Or . . .
"That's my brother! He don't claim!
That dude's gone be in the hall o' fame!
Jus' remember where you come from!
That's our only request!
Now, go ahead brother and be the best you can be
Make us proud as you go on to victory!"
So for many, sports was the only option
They could see
To college, to the pros, to prosperity, though it takes
Hard work, teamwork, humility
Discipline, diligence and tenacity
Sports IS home for many!
And it's not just about the accolade,
The sexual opportunities or even the money
It's about challenging oneself
And it might sound funny,
(continued)

What is an Athlete? *(continued)*

But it's about beating your own personal best
About achieving something you always knew
You could achieve
Meeting your own high standards
Because you believe in yourself!
And stay true to yourself
At every game and at every meet
At every opportunity
Even on the street
Maintaining the same high standard of integrity
Of a great competitor
A role model who demonstrates
With every fiber of being what it really takes
To be a superstar
So that the majority of society who will never make it
In quite the same way
Can have the athlete to emulate
Encouraging the personal resolve it takes to acquire
Success in one of the other 40 thousand legal ways
There are to live; and sports is only one way
And for many it will *only* be an avocation or a dream
So, the athlete is a talented person
Who Is much more than what is seen on TV
The athlete is strong, intelligent and wise
A business-minded strategist
With an eye to the prize
Not just someone who could
Hit it harder; throw it farther
Hook it; dunk it; run it faster
But someone who eventually comes to master
Self, becoming the MVP of his or her own life,
The most important game of all!

~Judy Sundayo

Judy Sundayo dancing with brother by another mother,
Hunter Carrington, *at Coolidge High School Reunion, Washington, D.C., 2010*

When Mashed Potatoes Was a Dance

When mashed potatoes

Was a dance

The spuds

Were *not* to eat

But they were squished and squashed

With joy

Beneath our dancing feet!

~Judy Sundayo

207

Peace

Peace

It's deceptive

It looks as small as a seed

But it grows into a massive oak

If only we'd believe

Peace

It's alive

And by death is not annoyed

As long as we nourish that seed within

Peace cannot be destroyed!

~Judy Sundayo

*Judy Sundayo (far right) with other attendees at **The San Diego Chapter of the Association of Black Psychologists** Retreat, including C. Kahalifa King (far left), Founder and CEO of Harmonious Solutions, http://www.harmoniouslifesolutions.org, Dr. Rochelle Bastien, Dr. Philip Raphael, Dr. Carl Clark, and retreat host, Dr. Carl Smith, Ramona, California, 2009*

*Judy Sundayo's long-time friends, **Jane and John Finch,***
Founders and Directors of the Self-Heal School for Herbal Studies
In Ocean Beach, California
http://selfhealschool.com/

Speaking of Truth

Speaking of Truth
Let it pour from you like a poem
Clear, resonant, deeply felt
Like a prayer
Like you're really there
On the inside
And all who truly listen, will come to believe
That your words are sweeter poetry
Than the mind can conceive
Blessed are the ears that can hear
The Word ring
With its melodic messages and inner rhythms
From the heart which loves to sing
Speaking of Truth
Let it pour from you like a poem
Of passion from the inside; a beatific vision in verse
For Truth upholds Beauty
And Beauty Truth

~Judy Sundayo

209

Compensation

Incomparable compensation
Pressed down shaken together
Over-flowingly bountiful compensation given
When you give to THE MOTHER
Mother Earth, GYIA. GBFG
However you feel her presence
Whenever you deposit into her account
Your compensation is amazing
Cuddled into her warm wet salty velvet depths
Comfort erupts, releases creative sparks
Returns dividends unimagined.
The prosperous wealth of being

~Alyce Smith Cooper

Alyce Smith Cooper, with prayer flag,
Bethel A.M.E Church, San Diego, California

*Judy Sundayo's niece, **Erin Allen** with son,*
***Emry Allen**, Baltimore, Md., 2012*

My Lion

A golden brown
Like any lion
Is the lion that I know
But his heart is warm as fire
And it shines as love aglow
Through a pair of eyes so gentle
Almost seeming sad and slow
Almost seeming that my lion
Could be any lion
Though
Mine is quite unique
For those who seek his eyes
Discover love
In all its ferocious splendor

~Judy Sundayo

Palate Cleanser

Milk

Ice Cold or wonderful warm
Refreshing milk
Chocolate chip cookies and milk
Food hot, spicy, bread and milk
Clean the mouth inside out milk

~Jaime V. Jones

Photo by Marina Shemesh, publicdomainImages.net

Holy Trinity

First two Photos by Junior Libby; Last by Peter Griffin; publicdomainimages.net

Like members of a brass band
Announcing their presence
With loud assertion
Come Onion, Celery and Green Pepper
Each one holding a different shape
Carrying a different flavor-sound
Yet all working together to create
Something quite profound
May this music within me play
From now until eternity
And I'll never forget the name of this band
It's called The Holy Trinity!
~Judy Sundayo

Onions are quite sweet as they are cooked if allowed to caramelize. Add to this the sweetness of green pepper and celery and you have what New Orleanians refer to as *The Holy Trinity*. Many add garlic and tomatoes to the mix and members of the wholesome trio do not complain. All work together to make GUMBO absolutely exquisite!

213

GUMBO Recipe Step 4:

Holy Trinity
(Onions, Celery & Green Peppers)

What You Need
Sharp, wid-blade chopping knife, or
Food Processor
Large 10-12 quart stainless steel cooking pot
Large wooden spoon

What You Gotta Get
1   Large White Onion
1 - 2 Green Bell Peppers
2 - 3 Stalks of Celery

(And if desired, add)
3-4 cloves of garlic, chopped fine
2-3 tomatoes, chopped
2-3 sprigs of fresh parsley, chopped fine

What You Do With What You Get
- Wash veggies
- Peel onion, discard skin
- Remove green pepper seeds
- Chop the onion, peppers & celery finely & evenly
- Add chopped veggies to the roux after it has reached the color you desire and stir for 5 minutes
- Add the roux mixture, including the Holy Trinity to the chicken stock and simmer altogether in the GUMBO Pot
- Simmer approx. 2 hours over medium heat
- Stir often. Veggies love to swim in the stock!

What You Bet Not Tell Nobody

- If the symmetry of the cut veggies does not matter to you, a food processor used in *pulsing* mode will complete the chopping in seconds, or

- Use *Salsa!* This senior's hands do not chop with grace these days. I buy a gallon jar of *Salsa Fresca*, which has all the flavorful ingredients, except celery. If you'd like celery, add it. My GUMBO is a delicious red because of the salsa!

- Garlic is often added after the traditional Holy Trinity, for a rich, mouth-watering aroma, not to mention flavor! Just chop it fine and add to the pot after the Holy Trinity!

- Tomatoes are often added to GUMBO. Just chop a few tomatoes and throw them in the pot after the Holy Trinity has been added!

- Another veggie that is commonly used in GUMBO in addition to garlic and tomatoes is parsley. Chop fine and add to the GUMBO pot to simmer. Save a half of a cup of chopped parsley to use as a garnish before serving. *(see Part 7 Seasonings)*

- Some chefs like to add shallots, a relative of the onion, and often indistinguishable, to their Holy Trinity for a distinctive flavor.

- After you add the Holy Trinity to the roux and are stirring the mixture, you will notice your onions will go from translucent to clear. Then, if you allow the onions to stick a bit to the bottom of the pan for a minute before continuing your stirring, you will find the onions will begin to brown a bit as they caramelize, releasing their natural sugars. If you repeat this several times, this will release a delicious aroma and add a definitively sweet character to your GUMBO. We call this the *"barely burnt-basting"* technique!

215

- Even though the "Seasoning" section is later on in this book, truth be told, the finest GUMBO chefs usually add the seasonings *(salt, black pepper, red pepper, thyme, basil, bay leaves, oregano, parsley, etc.)* just after the Holy Trinity has been added to the roux, and a little more (to taste) after the roux has been added to the stock. This allows all the spices time to really "settle-in" with the flavors of the stock, sausage and poultry. Feel free to add your seasonings all along the way as you are making your GUMBO! There is no need to wait!

Introduction to the Sweet Poems

The use of onions, peppers and celery in GUMBO, as well as in most Louisiana cooking, is so essential that these three are referred to as *"The Holy Trinity."* In other words, these ingredients are so important to Louisiana cuisine that that have taken on a quality that is well-nigh sacred to the preparation of most Creole and Cajun dishes, especially to the preparation of GUMBO. Onions particularly take on a quality of sweetness as they are allowed to stick and brown a bit on the bottom of the pot after being added to the roux. The technique that we have referred to as *"Barely-Burned Basting"* allows the onions to caramelize, releasing the sweetness, which we all know onions possess. This requires some care and attention so as to allow all of the sweetness of the Holy Trinity to be released without burning these sacred ingredients.

So, too in our lives, we try to arrange our circumstances so that as much sweetness can be released as possible. We turn up the heat on our relationships often to see if we can extract that which will add just a little more sweetness to our lives. In this section, we associate the flavor of sweet with those things in our existence that make life especially tantalizing, like dating for mating, idealized love, marriage, babies, children and families. The sweet in life also includes those things that support these realities, like weddings, births and the love, joy and happiness that ensue from our loving family relationships. So, as your Holy Trinity simmers sweetly in the roux, sit back, relax and open your heart to our *Sweet Poems*!

*Authors' friend, **Rev. Dr. Asha Mawusi Bell**, with **Marla Gibbs**, seasoned Hollywood actress, best known for her role on **The Jefferson's** and for her own T.V. show, **Room 227**; Photo taken at the African American Women's Conference, California, circa 1990's; Photo courtesy, Dr. Asha Bell*

Sweet

The Grace of God is truly great
A sweetly satisfying tasty cake
The best thing about this cake is
It is mine!
Next best thing?
I eat it anytime!
Not only delicious,
I gain not one pound!
In fact, it's nutritious,
My soul has found!
And I eat, and I eat
And I never get full!
Only grateful!

~Judy Sundayo

Sweet Baby Lullaby

Sweet baby growing by the river's side
Sweet, kind angel
Black against the evening sky
Young fruit
Bright, unspoiled Afric's pride
Grow brighter under rising moon
Sleep slowly less you grow too soon
Sweet, Black babe
Nurse the richness of the land
Dark child angel
One day you'll become a man
Young baby, let me grasp your strengthened hand
God's blessings on your soul today
That gift can ne'er be taken away
Sweet growing child

~Judy Sundayo

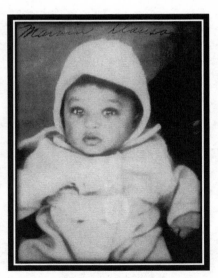

Judy Sundayo's cousin, **Mervin Dawson**
Photo taken, circa 1950's Washington, D. C.

*Judy Sundayo's oldest brother, **Leon Allen**,*
Washington, D.C., circa 1950's

Putting Away Toys

When my mom says,
"Girls and *boys*, it's time to put away your *toys*,"
We figured out how we could *play*
A game of counting toys *away*

We start by counting number **1**
And put up things that roll or *run*
Like choo-choo trains and trucks and *cars*;
That little robot we launched to *Mars*
Then, we put away the *trike*, our soccer balls;
And big-boy *bikes*

(continued)

Putting Away Toys *(continued)*

When we count to number **2**,
We catch some animals for our *zoo*
We capture a lion and a tall *giraffe*;
We even catch a monkey; that makes us *laugh*
We capture a tiger and a little yellow *duck*,
A giant whale and a parrot that *squawks*!

When we count to number **3**,
It's time for a miniature person par-TEE!
Invited are soldiers and *astronauts*;
Baby dolls, and a *jack in the box*
Doctors, nurses and firemen *run* to the toy-chest party
To have some *fun*!

By the time we count to number **4**,
We get what's left upon the *floor*
Building blocks and stacking *toys*;
Coloring books for girls and *boys*
Crayons, paints and modeling *clay*,
And books we've read throughout the *day*.

And when we get to number **5**,
I become inspector *Clive!*
I make sure everything's in *place*
With a very stern and funny *face*!
Until I'm certain that throughout *Play-land*,
Everything is *spic and span*!

By the time our counting's *done*,
We have had a lot of *fun*
My mom looks happy and we do *too!*
And so, we yell, *"Whoop-de-doo!"*
"All our toys are put *away*;
And ready for another *day*!"

~Judy Sundayo

222

*Judy Sundayo's grandniece, **Dylan**, daughter of*
***Christopher Allen** and **Asia Pendleton**,*
Photo taken in Baltimore, Maryland, 2014

Just Pretending

On Mondays,
I'm a monster with bright blue hair

On Tuesdays,
I'm a red ant and I don't play fair

On Wednesdays,
I'm a yellow walrus
And I love to swim all day

On Thursdays,
I'm a purple penguin
And I waddle, waddle, waddle away

On Fridays,
I'm a green giraffe
Nibbling the tops of trees

(continued)

Just Pretending *(continued)*

On Saturdays,
I'm an indigo bear
Sharing honey with the bees

On Sundays,
I'm an orange cow
And flowers make me sneeze

Pretending is fantastic fun
As you can clearly see
But the greatest time I have is when
I'm just being me!

~Judy Sundayo

*Judy Sundayo's nephew **Christopher Allen**,*
Asia Pendleton** and their daughter, **Dylan
Baltimore, Maryland, 2014

*The wedding of Judy Sundayo's maternal aunt **Ruth** to **William Ray** (center; Judy's aunt Helen (far left), her mother, **Thomasia** (2nd from left), her grandfather, **Emmett Smith** (2nd from right), her uncle **Leonard**, (far right) and her cousin, **Sandra** (bottom center), Washington, D.C., circa 1940's*

Sacred Wedding Dream

They walked together and climbed the mount
And mother led them to the fount of joy
And somehow all the children were there too
The waters and their own hearts' pounding knew
It was so right, so beautiful, so free
And mother bestowed her gifts
And they consumed
Their own most ancient and sacred adventure
Resumed
They walked together and spoke the word
And all of God's creation heard
And blessings poured down on their heads
And children danced and mother cried
And everyone felt good inside
We sent them wishes one by one
For health, and wealth and inner sun
And even before their words had come
Yebo! Yebo!
And it was done!

~Judy Sundayo

225

Address to Happiness

Happiness appears slippery,
Sly, shy, like me
A happy thought. . .
I have the address to happiness
Come, come see
Latch onto happiness,
Ride it, slow, fast,
Free
Catch up with happiness
I can hardly wait,
You agree?
Don't have to wait long
'Cause happiness lives inside me
Along with her brothers and sisters:
Joy, love, peace, abundance
All reside here
Beautifully
The address it is so easy, it's 1-2-3!
Happiness resides wonderfully
Inside of you and me!

~Jaime V. Jones

*Jaime V. Jones' nephew, **Derek Jason Watson**,
As a baby, San Diego, California*

*Friends of the authors' **Geneva Robinson Darcuiel** with her husband **Faruq** (left) and their children, **Damien** (upper right), **Nahla** (first row center), **Azra** (top center), and **Asia** (lower right); Professor Darcuiel teaches at San Diego Mesa College as well as San Diego State University*

Families

Families come in all shapes and sizes,
All colors and compositions
It's time to move past all those ancient suppositions
And celebrate
Families
Who share in love and laughter and support each other
Who could never imagine being in
Any other family
But their own
Yay team!

Being perfectly aware that it might seem strange
To some
But for families in love
It's just another blissful day done
Though sometimes filled with conflict, tears
And compromise

(continued)

Families *(continued)*

Families form forgiving spaces
Where love can safely rise
To the top
Families come in all shapes and sizes,
All colors and compositions
It's time to lose all those mean impositions and
Accept that even our own families are part
Of a larger band
And all of us throughout the globe
Are members of that clan . . .
The human family
At last
And if we look in *that* mirror
There's no need to fuss
'Cause what we see about families is
Them is us!

~Judy Sundayo

*Judy Sundayo's colleague, **Laura Mathis** (third from left) with her wife,*
***Wendy Hanna** (far left) and their two wonderful boys,*
Sheridan (second from left) and Kikay (far right); Professor Mathis works in the
Counseling Department at San Diego Mesa College

Dr. Johnetta Cole, (left) former President of Bennett College, Greensborough, North Carolina, with Alyce Smith Cooper

Fashion Valley Mall

All the high end high priced stores
At one end
Bloomingdales, Neiman Marcus
Jimmy Choo, Salvadore Ferragamo,
Williams Somoma, Crate & Barrel
JC Penny's at the other

Screaming toddlers limping along
behind determined to-be-hip mamas
Tight jeans sagging bagging ripped
Dogs walking people talking sleeping
dreaming scheming selling buying trying
to be a part of the fiber of today
in this USA

8-inch heels 4-inch platform
No heel no toe shirt off tattoos screaming boots hip hi tennis
shoes abound
no body playing tennis
Baby filled strollers allow for family outing walkers let the old
ones come
To the mall on a sunny Sunday afternoon

(continued)

Fashion Valley Mall *(continued)*

Music from another era
Unappreciated
by conventional culture
then used now to fan open wallets
blow up credit cards

Reluctant evangelist passing out tracts
stuttering
knees knocking
Witnessing all the same
All races all creeds all colors all sizes all ages
every fashion statement
Every capability from Mensa to Savant
midget to giant
All are welcome to Sunday afternoon
at the Mall!!

~Alyce Smith Cooper

Alyce-Smith Cooper in Toxic-free make-up
San Diego, California

*Judy's friend, **Nell Cotter** and Nell's husband, **Doug**,
Long Beach, California, 1990's*

The Castle Door

No waif or prince
Could make a home so warm
Could make a marriage bed so hot
That sizzles seep up
Through the hardwood floors

Edith and Clowanna know
That there is more to getting all dolled up
And finding oneself in strange positions
Than one might think

Perhaps it's the quest,
The challenge or the plan to reclaim power
Perhaps it's the knowledge
Found reading between the lines of life

Perhaps it's the painted porcelain face
Posed just so. . .
That smiles in recognition of the fact
That love IS there!

(continued)

The Castle Door *(continued)*

Somewhere between the tease and the temptation,
Between the bedposts and the bottom line
Love oozes out

No paltry treasure; No princely bauble
But something serious
Cementing commitment
Inscribing this message,
Tacked to the castle door. . .
"Love Endures."

~Judy Sundayo

*Judy Sundayo with long-time friends, **Candace Smith** and **Nell Cotter**,*
Long Beach, California, circa 1990's

*Judy Sundayo's daughter, **Aurora**,*
San Diego, California, 1981

Oh Life Before all Worlds

Oh Life before all worlds
How you make me smile
Truth be playful
In your face
I kiss you there

I know dance in your eye
Powerful one
It be dance of Love
Where every movement
Has meaning
Every glance has rhythm

(continued)

233

Oh Life Before all Worlds *(continued)*

Love you more, oh Life
Than what stars can shine
Than what moon can glow
Than what wise men know

Love being with you
'Cause you be walking me
Where realness go.

~Judy Sundayo

*Judy Sundayo's grand-kidlets, **Rachel** & **Alexander**,*
Florida, 2014

Alyce Smith Cooper and her grandchildren

GBFG's Rap for My Children

I'm crying for you for you are dying
You are running after the funeral car
Wearing your pants below your IQ
Telling the world what you want them to do
You want them to kiss what you show
But they will kill you, don't you know?
They will hunt you down behind your shades
Under your hoodie
Then trip you over your lowered pants
Leaving us to cry guilty hot tears
Because we did not insist you learn
who you are
Because we did not demand you learn
And know
Whose you are

(continued)

235

GBFG's Rap for My Children *(continued)*

KINGS-QUEENS-EMPOERORS-ARCHITECTS
Of empires, cultures near and far
KNOW WHO YOU ARE,
KNOW WHOSE YOU ARE!
GET WITH THE REAL!
I AM has created you with Spirit
And will choose the upward way
Choose whom you will serve this day

Choose another profile
Walk in the light
Cast a long shadow filled with
GOD'S POWER AND MIGHT
Use Your African Genius
To fight the good fight!
I'm crying for you this day
Don't let my tears be in vain
Put on the belt of truth
You are all GOD'S children
Let me be proud of you my youth
Let us be proud of you our youth
Let GOD be proud of you my youth!

~Alyce Smith Cooper

Jaime V. Jones, La Jolla, California, 2010

Love Tested

Love emerged emerald unexpected
Love lingered in eyes disconnected
Love warms wasted smiles resurrected
Love runs faster further undetected

Love elevates empty emotions painfully corrected
Love searches hearts not performances perfected
Love pours over cheerful children collected
Love heats up hearts intensely inspected

Love lights up when royally respected
Love restores, refines all in time when expected
Love remembers it all when connected
Love meets you wonderfully wherever directed

Love refuses to wait until we become disinfected
Love shows up the magic over time neglected
love searches for us who will accept it
Love delivers all you think daily manifested

Love won't be easily or quickly rejected
Decide daily love or fear be invested
Love delivers personal power resurrected
Deliver all your thoughts and words love tested

~Jaime V. Jones

Love Absolutely

Honestly I trade fear in for love,
Love is more my type
Daily I shower with love,
So love is never far from reach
Nor out of sight
I laugh at love, with love,
For love till loves eyes shine bright
I love to cuddle up with love on cold rainy nights
Daily I drink a cup or two of love
Hmmm warm, creamy ,light
I swallow down tasty, large morsels of love,
bite after bite
I sing love, about love, love I love to write
As I sit thinking, drinking, eating love, I giggle,
I grin in spite
Of all this world's daily news of doom and gloom,
oh such negative hype
No need to argue, no need to curse scream or fight
No need for you to be wrong so I can be right
Thanks to love
My future looks mighty bright

~Jaime V. Jones

Alyce Smith Cooper's great, grandchildren

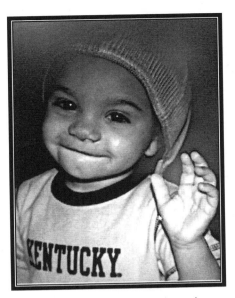

*Judy Sundayo's grandson, **Alexander**,*
California, 2012

Soothing Coos

A soft, awe-filled dreamy-eyed delight
Touched me that night
One wispy glance and a half-opened eye
And my heart was captured and I know why
It was those tiny fingers that reached up
Like they had a perfect right to
That wrested from me something like heavenly light
And with reverence, I surrendered
To the love that thickly filled the room like a blue cloud
The silence was not silent
I could sense that angels were singing
Somewhere in the vicinity of the yellow frog
And the blue bear

(continued)

239

Soothing Coos *(continued)*

You must have heard them, you were there!
And I, in bliss enfolded
Sang along with the heavenly muse
Sounds of welcome, soothing coos

And you in robes of terrycloth and down
Held court in princely compassion
And in quiet reserve you listened
To all kinds of supplications
Nonsensical babblings and silly sounds

Quite difficult to understand, I'm sure
And yet quite the gentleman,
you listened on some more
Until all was said

And then we gathered 'round the bed
And just breathed in
The breath around your royal face
As if you were some exotic natal flower
Full of sweet intoxicant

We left your side unwillingly
Inebriants of love all of us,
Bowing humbly to each precious moment
We had partaken in your presence
So full, it seemed our hearts might burst
For of all the royal grands, my love
You were the first!

~Judy Sundayo

Alyce Smith Cooper's great, grandson,
Little Dajuan

Love

The second stanza of my poem
The place where dreams are born
Then bloom living a full life
Feeding bees
Giving joy
Forming seeds
Dropping the fruit
Fertilizing the earth
Feeding the seed
Bursting open
Labor ushers in the sprout
Which breaks the soil
Springing into the atmosphere
Shining forth as another generation
Of love
~Alyce Smith Cooper

Every Woman - NOT

Seems like I'm called to do it all
Called to be daughter, mother, wife
Auntie, cousin, provider, nurturer, healer,
Counselor, mediator
Everything hovers over my head
Screaming into my ears
Accomplish, conquer, overcome, be
Every Woman – **NOT!**
You are required to accomplish much
You are not required to do it alone
You are not alone - - **Not now, not ever!**
In your mother's deepest parts
Planted and formed,
You were not alone
A plan vision purpose there for you
You are not alone
Every woman...NOT...
A UNIQUELY FORMED BUILDING BLOCK
OF THE KINGDOM . . . YES!
Join in, step into your vision
Be your life in CREATOR . . .YES!

~Alyce Smith Cooper

Alyce Smith Cooper with grandmother, **Theresa Merriman**
*And mother, **Anita Smith** at the occasion of Alyce's Graduation Party
for her Master's Degree, United Sates International University, 1976*

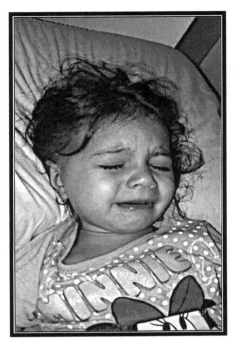

*Judy Sundayo's granddaughter, **Rachel**,*
Florida, 2014

On Putting the Baby to Bed

That deep, slow hesitant breath comes
And the fight begins
A cranky onslaught of grimaced tears
Flood the battleground

And I, your most loving and unwilling enemy
Watch
As you stockpile your arsenal against me
Frowns and pouts in tantrum'd force
Are hurled in my direction

(continued)

243

On Putting the Baby to Bed *(continued)*

But I am well armored in my compassion,
Little one
I am on guard and much more patient
Than your few years could ever comprehend

Slowly, my bedtime stories
Wear down your defenses
My soft, soothing voice disarms you
Without your ever knowing

And in one final assault,
My lullaby has captured you
You are my prisoner
Though you have fought well,

Your eyes have surrendered,
Laying their lashes down
On moist cheeks

The fight is over for a time,
Rest now my baby
May your sleep refresh you for tomorrow,
When once again,
We will be the best of friends
~Judy Sundayo

Alyce Smith Cooper with Graduate School Fellows,
San Diego, California, circa 1975

Extended Family

The family of the human experience
Is extended far beyond blood ties or national boundaries
Not just my four and no more
That was never the intension in the village
The entire planet is our village
The genius endowed within the souls of all folks displayed in
the beats the songs the dance the classical accomplishments
The clothing swag the language evolution
The explosion of quantum physics the expansion of
governmental systems
All the family is invited encouraged
Drop your nuggets into the cauldron
Transform ideas into reality
Create the things from the thoughts
Manifest from the source
From the mind of the CREATOR
Extended Family
Do your natural thang!

~ Alyce Smith Cooper

The Thing About Love

Here is the thing about love, see

Love lives, laughs inside you and me

Now because of what I know

I love it that love is with us

Everywhere we go

~Jaime V. Jones

Jaime V. Jones as a young girl, San Diego, California

Historic church in France, Photo by Judy Sundayo

Getting Married On Saturday?

So I am asking you my Sister-friends
how long do you and your man or boyfriend
Find spending time together amazing and great?
The shorter you know each other or the longer you date?
Do you find you are spending more time, less time or can
hardly wait
to see each other again or are you in a hurry to separate?

My man he keeps asking me, "Where are you going to be,
come Saturday?"
"Why you want to know/" I always say
Because, I want to hang out with you is that okay?
So the questions begin, I fire away
Am I your sweetie, your girlfriend of 4 years?
Am I your best friend your lover, your beloved blood sweat
and tears?
Yes, Yes, winking his eye, yes you are my darling dear

(continued)

247

Get Married On Saturday? *(continued)*

So now whom did you say is taking your girlfriend out on
Friday night?
I am taking my girlfriend, you sweetie out as always, that is
right.
More questions; Then Babe, who you spending all day
Saturday with much delight?
Well, sweetie if you must know let me put it to you this way
I want to spend the whole day, all day Saturday
With my girlfriend, my lover, my beloved on Saturday we play
I plan to spend Saturday evening doing what you want,
whatever you say
As long as that night in bed with my lover I get to stay
So, I am your best friend, your beloved blood sweat and tears
you say?
Yes, he answered, love you are all that night and day
I am your lover, your woman, can't live without me would
you say?
Yes, yes, I would because I have been blessed that way!
Honey, then if you were to ask, if you could find some way

I am wondering how much longer before you would say
I think we should get married on Saturday
Babe, if you ask me in the next 28 days
I would and will be delighted inclined to definitely say
Yes, I will marry you without delay!
What do you think now my man? Let's do this before we get
old land grey
So tell me my lover and best friend; am I who you will be
marring come Saturday?

~Jaime V. Jones

Alyce Smith Cooper's granddaughter, **Diona**
With husband, **Adam** *and their children, San Diego, California, 2012*

Wedding

A new family joining community
All protocols have parallel function
Who is actually in charge
Does age and wisdom have position
Not that young love needs wisdom
It only wants the freedom to exist
Charting its own course is its final destination
Only when it gets there
Does it need the wisdom of age
And unto thee do I pledge my troth

~Alyce Smith Cooper

Endure

Endure the solace of gentle peace
Take in the silence
Let it wash your soul
Endure the opening of joy in a heart
Filled with doubts, fears and pain
Endure the opening of your once guarded heart
To the unconditional love
Available from the sender
From the creator
From the giver and lover of life
Endure the syncopated beat of the heart
Of the universe
As it sings in a loud voice, "I Love You!"
~Alyce Smith Cooper

*Alyce Smith Cooper's father, **James Frederick Smith "Bosco"***
in his youth, Santa Barbara, California, circa 1940

*Friends of the authors' **Dr. Maria Nieto Senour**, Trustee, San Diego Community College District and Retired Professor, Community Based Block Program (CBB), San Diego State University, with dear friend, **Ernie McCray**, Retired Educator and Principal, San Diego Unified School District; Author, Actor, Advocate for Social Justice; Photo taken Valentine's Day, 2015, Courtesy of Maria Senior*

Just Love

Love anyone, everyone
White, yellow, brown, red or black
Love them all, skinny, funny, short, tall, round
With or without a hat
Love them especially if they reside across the tracks
Just love people until they all come bouncing back

Don't let anyone tell you love never hurts
That's just crap
But it's nothing we can't handle even when love is messy,
Painful and full of verbal smack
Mostly love is kind, respectful, forgiving and honest
Matter of fact
Love is fun, passionate, wildly wonderful,
Especially if you're starting from scratch
Love inside, outside in the warm night air

(continued)

251

Just Love *(continued)*

Love upstairs, love downstairs,
Love with your own personal flair
Love friends, family, especially yourself
Anytime, anywhere
Speak, think words of love,
Let love go with you everywhere!
Love Saturday and Sunday; Monday through Friday too
Love to motivate, bring out the best in you
Love with all your emotions; love without abuse
Look, listen and learn these words:
I do love you!

Just find a place and start
Just love with all your heart
Just love without excuse, sweetheart
Just love, accept love as art
Just love, appreciate that love is smart
Let's just love each other until life us departs

Our most powerful state, love all around
Love is everywhere, forever and always profound
Love uplifts, inspires never brings down
Here on earth, yes, love is easily found

Love with a purpose and a loving view
Love passionately, remember first love you!
Love the good the fun, the beautiful and true
Love just because it is so good for you

If love you seem to never see
Look around, breathe and maybe
Love is waiting ever so gently
Love, sigh, again breathe deeply
Love full of wonder, love full of mystery
Just love until love is no longer history!

~Jaime V. Jones

Alyce Smith Cooper's great, granddaughter,
Lisa Jada

Your Own Self's Valentine

Comes a time in everybody's life
When you have to be your own self's Valentine
It goes something like this:
On February 14th (whatever the year)
You get up early that morning,
Rush to the nearest mirror
And throw yourself the biggest kiss
You can manufacture!

(continued)

253

Your Own Self's Valentine (continued)

Then you put on your best outfit
Topped off with your favorite hat
Cocked ace/duce!
*('cause nobody - - but **nobody** loves you more than you do!)*

You step out of your door going wherever it is you must,
With a big smile on your face - -
Knowing that yes, you **will** receive roses and candy,
'Cause you will send them yourself
To your favorite Valentine - - **You!**

A great way to get exactly the color roses you want
And your favorite flavor of candy
Sounds foolish, you say? Not so.
Next year or the year after,
There will be another lover. . .

But for now - - learn to love yourself. . .
What better way to stay in practice
Than by being
Your own self's Valentine!
Happy Valentine's Day!
~Alyce Smith Cooper

*Judy Sundayo with cousin, **Falilah Bilal**, San Francisco, California*

Mirror-Mirror

Mirror, mirror on the table
Tell me that I'm truly able
To be the woman I'm meant to be
Patient, kind, forgiving, free

Show me every wrinkled line
The pain of all I've left behind
And wisdom just behind my eyes
For courage to confront my lies

Show me a true and loving smile
My willingness to sit a while
And wonder if I've got the strength
To persevere with unwavering faith

(continued)

Mirror-Mirror *(continued)*

Show me a woman walking as she should
With presence toward her highest good
I see her and I know her name
Beyond this Mirror-Mirror game

And what I see has warmed my heart
And brought together every part
Into an integrated whole,
Bound by light of inner gold!

~Judy Sundayo

*Friend of the authors' **Pearl Jones, Mental Health Counselor** at*
***Mental Health Systems**, a non-profit agency committed to cost-effective Mental*
Health Services and Drug/Alcohol Recovery;
*Pearl is also Owner of **Pearls of Wisdom**;*
This Poem was written at a Pearls of Wisdom Women's Workshop;
Photo taken with her son Eddie at Pearl's Birthday Celebration,
San Diego, California, 2015; for more information, see
https://www.mhsinc.org/

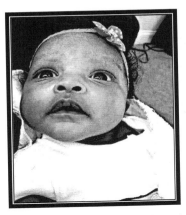

Alyce Smith Cooper's great, granddaughter,
Zya Bridges

Extra Crispy- Extra Chunky

I will tell you friends, I am happy, healthy, loving
Extra crispy, extra chunky
My friends crack up, laugh and they point at me
I laugh too cause I am definitely deliciously extra crispy
And extra chunky
This is who I am right now big beautiful and pretty
Never a week goes by without a comment
Or compliment About my beauty
No matter how small I appreciate them all;
Behind my back it is not my duty
To care about what others think or say
About my big fine booty
In fact I am laughing and giggling right now
'Cause I do not care what you think
Imagine that holy cow!
I enjoy being God confident, highly favored,
Blessed and wow!
I am old enough now
I live not to worry; learn not to worry my friends - how?
(continued)

Extra Crispy- Extra Chunky *(continued)*

Well, if God is for you, then who cares who is against you,
That is a slam-dunk!
Remember God made you and God don't make no junk!
A toast to you, on beauty, health and love stay daily drunk
Be intoxicated on joy, peace and kindness
Store these in your spiritual trunk
Whatever you do don't lose your fire your spice and spunk
Do not let anyone define for you if you are too little
Too much or socially sunk
If you are happy and healthy why pretend
That you wish to be slim or trim
Enjoy as you get older how you are,
Where you are and then
Daily you get to focus on being irresistible, intelligent
women and men
Along with delicious funny, adorable sweet
and decadent my friend
Loving, forgiving, fun, generous, successful, adventurous then
Alive, aware and alert go on set your own trends
I encourage you focus on you, live life filled up whole,
complete lacking nothing and then
Go find someone to love you that you consider a Ten !
This can happen anytime, anywhere, to anyone,
I want this for you, especially when you allow yourself to
know, to like, loving you believe me , this is your win/win
I encourage you focus on you, stop comparing or competing
be your own best friend
I am living, loving and laughing extra crispy, extra chunky - so
I win
Without judging, criticizing, whining complaining
let me say it again
Focus on what you want and be grateful for what you do have
big or thin
~Jaime V. Jones

258

Rev. Alyce Smith Cooper, Dr. Judy Sundayo and Dr. Rochelle Bastien; Dr. Bastien is a Licensed Clinical Psychologist in private practice and the past President of the San Diego Chapter of the Association of Black Psychologists; Photo taken at The International Convention of the Association of Black Psychologists, Washington, D.C. 2010

Love is Thicker Than Blood

They say blood is thicker than water
So relatives rule

I say love is thicker than blood
So if a relative is a fool
Best get yourself out of harms way immediately!

Don't be trusting some family nut
Who instigates repeatedly!

Love is thicker than blood
This chemistry lesson rules!

So bond into family those you love
And, at arms-length, keep the fools!

~Judy Sundayo

A Moment Called Now

It's time to set sail on the winds of adventure
To pack all our memories and say our goodbyes
It's time to set sail for a truer tomorrow
On oceans of promise, we sail on blue skies

It's time to let go to a new inspiration
A sense of contentment, as fears fall away
It's time to let go to a new way of being
To trust in the rhythm we're feeling today

It's time to return to what seems so familiar
The safety and joy of that place we call home
It's time to remember the faces of family
The knowledge that somehow we're never alone

It's time to envision a different dimension
The hearts of our children have taught us somehow
It's time to conceive a new song of tomorrow
By being in love with a moment called now

~Judy Sundayo

*Judy Sundayo's cousin **Garval** (In the Presence of God) **Palmer**, who
Graduated with his degree in Dental Hygiene in June of 2014, next to his daughter,
Sommer (center) and his wife **Ingrid** (right)
Photo taken in Maryland, circa 2015*

*Judy Sundayo and daughter, **Aurora**,*
Accra, Ghana, 2000

If I Call You?

If I call you mother will you wipe away my tears?
Will you comfort my sorrows and ease my fears?
If I call you mother, can we agree?
That there has been pain for you and for me?

If I call you father, will you look in my eyes?
Without conviction or surprise?
Will you call me daughter and shelter me from sorrow?
Would you risk your own life for mine tomorrow?

If I call you brother, have you got my back?
Regardless of whether you're white or Black?
Can we help each other to advance?
Will you teach me your songs and invite me to dance?

If I call you sister, will you braid my hair?
Will you share your secrets and *let m*e care?
If I call you sister, will you never forget
We must leave in the past all our fears and regrets?

(continued)

261

If I Call You *(continued)*

If I call you daughter, just wait and you'll know
That I've been your mother since eons ago
And all of my children, my daughters and sons
Are called by the ancestors, claimed by the drums

If I call you son, who can say it's not so
Sunrise over African soil we all know
That our mothers and fathers, our daughters and sons
Are all *root-connected; we're* a family as one!

So, mother, my mother
My father, my own
I'll call and you'll answer
My sister, I'll phone
My brother, you'll help me
My daughter, you'll see
My son, we're connected
For eternity

~Judy Sundayo

*Judy Sundayo's son, **Hasar**, La Jolla, California, 2013*

Alyce Smith Cooper and her grandmother,
Theresa Wiley Merriman, *San Diego, California, Circa 1970*

Classy Ladies

A long line of proud descendants is my family tree
Proud beautiful talented women we
Heads tied in clean white cloths
Big house cooks you see
Gathered the best food, cooked and served
Nursed the Captain and his wife;
Birthed his children and hers
Suckled hers and mine while my man looked on
And sucked his teeth
Well-suited for this job, we came to polish the silver
Iron the linens and lace back from gleaming silver platters
Reflects my ebony face as once it did from platters
Of gold taken from the Dark Mother's womb
Yes, who could be more suited to handle the finery of
Another time, another place than an heiress
Of a Royal House, stolen and sold,
Yet Royal still

~Alyce Smith Cooper

Dating

Pleasantries at a distance keep
He and she are dating
A slow advance of words that steep
A brew of love for mating

He acts silly; she acts cold
He responds with gifts a bearing
She feels giddy; he feels bold
She prepares a meal for sharing

Nicely he behaves and she
As sweetly takes his arm
Her lips a focal point for he
For she, it is his charms

Wordless moments glisten eyes
Blissful chills, endearing sighs
As slowly love entreats
At last she opens up her heart
To him whom she completes

~Judy Sundayo

*Judy Sundayo with fiancé, **Al Washington**,*
Benton Harbor, Michigan, 2007

Promise, Promised He

Love you, giggled she
Do you? questioned he
Oh, yes! sighed she
How much? asked he
Every minute! chimed she

What about tomorrow?
prompted he
Don't push it! smiled she
Me too, responded he
Me too? questioned she
Let it be! smiled he
Talk to me, said she
Walk with me, motioned he
How far? asked she
To me, winked he
Too far! laughed she

Come here, said he
Kiss me! said she
With pleasure, said he
Love me? asked she
Marry me? asked he
Imagine that! said she
Imagine what? questioned he
We, you, I? asked she
Yes, forever! promised he

Happily ever after? asked she
Forever, forever! responded he
Promise, promise? asked she
Promise, promise! promised he

~Jaime V. Jones

That Part of Me That Has to Do With Love

That part of me that has to do with love
I give to you
It's the song-singing, tear-flinging, desire-bringing
Part of me that you have captured with your
Loving ways
It's those sunny-day, drowsy between the sheets
Early in the morning thoughts of you
That make me feel this way
In a purple plaid maze of royal blue fantasies
Buried deep in my heart
I give to you, completely
That part of my life that has to do with love,
And babies and soft eyes and warm kisses and
Bright, sincere, straight from the soul smiles
That part of my life
Is always redeemable by you
For any similar insanity!

~Judy Sundayo

*Judy Sundayo with fiancé, **Al Washington***
La Jolla, California

Palate Cleanser

Pickled Ginger

Just a little on your plate
Pickled ginger clean
plus adds taste
Too much,
An eye and mouth-watering mistake
Between sushi, oh it's great!

~Jaime V. Jones

Alyce Smith Cooper's great, granddaughter,
Lyric Adriana

Rice

Photo by Ian L, publicdomainImages.net

I think rice is very nice
With chewy kernels so very small
It won't take long to cook at all
When served with GUMBO the flavors touch
And some folks may not like it much
But, I think rice is nice!
~Judy Sundayo

Although some people debate over the best type of rice to use for GUMBO, remember, the main dish is the GUMBO! Make the rice YOU prefer to use. GUMBO is so flavorful and spicy that you will find it will likely overpower ANY type of rice you cook, even *(Heaven forbid!)* jasmine or wild rice. We believe the purpose of rice in this dish is as a complement! Folks don't eat GUMBO for the rice! They eat it for the GUMBO. Rice is a starchy sidekick to the spicy proteins in GUMBO. Traditionally, most Louisiana cooks used whatever rice was handy and economical! For most families in Louisiana, that was usually long or medium grain white rice in bulk. So experiment, and then choose the rice your family enjoys most with their GUMBO. We suggest long or medium grain white rice as a compliment to GUMBO. But whatever you decide, remember if your family and friends are talking too much about what type of rice you are serving with your GUMBO, maybe your GUMBO ain't saying nothing!

GUMBO Recipe Step 5:

Rice

What You Need
- A Rice Pressure Cooker, or
- Large 4-6 quart Stainless Steel Saucepan
- Large netted colander

What You Gotta Get
- Two cups of rice *(we suggest long or medium grain white rice)*
- Water *(twice the amount of the rice by volume)*

What You Do with What You Get
- Wash the rice in the netted colander
- Boil the water on medium high heat
- Add the rice to boiling water
- Lower heat to low
- Cook the rice, 20 – 30 minutes, until most of the water has evaporated and the rice is soft

What You Bet Not Tell Nobody
- I like to add 1 or 2 vegetable bouillons to the boiling water before adding the rice to increase the flavor and nutrient value of the rice
- A Rice Cooker will cook perfect rice every time, without any bother
- It's best to cook the rice right before serving the GUMBO

Introduction to the Sour Poems

As an adjunct to the wonderful dish of GUMBO, there are extras that go hand in hand with the traditional GUMBO ingredients. The most important of these is rice. Rice is typically served with all GUMBO dishes. It is usually scooped into a bowl and the GUMBO is ladled on top, or it is scooped and placed on top of a bowl of GUMBO, and just to one side. Another adjunct to GUMBO in many quarters is potato salad, a cultural contribution many believe of the Germans who settled in Louisiana. We all know that potato salad has a slightly sour flavor, owing to the mayonnaise or salad dressing that is used in its preparation. But rice too has a bit of a sour undercarriage due to the milky content of its grain. The naturally sour foundation of these foodstuffs adds to the overall flavor of GUMBO. Taken alone, sour would overwhelm the dish. But in combination, the sour flavor is a wonderful balance to the sweet, salty and bitter flavors of other ingredients.

Similarly in life, we have experiences that alone might overwhelm us. The experiences of death, loss, grief and fear can have this affect. But blended in with the support of family, friends and spiritual purpose, these experiences provide balance by helping us to see the big picture and experience gratitude for our collective blessings. The poems in this section speak to the experiences that are startling, painful or difficult when experienced alone. We hope the poems in this section will encourage you to simmer your sour experiences in the collective GUMBO pot of your life!

*Judy Sundayo's paternal aunt, **Esther L. Moore***
*Holding Judy's daughter, **Aurora**; photo taken by Judy Sundayo in*
Old Town, San Diego, California, 1981

Sour

The flavor sour is quite dour
Puckering the senses
By the hour

Like news of sadness
It gives us a fright
Though it never seems
To sit quite right
With us
We're left to grieve

And our contorted faces
Conceive
A bleak tomorrow

Let's bury the dead!
That being said,

Pucker up!
And kiss away your sorrow!

~Judy Sundayo

273

Grieving

Seed sifting in Ellen's garden

Comfort to a battered heart

Well acquainted with anguish

Too well known to piercing loss

Not that death means not knowing

It means not having the familiar

The warm embrace

The haunting smile

The taste of Lemon Bars

It means paying more attention

To what we have in now time

To the presence of today

To the people we love

Sifting seeds in Ellen's garden

Will give/get/share comfort for today

Today is what we have

PRAISE GOD for today's comfort

~Alyce Smith Cooper

*Judy Sundayo's cousin, **Rafiq Bilal***
Activist and scholar, San Francisco, California

274

*Judy Sundayo with brother of another mother, **Marc Halberg,***
Ivory's Rock Conference Center, 2012, Ipswitch, Australia,
shortly before his transition in San Diego, 2012

Miss You

Miss you brother, all the time
My go-to techy, genius sublime!
I miss your smile wide as tomorrow
Your wit; your charm, now fodder
For sorrow

I *think* you're in a better place!
I **KNOW** you're at the feet of Grace
And Truth and Love and Peacefulness. . .
So, I will count myself as blessed
To have had a brother as cool as you
A friend to hang with at Amaroo

Now once again I pray for serenity
To accept that your death, which I cannot change
Has freed you for eternity!

~Judy Sundayo

275

Against the Cold

Fabulously forlorn, and downhearted, I decide
My course anew . . .
Face to my inner sun
For there is no other in this bleak winter
Best dress my mind against the cold
And keep moving
Step by step
One breath at a time
Best secure my slow advance
With deliberate purpose
Less the stony road hewn with disappointment
Defeat me
For much has been suffered
Bare feet against the painful pebbles
Of a wished for love
But hope has not died
It has only been transformed
Step by step
One breath at a time
Into the sturdiest of walking shoes
~Judy Sundayo

Judy Sundayo's friend, **Dr. Lawana (Firyali) Richmond**
Sr. Business Analyst, University of California, San Diego

Fear Factor

On top of the shame
Against the blame
Between the pain
Forget the fame

Under the guilt
Beside the doubt
Near the worry
Lies fears story

Up the fear
Behind the tears
On top of the years
Respect disappears

Between the shame
Over the blame
Through the pain
No compassion gained

Up the worry
Near the guilt
Across the doubt
Anger screams out

(continued)

Fear Factor *(continued)*

Up the shame
Down the blame
Across the pain
It's all the same

Around the guilt
Into the doubt
Beside the worry
No need to hurry

Above the fear
Beneath the tears
Between the years
Love just ain't here

Around the shame
On top of the blame
Down the pain
No power gained

Into the worry
Beside the guilt
Under the doubt
Hate leaped out

~Jaime V. Jones

*Judy Sundayo's maternal family, Judy's mother, **Thomasia** is seated on the far right; Seated in the center with folded arms is Judy's aunt **Jean (Smith) Palmer**, Thomasia's youngest sister*

A Life on Loan
(At the death of Aunt Jean)

A wide expanse of field
Endless blue skies full with sun
Dawn, in unassuming glamour waits,
Arrives and sings
And all my tears become dew
Refreshing the morning lawn
All my nights' misery has been relieved
With the fullness in the light of daybreak
Oh, my heart, whoever taught you how to pray?
No one, and yet you seemed to know all along
About those things - - God and sunsets and piercing
Sea breezes on empty beaches
Inner cries and remote twinges concerning
The omnipotence of Love

(continued)

A Life on Loan *(continued)*

And the restfulness of Peace
When the soul comes into its own

No one had to say, there's something there
One just knows. . . there's something in a baby's smile
In a child's clumsy innocence, in birth, in death
In the farthest reaches of the night's velvet blackness
In the soft intricate weaving of the rose
Something, in its immaculate bouquet. . .
And my heart, you've known it all
You've watched all the stars that roam the sky in idle rest
You've taken note, and roamed and done your best
And now I see you have a pleasing smile
I recognize we're friends and do acknowledge this. . .
In all the earth's moving from one expanse
To another
I love you

And thusly said, it is enough
For hearts know what men cannot
And hearts sing, when men,
With all their earthly concerns and thoughts of self
Have long forgotten how
Oh, God, bless the inner beggar of Truth
Who knows, and rejoices and beseeches
Each moment's breath of life
Oh, most precious gift,
On loan
~Judy Sundayo

Friends of Alyce Smith Cooper on a mountain hike

In the Face of My Pain

The sun had the unmitigated gall

To rise

And shine daily

In the face of my pain!

How can this be?

Well, if it stopped

For each heart's pain

It would never rise or set again!

~Alyce Smith Cooper

There's a Peace

Behind that blanket of blue sky
There's a little one
Asking why
Beneath the deepest, coldest sea
There's a meaning
Searching for me
Up and beyond the highest peak
There's a wisdom
That I seek
Between my breath coming
Soft as air
And my breath going
Without a care
There's a feeling
Waiting there

~Judy Sundayo

Judy Sundayo's long-time sister-friend,
Jane Richmond, *San Diego, California*

Jaime V. Jones, Judy Sundayo and Alyce Smith Cooper, La Jolla, California

Opportunity Knocking

I went for a worship walk

With my God, our God I wanted to talk

During my spiritual time during our relationship

I asked my creator, "What is all this hardship?"

I'm feeling unimportant, unmotivated,

Financially ill equipped

Lord, I want, I need to get a grip

Mother, Father, God help me with all of this

God reminded me it is opportunity knocking,

Better answer quick

I woke up today feeling broken, unhealthy,

pulled in many ways

I asked my creator,

"Why am I like this these days?"

(continued)

283

Opportunity Knocking *(continued)*

God reminded me opportunity knows
You want it to come and play
Better open up, clean up my attitude
before opportunity gets away

All around me everyone seems to live in fear
I asked my creator, "Why all the suffering, trials and
tribulation this year?"
God reminded me
It is only opportunity knocking, dear

Be courageous, no matter what happens
Especially through all the tears
Fear not, in spite of all the bad news,
Nagging, complaining you hear

I went for a worship walk
With God, I wanted to talk
About all the opportunities knocking, knock, knock
Thank you God
Thank you a lot!!!

~Jaime V. Jones

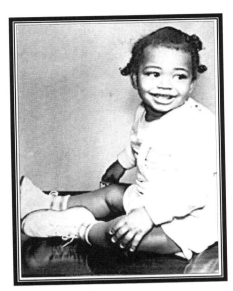

Judy Sundayo's brother, **Kelvin F. Moore,**
Washington, D.C., 1954

For My Brother, Kelly

Kelvin, you started life
Quite the funny one
The biggest grin one ever saw
Would quickly span from ear to ear

The biggest, roundest, laughing eyes
Were quick replacements for a tear
But mostly, one would recognize
That smile, then later on
That striking Kelly-green style
In long, good-natured strides

For those who knew you well inside
Would surely know
You had the best of hearts
The kindest face
(continued)

285

For My Brother Kelly *(continued)*

The greatest compassion; the fullness of grace
The best of humor; the most of trust
For you, forgiveness was not too much to share
I loved you for your kind and loving smile
I loved you even those few times
You didn't love yourself
Or care for kindness or want for justice
I loved you just because. . .
You were you!
Too quickly, you grew to be a man
Big and bristly-faced, fierce and gentle
Kind and complicated
Your smile is still what we will remember
Gap and all!
To me, you are still that same smiling child
Eyes open, heart full of innocence
And well I know that this, your last journey
Is *not* an ending
But the beginning of new realms to explore
A well-earned peace for you to enjoy
In this, I am content and wish you well, my brother
And God's speed!
~*Judy Sundayo*

*Judy's brother, **Kelvin F. Moore***
Washington, D.C., 1987, two years before his death

*Judy Sundayo's older brother, **Granville N. Moore, Jr.***
Billings, Montana, 2011, two years before his death; Photo by J. Sundayo

A Melancholy Poem for All Seasons

A small puddle was on the ground
And all around were red leaves
And people squished through under bare trees

A woolen cap lay on the ground
And all around were dashing sleds
Never aware of one bare head

A little red ant was on the ground
And all around were grains of sand
Being trampled on by feet of man

A soft pink petal was on the ground
And all around were purple and red
Cool breezes blew
The ones that were dead

~Judy Sundayo

Hovering Death Angel

Wings wide strong and deft
Hovered over Uncle Possum
Just before he left
Family gathered saying tearful good byes
Praying hopeful prayers
Recalling family gatherings
Reliving laughter shared
The Bar-B-Q that fell off the bone
Teens who could not let go the phone
That wild young one who has found THE LORD
Prayers answered
Uncle Possum has his reward
With family gathered
Tears laughter prayers shared
Death Angel hovers no more
Swiftly softly with a gentle grasp
Gathers Uncle Possum free at last to fly away
To his home in glory
To be welcomed by Daddy Mama
The heavenly choir singing
Welcome home dear son
You job is done.

~Alyce Smith Cooper

Photo taken by Judy Sundayo of Garden in Paris, France

288

The Great Wall of China, the length of which is over 13 miles long
Photograph by Judy Sundayo, 2007

Journey

The days are long my soul
Find your mountain stream and quench your thirst
Our journey will be long
But our destination far surpasses anything
We've seen along the way

My head hangs heavy on my shoulders
When I think of love
And my feet drag as if they would pull me down
To grobble there in the dust
With only tears to refresh them
But, I turn my face to the sun
From it I gather strength
to keep its brilliance always in my mind's eye

(continued

Journey *(continued)*

And the warmth of the world in its light
Is far better food for you my soul
Than all the heat of passion

The days are long my soul
And this body has a difficult road to follow
But we will rest one day by the stream
in your homeland
And you will drink till you are filled
And I will sing a love song

~Judy Sundayo

*Judy Sundayo and **Al Washington** at the Great Wall of China, 2007*

*Alyce Smith Cooper and granddaughter, **Lisa Jada***
San Diego, California, 2013

Mind Gumbo: Sorrow's Baby

Watching my 7-year old great, grand daughter
Write a poem about what it takes to be a friend
What hitting others does to friends?
What constitutes bullying?
How harsh words can hurt too

Reaching out to a hurting 7 year old
with big front teeth
Smiling through hot tears of rejection
By a longed-for-dead-beat-dad.

Stirring the RED HOT POT of mixed emotions
With a chicken foot of bitter responses in the gut
Ugh! That don't taste good!
Stir in some playful hugs, sprinkle in
some blessed oil

(continued)

Mind Gumbo: Sorrow's Baby *(continued)*

Shake in some spiritual herbs aka Proverbs
Speak the words of FAITH HOPE JOY PEACE
Aka THE GOLDEN RULE
Turn up the fire of THE HOLY GHOST
Boil that fiery pot!!
Chop up the onion of desire
Mince the garlic of dis-par-ate emotions
Greed guilt hatred foolish thoughts of
self-reproach
CHOP IT CHOP IT CHOP IT CHOP IT CHOP IT
CHOP IT!
BOIL IT BOIL IT BOIL IT BOIL IT BOIL IT BOIL IT!
Into the Gumbo Pot of a broken heart
Does not go a broken spirit
The Spirit-The Breath belong to
THE I AM GOD
Belong to THE LORD OF HOSTS
The Angels of LOVE

BE GONE forces of anti-love
GOD'S child resides here
And the authority is established
All the forces of dark feelings must go
The Whole Armor of THE I AM GOD is the pot
Stirred by the Sword
WORD
No weapon formed within or without
Will succeed
Yield to the fire of the HOLY GHOST!

(continued)

Mind Gumbo: Sorrow's Baby *(continued)*

Become a testimony of healing!
Transform into a fruitful incorruptible stew!
Great Grand Ma's voice declares and decrees
Darkness and all attempts to dis-courage
Are bound, cast down and boiled into nothingness
That this child walks in LOVE
In the footsteps of JESUS!
Is guided by the HOLY SPIRIT!
Is healed whole and flourishes!

She knows THE I AM GOD as her real FATHER
As GOD'S PROPERTY
She is long lived stable incorruptible
As the hedge of protection placed all around her
Sprinkle in a little salt drop in the okra of
Great Grand Ma's Godly Wisdom
BOIL IT BOIL IT BOIL IT BOIL IT BOIL IT!
Taste again . . . UHM HUM
'Gumbo mind come into submission
to the WILL OF GOD!

~Alyce Smith Cooper

Alyce Smith Cooper as a child

Still in Death

Black moved on the night
Moved on slow and cold
It grabbed the earth
With strong black fingers
Sam died
It gripped the soul
Why Sam?
The biting wind offered no release
For hearts that bled burning tears
Tears that burned through death and sorrow
That burned out love in the face of the cold
I remember the time
I saw him and was glad
To see his face aglow with joy
To see his sly smile
And his love for the people
The hearts whose blood would run together
As the blackness squeezed the emptiness out
Out of our minds
And out of our lives
Was it his hope that we might find
A bond between us?
The earth is chilled and quiet in the moonlight
But the darkness lingering in the midst of the night
Never releases its hold on the earth
Completely

~Judy Sundayo

*At the gravesite of **John Gregory Chedester, "Greg"***
*Beloved brother of **Richard** and son of **Cheryl** and **John,***
Judy Sundayo's in-laws, London, Kentucky,
Photo taken in November, 2014, courtesy C. Chedester

Mourning Clothes

How many days have passed?
And still I've nothing but my tears
Hold onto memories, I gasp
Yet comfort never nears

Lonely in a crowd am I
So, inside will I weep
Forgotten are those happy days
When joy woke me from sleep

This grief in all its territory
Rules with ironclad fist
And I in mourning clothes conspire
Freedom from its kiss

(continued)

Mourning Clothes *(continued)*

Long are the days my heart stands still
And longer still the fires
That burn the lakes of innocence
And make of roses, liars!

~Judy Sundayo

*In honor of **John Gregory Chedester, "Greg,"** a soft-spoken,
kind-hearted and kind-spirited individual, who was quick to help
others in need, slow to anger and full of the quest to live life fully;
Will be deeply missed by family, as well as by his many friends;
Photo taken in London, Kentucky, 2013, courtesy C. Chedester*

Gone too Soon

Gone too soon
Shoot the moon
For shining in this dark
Death has stung
Its poison flung
Our grief
The stinger's mark!

~Judy Sundayo

296

Alyce Smith Cooper with *Jacqueline Hughes Mooney,*
Renowned African America quilter

Seed Sifting

Seed sifting in Ellen's garden
Comfort to a battered heart
Well acquainted with anguish
Too well known to piercing loss
Not that death means not knowing

It means not having the familiar
The warm embrace
The haunting smile
The taste of Lemon Bars

It means paying more attention
To what we have in now time
To the presence of today
To the people we love

Sifting seeds in Ellen's garden
Will give/get/share comfort for today
Today is what we have
PRAISE GOD
For today's comfort!

~Alyce Smith Cooper

297

Killer Fear

Fear kills dreams

Like Stearn's electric paste kills roaches

Dead as a doornail

Wake up one morning

Find your dreams strangled in the nest

By fears, saying. . .

You are too this!

There's not enough of that!

What you say today. . .

Tomorrow, when you wake up. . .

Will be true!

~Alyce Smith Cooper

*Quilt by renowned African American Quilter, **Jacqueline Mooney***

*Judy Sundayo with childhood friend, **Nancy Caliman**, (right)*
Chemistry major, University of Maryland,
Photo taken in Washington, D.C. circa 2000's,
Just a few years before Nancy's transition

A Winter Sadness

It's cold and oh the leaves fall
My breath is a slow painful, winter wind
Empty of leaves and life
My heart ceases to question
It's tired and
Has done its best
My mind ceases
To care and all the rest
Stops for a time
Waiting, waiting
A winter sadness waiting

~Judy Sundayo

Dust to Dust

Lying there ash to ash

Recalling the years;

Now smothered embers slowly smoldering

Being there dust to dust

Tasting moist dirt

Consecrated by tears and

Flavored of blood

Feeling bare, flesh to flesh

Striped of my soul and indignant

I cursed . . . my last sin

With death as my sacrament, smiling

The earth took me in

~Judy Sundayo

Photo taken by Judy Sundayo in Kemetic Temple

*The authors' friend, Rev. **Dr. Asha Mawusi Bell**, Prayer Warrior, With Judy Sundayo, San Diego, California, circa 1990's; Photo Courtesy, Rev. Dr. Asha Mawusi Bell*

Black Psalm

My mind just runneth over
Like they say about that cup
This bum raps bought and paid for
With the interest piling up
From unforgotten sorrow
My head's hanging heavy-low
With unwashed tears, I watch my feet
Continue going slow
From high noon until midnight
From sunset until dawn
I haven't got my have-ta-gits
My bin-gots done bin gone!
My mama's done her crying
My daddy's done his best
Theys aged and wearied from the years
The world has did the rest
Well, my hopes still lie in heaven
They'll be resting there until
All our cups are running over
And we finally get our fill!

~Judy Sundayo

Pine Swept Moss

My love laid me down on pillowed beds
Of pine swept moss
Nature's coquettish greenness blossomed
Her teardrops hung from every flower
And touched my soul, her child
A silver web was spun around our hearts
In marriage of that moment with our lives
Happiness was the word in my existence and my being
It seems so long ago now
My love left like the spring
All the world withered and grew cold
Barren branches holding me
Is the memory of his arms
My love laid me down on pillowed beds
Of pine swept moss
And buried me there
~Judy Sundayo

Photo by Judy Sundayo, La Jolla, California

*Judy Sundayo with friend, **Jane Richmond***
On the River Seine, Paris, France, 2008

Renewal

I have left my old skin

By the rocks near the river

It crumbles . . .

Bleached transparent by sun and rain

My new skin is dark and vibrant

It sparkles like jewels

Once again, I plunge

Into the waters

~Judy Sundayo

Have You?

Have you ever been disgusted?

Feeling a hate so deep within your heart

And in the end . . .

Pity?

Have you ever felt desperately alone?

Scared to tears

Yet warm and secure between cool sheets?

Have you ever loved with a love meant only for eternity?

Then watched eternity . . .

Pass you by?

~Judy Sundayo

*Judy Sundayo and brother, **Granville**, as toddlers,
Washington, D.C., circa 1950's*

304

*Photo taken during a memorial hike for **Ed Mercaldo,** Highline Trail in Glacier Park, Montana, 2014; Photo courtesy Ed's wife, Karen Mercaldo*

In the Spreading of his Ashes

In the spreading of his ashes

Angelic Guides threaded rainbow radiance

Through light beams

Creating a royal tapestry

Rolled out before his essence

Welcoming him back home

To THE SOURCE

Remembering Ed Mercaldo

As a generous spirit – a loving man

~Alyce Smith Cooper

The Other Side

Ah, as the billowing stream rushes
The honey-filled buttercups start to cry
And there is no place for a tear to rest
'Till it reaches the other side

It's late in the afternoon now
And the towering trees sweep the sky
And sun-drench dust lines the footbridge
Which leads to the other side

See how the birds whisper melodies
Updraft and downdraft they fly
And each one drops a buttercup
To the grass on the other side

The cool night harbors it's own moon
And we dance in its light from on high
And only the purest of lights touch our souls
As jewels on the other side

~Judy Sundayo

*A five –generation photo of Judy Sundayo's maternal family; her great,
grandmother, **Eliza Harris** (far right), her grandmother, **Florence Smith** (top
center), her aunt, **Helen Dawson** (far left), Helen's first daughter, **Sandra
(Dawson) Summers** (Center left) and Sandra's first Daughter, **Torii** (Center right);
Photo taken Virginia, circa 1900's*

*A friend to all, **Maryam Sulliman** (1958-2014); A tremendously talented chef, entrepreneur, businesswoman; Kind to a fault; Well respected; admired by all who knew her; Charitable to the community & anyone in need; Originally from Eritrea, Maryam became well known for her Sambussas which were savored throughout San Diego; Her memory will be cherished*

Maryam

A kind soul
A wonderful cook
A loving smile
And a certain look
That said,
"I've known troubles,
but I don't let it show
I left that behind me a long time ago
My life has been full
Of service to others
My family, my friends
My sisters and brothers
I think they know
When we're apart
They still hold the best part
Of my heart
So, I rest content in who I am."
Rest well, then
Dear sweet, Maryam!

~Judy Sundayo

307

Treasure Chest

I recollect there was time
It hurt more
I still wince at memories
Still catch a sob trying to flee
From my heart to my throat
Or from my throat to welling eyes
And then again, sometimes
I catch myself with a thought that makes me smile
Or laugh out loud
At some small thing that reminds me
Of a precious moment past
I know I'm left with something
A collection of thoughts and feelings
A treasure chest, really
Of all the moments my heart holds dear
I pull out one memory or another
At times to reminisce or share
My friends smile sweetly and nod
In genuine acknowledgement, but
I fear no one truly knows the value
Of these my precious treasures, but me
I'm left with my collection to comfort me
A wealthy pauper

~Judy Sundayo

*On left, Judy Sundayo and **Toi Ethridge**, former participant In the Rites of Passage Program for African American Girls; on right, Toi's mom, **Joann Marie "Duchess" Ethridge**, who made her transition in 1999, but was a wonderful, mother, friend, childcare worker and advocate for social justice in San Diego; Photo, Judy Sundayo*

I Can't Breathe

Rumain Brisbon, 34, father of four, shot to death
When police mistook his bottle of pills for a gun
Tamir Rice was playing with a toy gun in a park
When police shot him dead. He was 12
Akain Gurley, 28, shot to death by police in New York
Police Commissioner called him a *"total innocent."*
For all the murdered innocents, devastated, I grieve
Weighing heavy on my spirit, Lord
I can't breathe! I can't breathe!
Yvette Smith, 47, was shot and killed after opening her door
To the police, whom she had called for help
Jordan Baker, 26, was shot by an off-duty officer who
Mistakenly thought he was a robbery suspect
Rekia Boyd, 22, was shot and killed by an off-duty officer
Who mistakenly thought he saw someone nearby with a gun
For all the murdered innocents, devastated, I grieve
Weighing heavy on my spirit, Lord
I can't breathe! I can't breathe!
Wendell Allen, 20 was shot and killed in New Orleans
Unarmed and without provocation
Aaron Campbell, 25 was shot and killed by police in Portland
while standing submissively with his hands behind his head
Only a drop in the bucket, are these our numbered dead!
For them and the thousands more
It's too late to get them back
All were killed by police
All were innocent
All were Black
For all the murdered innocents, devastated, I grieve
Weighing heavy on my spirit, Lord
I can't breathe! I can't breathe!

~Judy Sundayo

Palate Cleanser

Judy Sundayo, on the Giza plateau in Kemet (Egypt);
Pyramids of Pharaohs Khufu, Khafra and Menkaura in background, 2010

Soda Crackers

Soda Crackers, Snap!
Thin and dry
Like a weathered map
That desert travelers find
And pluck from sand
Scorched and crumbling
Color bland
Like nomads
Brittled by the sun
Yet, no less ready
One by one. . .
Head and heart and hands
All steady
To find that oasis within,
Snap!
Like the crisp bite of dry crumbs
Sweeping the palate
Drying the tongue
Soda Crackers,
Treasure won!
~Judy Sundayo

Seafood

Photo by Jon Sullivan, publicdomainImages.net

Shrimp, crab, crawfish
Crawl in the pot
If pre-cooked
You won't need to simmer a lot
We're really not trying to cause you trauma
But 'cause of you, this GUMBO
Gone make somebody
Slap they mama!
~Judy Sundayo

Seafood is at the heart of almost all GUMBO recipes. Whether it is Chicken and Sausage GUMBO, to which shrimp is traditionally added, or an all Seafood GUMBO, where shrimp, crab and crawfish are happy to jump in the GUMBO pot together. Seafood GUMBO is common in New Orleans, given its proximity to the coast. Cajun chefs especially revel in making a GUMBO of sausage and oysters. Seafood gives GUMBO that deep savory ocean flavor. It's always preferable to use fresh seafood, but if not available, frozen will work just fine!

GUMBO Recipe Step 6: **Seafood**
(Shrimp, Crab Legs,)

What You Need
- Covered bowels for cleaned seafood
- Sharp paring knife
- Short bristled brush
- Kitchen shears

What You Gotta Get
- Shrimp
- Crab legs

What You Do With What You Get
- Peel and devein the raw shrimp washing thoroughly.
  (They live in the sand and tend to be gritty.)
- Scrub crab legs with short bristled brush.
  (They tend to be hairy and gritty too.)
- Using kitchen shears, cut crab legs into 2-3 inch pieces.
  (They fit nicely into your bowls and more people get a piece.)
- Add the crab legs and raw shrimp to the hot GUMBO pot 15 – 20 minutes before serving.

What You Bet Not Tell Nobody
- Fresh shrimp is expensive but it may be worth it if you want a nice shrimpy flavor.
- Powdered dried shrimp is less expensive and is still flavorful. Add a 4 oz. bag to your stock to zip up the shrimpy flavor.

- Pre-cooked frozen shrimp will work in a pinch. Just don't add to the GUMBO until the last 10 minutes before serving.
- For a Seafood GUMBO, in addition to the shrimp and crab legs, you may add 1-2 cups of crawfish tail meat; allow to simmer in pot 25 minutes before serving or only 5-10 minutes, if pre-cooked

Introduction to the Savory Poems

Seafood has a wonderful effect on GUMBO by virtue of a magical blending of several flavors: salty, bitter, spicy, sweet and sour. Anyone who has eaten shrimp, crabs or crawfish knows exactly what we mean. A blending of all of these flavors results in what we believe is savory by definition. Savory represents a richness and a fullness of flavor, which encompasses all of the other flavors simultaneously. Some say GUMBO is synonymous with the flavor savory.

In our lives, savory represents the wisdom that comes from all of the other experiences in our lives. It represents knowing how to make sense of our youth, our history and early lessons, our talents, our shortcomings, our relationships, our children, our families and our friendships so that we can find fulfillment. The savory poems are the wisdom poems. These poems represent what we have come to believe and understand about ourselves, our experiences and about life in general. They speak to our philosophies, our values, our character traits and those of our friends and allies who have helped us in the development of these belief systems. Like seafood, the savory poems have a sprinkling of the saltiness of youth, the bitterness of young adulthood as we learn the abrupt early lessons of reality, the spiciness of our infatuation with the earth, food, music, dance, poetry, the sweetness of idealized love and joy in our children and families and the sourness of loss and grief. The result is a thick, rich and savory experience, which we hope you will enjoy in the *Savory Poems*.

Judy Sundayo and childhood friend, **Michelle Henderson,** *Mathematics Major, Boston University, Photograph, San Diego, California, circa 1975*

Savory

Well-seasoned,
Like a simmering, soulful, soup,
The scent of savory
Salutes at the door
And scintillating herbs
Soothe the soul to the core
Savory . . . *satisfies*
With warm and wizened sage
Like a full-bodied friendship
Savory
Betters with age

~Judy Sundayo

New and Time Tested

Friendship
The reality of another Being
Entered into, Shared, Sacred
Value-laden
Based in deep wells of desire
To be included
To experience the power of fellowship
To know the joy of the dance
The freedom of self-exposure
To know no fear of rejection
Friends love simply
Because you are my friend
Thank GOD for new friends
And the time tested ones

~Alyce Smith Cooper

Alyce Smith Cooper *with friends* **Jan Philips** *and* **Judy Sundayo**

*Judy Sundayo with **Vickie Butcher, J.D.**, and Vickie's sister, **Tabor Knight**;*
Vickie and her husband, Dr. Richard Butcher, former President of the National
Medical Association, long-standing, trusted Medical Doctor in the
*San Diego community co-founded **Water for Children Africa, Inc.***
to provide safe drinking water and sanitation for children in Africa;
Kwanzaa, at the Butcher's home, El Cajon, California, 2014

Kwanzaa at the Butcher's Home

Warm hearth, warm hearts, no need to roam
It's Kwanzaa at the Butcher's home
I search the faces gathered 'round
Glowing joyfully, Black, White and Brown. . .
"Habari Gani!"
"*Umoja*, Habari Gani!" The reply is called out!
And the principle of Unity is read about
Each subsequent day, a new principle is read
And each guest finds meaning in what is said

Kujichagulia, yes, we'll determine for ourselves
Our own fate!
Ujima, whatever work we do, let's cooperate!
Ujamaa, we pool our resources for prosperity
So our *Nia* will purposefully serve the community
Kuumba, yes, we're creative in the extreme!
And *Imani* is the reminder that God leads our team!

(continued)

Kwanzaa at the Butcher's Home *(continued)*

The mood is sincere as heads nod and eyes glisten
Each person shares, while the others listen
Three decades of celebration,
Yet each year we still learn
We must bury the past and the future affirm

By the time the evening is brought to a close
"Harambee!"
We've all pulled together even those
Who had never known what Kwanzaa was about
Are embracing strangers before going out
Warm hearth, warm hearts, no need to roam
All are welcome to Kwanzaa at the Butcher's home!

~Judy Sundayo

*Vickie Butcher, J.D., has been honored at the San Diego Women's Museum, for her community service in an exhibit of African American Women entitled, **Beautiful, Brilliant & Brave**: A Celebration of Black Women, March 2014; Vickie is Co-founder and Executive Director of **Water for Children Africa, Inc.**, a non-profit organization, which provides children from the poorest of African villages with clean well water and sanitation equipment; 30,000 children die each day from contaminated water; 85% of all diseases in African children under the age of 5 are caused by water-borne illnesses; Photo courtesy of V. Butcher; for more information, go to http://www.waterforchildrenafrica.org/*

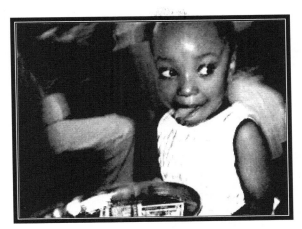

*Alyce Smith Cooper's great, granddaughter, **Lisa Jada**,*
San Diego, California

Compassion

With a wide open heart
Be ready for anything
When the wild fires burn
Pray for changing winds and rain
If the money is low
Eat the fruit off neighbors' trees
The world turned upside down
Look forward to the next
Leap of cosmic consciousness

~Alyce Smith Cooper

Alyce Smith Cooper's A Street House & Community
Gathering place around the kitchen table, Golden Hills, California

Friendship

So what does it look like
This friendship we entertain?
Does it flow in tandem
Like silken banners in summer breezes
Or rustle like oak leaves pelted by rain?
Where does it meet
To satisfy curiosity
To commune
To adorn with gayety
compassionate hearts.
Facile minds sparkle with contentment
At thoughts that enter
With the notion of being your friend.

~Alyce Smith Cooper

Alyce Smith Cooper and friends

Jackie Bachlor and *Judy Sundayo's mother,*
Thomasia (Smith) Moore, *Washington, D.C., circa 1940's*

Since Second Grade

Since second grade you were my friend
We hung out hand in hand
We stayed that way until the end
For friendship, took a stand!

We walked together home from school;
My freckles, some would hate,
If they messed with me they had to be fools;
Your fist would set them straight

We stayed like sisters as we grew
Through good times and through strife
Our daughters became good friends too
As mothers in married life

Though death now has a distance made
You're still my sister-friend!
A blessing since the second grade!
Thank the Lord, Amen!

~Judy Sundayo

323

I am Up

Slowly sweetly merging
Feet — gratefully grounded
Legs – Up; knees- Ouch!
Thighs twittering thunders
Hips high helping
Internal organs ready recharged!
Heart hopeful happy
Lungs lightly loaded
Stomach silently shouting
Chest celebrated, neck noble
Head, honest, humorous; eyes eager
Eyes engaged energized, lips laughing
Human body, all systems unfold
I am up, best day ever; Told you so!
Seek first the kingdom
I gotta go!

~Jaime V. Jones

Jaime V. Jones and friend, *Mary Higgins,*
San Diego State University, San Diego, California

*Long-time friend of the authors', **Denis Newsome**, technical advisor and Fight choreographer for "Lethal Weapon;" Master teacher of **Capoeira,** Capoeira Angola de Sao Bento Grande in the Hood; dedicated to passing on the Art and tradition of Capoeira to the next generation; Photo courtesy of D. Newsome http://malandros-touro.com/about.html*

Courage

Courage~
The lion has it, right?
A strength beyond strength
A power beyond power
A knowing~
Like a feeling of reliance
On inner stuff
Courage~
Like a heart beating
Faster than fear
You have it, right?
A certain persistent breath
Beyond your breath
And nearer than near

~Judy Sunday

Things That Take Me Back

There are sounds
That are familiar sounds
There are places
That touch my heart like home
There are smells
That take me back to the summertime of '62
And all the words I utter
Are not new words . . .
Just an old soul remembering

~Judy Sundayo

Judy Sundayo and Al Washington at the home of Stevie Wonder,
Los Angeles, California, 2001; Photo courtesy of J. Sundayo

*Long-time friends of the authors', **Conley Major**, veteran,*
Artist, videographer, community activist, historian, and strong proponent of social
justice; Photo courtesy of Conley Major

Unity

Not just a word
A meaning to be heard
And felt and remembered

UMOJA
Tied to history and a glorious past
Let's all pull together
And decide at last
Our destiny

UNITY
Portends success and power
Let's all remember
This week, this day, and hour that
UMOJA RULES

But it starts with us
And this will have to be a must
To be united we must understand
It starts with me to take a stand

(continued)

Unity *(continued)*

I know who I am
I'm not afraid
To admit when I'm wrong
To let my agenda fade
For the good of the group
For the good of us all
UMOJA is UNITY
And if you recall
It's not all about me
It's about our history
And our family
It's about cooperating
For our destiny
UNITY is not just a word
It's a profoundly significant meaning
To be heard
And felt and remembered and acted upon
For UNITY is realized
When we act as one
~Judy Sundayo

*Judy Sundayo's brother-friend and colleague, **Michael Temple**, Professor, Counseling Department, San Diego Mesa College, Coordinator of the **Mesa Academy - UMOJA** (Kiswahili word, meaning "Unity") **Program**; Photo taken with **Alyce Smith Cooper** & **Jaime V. Jones** at The **Annual UMOJA Conference**, San Diego, California, November 2014*

Alyce Smith Cooper San Diego, California

When the Going Gets Tough

Some folks say
Crumple up in a heap of tears, worry,
And frustration
When the going gets tough
An accident . . .
Someone gets sick . . .
Not enough money . . .
Some folks just go into a shell
Fold up like a broken umbrella
Or the light in their eyes flickers
And dies

Now, my grandma used to say
"When the going gets tough,
The tough get going."
But, what I say if this . . .
"When the going gets tough,
The tough dress up!"

(continued)

When the Going Gets Tough *(continued)*

It goes something like this . . .
The unhappy event has taken place
The tough time is here
Now what?
I can grab a chocolate bar
A drink of gin
A telephone or a bible
Or drop to my knees to pray
On my knees I'm looking up
To see a sky still blue
A sun still shining
Before I know it
I'm thanking God
For breath, sight, the movement of my limbs
A mind to think
And a heart that still pushes warm blood
Through my body

By now, my knees are aching
And I'm thinking
Kinder, gentler thoughts
Where do I go from here?
Whatever the problem
Once I've prayed about it
It no longer belongs to me
I'll have to think a new thought
I'll go a new direction
Leaving the bad behind
I'll put on some *"Problem-solved!"* clothes
'Cause when the going gets tough
The tough dress up!

~Alyce Smith Cooper

*Friends of the authors, **Makena Hayes-Gorgonnu** and **Auset Price**;*
*Makena is a Social Media Marketing Strategist at **Celebrity Events** by Makena G.*
*as well as Live Event Producer at **Ashaye Soul Productions**,*
https://www.facebook.com/makenag
Auset Price is a natural hair stylist, educator and massage therapist,
https://www.facebook.com/auset.price

My Sistahs

My Sistahs come in many sizes
Many forms and shapes and shades
My Sistahs could win beauty prizes
For their stunning wraps and braids

My Sistahs got that intellect
That keeps them on their toes
My Sistahs seriously protect
Their children, heaven knows!

(continued)

My Sistahs *(continued)*

My Sistahs are creative
And hardworking to extremes
My Sistahs so tenacious
Never give up on their dreams

My Sistahs, it's a blessing
To have you by my side
My Sistahs teach me lessons
Which fill my heart with pride

My Sistahs, my Sistahs,
My Sistahs I must confess
As family, friends and confidants
My Sistahs are the best!

~Judy Sundayo

*Longtime friend of the authors, **Gwana Ajibola**, one of the
Original elders in the first Rites of Passage Program for African American Girls in
San Diego County, with daughter, **Kiki**, Gwana is also Managing Consultant at
Great Works Enterprises, for personal and organizational consulting; Photo
courtesy of G. Ajibola; for more information contact Gwana at
g.works.enterprises@gmail.com*

Jaime v. Jones with sister, **Marilyn R. Jones-Sims** (Cookie)
And **Aunt Sharon Jones**

Testing!

Do me a favor, check this list
Sometimes your words strike hot like a fist
Feeling discouraged, excluded and dismissed
Put all your words and thoughts to this simple test

Encouraging? Including?
Me and you plus all the rest?
Do your words encourage me to be my best?
Leaving me proud with a celebrated chest?

Do your words evoke dignity, love and respect?
Even though I know I too sometimes forget
To put my words and thoughts to this test
Then my words end up creating resentment
Oh, heck!

(continued)

Testing! *(continued)*

I pray someday to reconnect
Family and friends I neglect
Creating a lot of regret
Now I surrender to any help I can get
Sorry for all the disappointment and disrespect
Working now, I fully accept
All the responsibility
For what comes next
This is not easy we are worth it I confess
Let's practice and daily check
That our words encourage and include respect
We are blessed and able to select
Our words and thoughts be sure they reflect
Love, compassion, forgiveness, appreciation
Intent to connect
Doing so, even your errors become correct
But we all got to stop and check
Our actions, words and thoughts put to this test
Think before you speak
Will your words deliver respect?
I pray may all your words return to you,

No regrets!

~Jaime V. Jones

*Alyce Smith Cooper's son, **Steven Stokes**,*
San Francisco, California, circa 1990

Serenity

Come along with me
Said Peace to Serenity
Over glens of misunderstanding
Boulders of ego, false pride
And plains of stupidity
Join me beside the still waters
Where truth and wisdom swim
Come rest awhile
Join the breezes
While they settle the dust

~Alyce Smith Cooper

Until That Day

There was a town the Word was spoken
They slept unsheltered
Even moonbeams touched their souls

Take this die I cast before you
Take this spirit off the grave
You who hear my words will listen
Days will rot and peel away
Cherish only what I give you
Till that one lamp lights your way

May days look on your life in favor
And nights bend down to give you rest
May Truth in all its Glory be
A bowl of Love, which fills your breast

Until that day when Light will guide you
To that place you once called home
Many burdens you will carry
And you will roam and roam and roam

~Judy Sundayo

La Jolla Cove, La Jolla, California;
Photo by Judy Sundayo

*Judy Sundayo with friends and jegnas, **Dr. Carrol Waymon** (left), her first Black professor in Graduate school; Community Advocate and Expert on Race Relations, Retired Professor, Author of the book, **"On Being Black in San Diego,"** Civil Rights Activist, Head of the Citizens Interracial Committee (CIC), which in 1964 became the first human relations agency in San Diego;*
*And **Dr. Carl Smith** (right), Retired Psychologist, Licensed Clinical Social Worker, Former Clinical Supervisor for Veterans Administration, Expert in Sex Therapy, Addictions, Biofeedback and Physiological Psychology and Research; All former Presidents of the San Diego Chapter of the **Association of Black Psychologists**, photo taken, San Diego State University, circa 2010, courtesy of J. Sundayo*
www.abpsi.org

To Educate

What does it mean to educate?
To inspire; to uplift
To change the fate of a people,
a nation, a world?
It means first of all . . .
To care enough to LOOK
Past the lecture,
The syllabus and even the book
Into the very heart of the would-be scholar
A piercing soul deep view to ponder . . .
And secondly, to LISTEN
Let your tongue silent keep;
Till you can finally hear the ancestors speak
Only then can a teacher truly teach

~Judy Sundayo

337

I am a Recovering Hypocrite

What I find to be most human
Humbling and true
Whatever, whenever I am criticizing
Finger-pointing a few
Judging, talking about, frustrated, complaining,
Nagging you
Somehow, someway, somewhere,
a closer look
I am doing that same thing too!
Once I am mature I introspect, I self-audit
Most of what I do
Then and only then I can realize darling, you
Have been walking a mile or two
In my little, too tight, high heeled shoes
Ouch, Ouchy, oooo!
Singing, co-signing the same ole judging,
Criticizing tore up from the floor up blues
I am a recovering hypocrite,
how about you?
Now, that you know
What you going to do?

~Jaime V. Jones

*Judy Sundayo's friend, Ric**hard Kenner,** Phoenix, AZ, 2014;*
Photo courtesy of R. Kenner

Purpose

Yes, I'm blessed to have a purpose
It's a masterpiece in jade
With dabs of dreams I clearly see
Though the colors sometimes fade
I tell myself I can create
Whatever my heart can hold
I paint; re-paint; let dry the time
To see what will unfold
Then, one morning something happened
As the Light awakened me
Unfolding layers from my eyes
So blessed was I to see
That each brushstroke lovingly applied
Beckons the canvas produce
And my purpose is a work of art
That time lets love seduce

~Judy Sundayo

A Thousand Tomorrows

The young build their dreams

Of a thousand tomorrows

A few as they age

Will have learned from their sorrows

Blessed be the elder

Or the wise child who knows

That today's missed moments

Are tomorrow's woes

~Judy Sundayo

Judy Sundayo *with cousin,* ***Garval L. Palmer***
Upper Marlboro, Maryland, circa 1980's; Photo courtesy J. Sundayo

*Jaime V. Jones' niece, **Evelyn Jones** (Mimi),*
as a child in Nordstrom Fashion Show, San Diego, California

I Wish I Were You

Sometime, somewhere, we hear, we see
Someone, we think, "Wish that were me!"
Life questions, "Oh, really?"
So you think you are willing
To pay the price
To live their life?
Everything in this life
Cost, Cost us, life has its price
The price we humans pay
To grow, live, laugh, learn everyday
Learning life lessons we call them by name
Wisdom is knowledge plus application
Here comes some pain
Passion produces opportunities for fame
Let me keep this simple, let me keep this plain
In every life there is golden sunshine
And pouring rain

~Jaime V. Jones

341

While I'm laughing

I want to die while I'm laughing
Man, what a great way to go!
Happy, full, content to the max
With that "had a great lifetime" glow!

I want to die while I'm laughing
After hearing the funniest joke
Feeling all the joy of my many years
'Round all my family folk!

I want to die while I'm laughing
Since we have to go anyway
I'll take my trip to the Pearly gates
Laughing all the way!

I want to die while I'm laughing
And with gratitude attain
The finality of life's promise
Having only my smile remain!

~Judy Sundayo

Judy Sundayo, La Jolla, California, 2011

*Long-time friends of the authors' **Paul and Denise Simms**;*
***Paul B. Simms, MPH**, is former Deputy Director of the San Diego County Health Department ; currently Visiting Scholar, Claremont Graduate University, investigating health disparities; also President and CEO of Simms Technologies, LLC, technology-related systems development with a focus on health care; **Denise Adams-Simms** is Interim Executive Director at San Diego Black Health Associates; Vice President of Operations, **Simms Technologies, LLC**; Photo courtesy, the Simms* www.sdbha.org/

Harvest Time

Harvest time, harvest time

Reap your blessings,

Celebrate mine

All that was promised, has come to fruition

In divine unfolding

What a holy condition

Harvest time, harvest time

Reap your blessings,

Share in mine

~Judy Sundayo

Co-Creating Friendship

Co-creating peaceful friendship
Began in softened earth
A stone revealed itself
Pulled out and placed in a light-filled chamber
Forgiveness laser is beamed for changes
Hope is generously applied
Powerful love enters
Stone returns to powder
Tears of understanding water tenderize
Earth opens to receive
Earth employs succulent forgiveness
Earth accepts herself transformed by light
Winds blow but are never able to remove
Loving intentions
For the growth, bloom and beauty of true friendship
~Alyce Smith Cooper

Alyce Smith Cooper and friends

344

*Judy Sundayo's son of another mother, **Jamaal Mason Walker**,*
Half Dome, Yosemite, California 2014; Photo courtesy of Jamaal Walker

The Marriage of Thought and Speech

Thought had the idea first
and determined, proposed
Speech accepted; her heart in love exposed
They sealed then their vows
with a passionate kiss
and soon awaited in the pregnant mist
for their child, Action, to be born
So blessed the day Action came to be,
a baby born by sacred alchemy
and Action set about to manifest all that
which Thought and Speech had sought to quest
Then, creation unfolded by virtue of Action's vision
Emblazoned by a course of clear decision
all Action dreamed took form from whence
Love's invocation breathed
and thusly are all destinies conceived
For Thought and Speech with passion plant the seed
What grows is raw potential to succeed
Vision and breath then guide and nourish
Whatever we plant and nurture will flourish!

~Judy Sundayo

345

Time

See how the years pass
Quickly brushing us aside
Scarring our knees
Not even leisurely enjoying these days
But hurrying on
Like a restless child in wild abandon
Here, climbing a tree
There, eating its fruit
Everywhere planting memories
As seasons dash by
And years race toward forever
Where are they going to~
These years so fast
To find a place to rest at last?

~Judy Sundayo

*Judy Sundayo with good friends and colleagues, **Kathy Robb** (left) and **Eadie Richards** (Center); both Retired Professors, Mesa College Counseling Department, San Diego, California, Photo courtesy of J. Sundayo, circa 2000's*

Taylor Thompson, at the time of her high school graduation, June 2014
*Taylor is the granddaughter of Judy Sundayo's friend, **Claudia Thompson;** Photo*
courtesy of Taylor Thompson and Claudia Thompson

Trust

(A poem for Taylor, written at the time of her coming of age)

Trust the love that makes you smile
And which gets stronger mile by mile
Trust the joy from simple things
Ladybugs; butterfly wings

Trust the gifts that have not price
And only folks who treat you nice
Trust those things, which bring forth life
The sun, the rain, a mother's strife

Trust the tree that gives you shade
And the food that nature made
Trust your mind when it is clear
And trust that God is always near

(continued)

Trust those friends who comfort you
And trust that you'll know what to do
When challenges bring you much dismay
Trust everything will go your way

For goodness and kindness pursue us with Grace
So, trust that you will find your place
And as you come into your own
Trust your heart, your inner home

~Judy Sundayo

*Long-time friend of the authors', **Claudia Thompson**, retired Counselor, Grossmont College Claudia was also one of the original elders in the 1ˢᵗ **Rites of Passage Program for African American Girls** in San Diego County; she advocated along with other Black parents in the early 1970's for images of Black babies on commercial baby Products; efforts like these helped bring about change, e.g., the first image of a Black baby on a box of diapers; Photo courtesy of C. Thompson*

Jaime V. Jones' mother, **Evelyn Jones**
And aunt, Arkansas, circa 1940's

The Internal House Voice Calls

The subtleness, the soundness, the soulfulness of it all
The spirit of our internal house voice yes she calls
From bright breakfast balconies of passion
She calls to us

From life's lighthouse of clarity we get summoned
From pretty porches of power we are gathered
Whispers from stained glass windows
Of colorful courage
We hear our names

From red painted roof tops joy connects
Commits our souls
From blessed brave bathrooms of fresh forgiveness
We are both challenged and changed
From beautiful bedrooms of belief
We boldly find our way
From deserving dens of affection, laughter reins,
Rings, loose and loud
(continued)

349

The Internal House Voice Calls *(continued)*

From kitchens of creativity
We consume wonderful wisdom
From delicious dining rooms of determination
We stand up
Full for every occasion

From living rooms of perfection we are delivered
Into possibilities, opportunities, potential,
The future fully discovered
Personal internal voices listened to, found, recognized
Uncovered like some lusty decadent lover
Voices unlike our fathers or mothers
That voice unlike anyone or any other
That voice that moves in, moves us, inspires
And resonates

That voice that artistically defines and vibrates
Who we are, what we are, why we are
This voice multiplies; It pulsates
This gift, our life contribution, our passion,
Our legacy with us originates

Yes, listen it is our authentic internal voice after all,
Come true
Spoken with eloquence spoken by you
Heard by we the multitudes, now
What you gonna do?
Daily witnessed that internal voice
Breaks shine through
Are you there? This call is for you
Your Internal House Voice is finally calling you
Hello. . . It is for you!
~*Jaime V. Jones*

Alyce Smith Cooper and great, granddaughter,
Lisa Jada

Which Original?

I cloned myself the other day for the 119th time!
A little ostentatious, you say?
Well, could be so
But I've so much work to do
Bids from all over the universe
Request my presence
To witness that love is all
Light conquers darkness
Peace is possible
All brothers/sisters under the sun/moon
Thank goodness all my sister-clones look like me!
The older ones prefer it so
The children know me by any costume,
Disguise or role
Ah well, all is joy
For I know—Which is the original!

~Alyce Smith Cooper

Wise Enough

I am not wise
But I thirst for peace
What a surprise that my mind should release
Me from all other obligations but that one
Even for a short time
This is perhaps a little more sane than usual
May my thirst be quenched in torrents of bliss
Niagara Falls-like Grace in downpours, like this flood
Drenching the confusion of dis-ease
Washing over all the wounds
My ignorance has left behind
Leaving me in born-again innocence
To ponder my condition
I know the cure is slow
And complete recovery more than not
Comes only to those few who know
That generally speaking
Life gives us more than one shot
I am not wise, but I hope to be free
I am not wise, but wise enough
To use my inner eye to see
This is indeed much more sane than usual
~Judy Sundayo

Judy Sundayo (center) jegna (guide/advisor) for these gifted young ladies, **LaWanda Weaver** *(left) and* **Charlene Black** *(right)*

Judy Sundayo's friend and jegna (teacher/guide) **Dr. Robert V. Guthrie,** *(1932-2005); Psychologist, Educator, Author of the seminal work,* **"Even the Rat Was White: A Historical View of Psychology"** *highlighting the significant work of Black Psychologists in the U.S., while refuting inaccurate and disparaging myths at that time common place in academia regarding African Americans*

Black Psychology

A monumental occurrence in history
Was established with Black Psychology
It started when the American Psychological Association
Treated Black psychologists with hesitation

When APA theories were racist in thinking
Blacks found a way to move through the stinking
Morass of myths and mis-education

So in 1968, one day, Black Psychologists broke away
In the middle of the APA convention
When demands were met with consternation
Black Psychologists just walked right out
To profess what Black Psychology was all about

(continued)

Black Psychology *(continued)*

And to help eliminate Black alienation
They formed their own association,
Fondly known as ABPsi,
They had the courage to question why
Even the rat was white,
And to see that Black Rage was something real
That needed to be reckoned with

And that we had positive traditions
To keep us sane in the face of insanity
And despite suffering
From Post-Traumatic Slave Syndrome, we found that when
we stuck together

And worked and prayed and studied and danced and sang,
And poured libation and voted and raised our babies,
And fed each other and taught our children and housed our
homeless and comforted each other and cared for our elders
Something happened,
Something ancient and enduring
Like mental health

And we learned it was good to be Black and
African and rich in melanin
And that we had a classical African culture
That had persisted through the hell of enslavement
And we refused to be studied and poked and prodded and
Pitied and pronounced pathological
We were the first,
The founders of civilization
And we only needed to be reminded of this
And of our Integrity
And our righteousness
And our worth

(continued)

Black Psychology *(continued)*

And these would be the substance of our healing
And Black Psychologists understood all of this
And they brought us back
To the source of all things
To an African worldview and all it brings
And to this day,
They've followed their mission
To serve the community
With a healing vision
~*Judy Sundayo*

Friends of the authors' **Dr. Norman E. Chambers,** *Psychologist,*
Professor Emeritus, SDSU, Director, **Carl Rogers Institute of Psychotherapy,**
Training & Supervision, *&* **Multicultural Counseling & Consulting Cente**r*,*
San Diego; Photo courtesy Dr. Chambers; For more information, go to
http://www.manta.com/c/mm8bnrw/multicultural-counseling

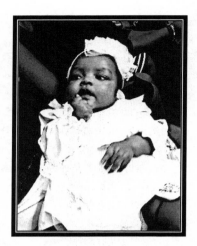

Alyce Smith Cooper's great granddaughter,
Zya Bridges

America's Next Top

Strut your stuff
Don't take no crap! Pose!
And take that picture, Snap!
The nation's watching!
The world is too!
Go ahead, do what you do!
You got what it takes
So, go 'head and flaunt it
The time is now
You know you own it!
Head back; chin Up!
Walk that walk!
When necessary, talk that talk!
No one's gonna cheat or caudle
Here she comes. . .
America's Next Top. . .
EXECUTIVE IN THE OVAL OFFICE
Pop the cork on THAT bottle!

~Judy Sundayo

*Plaque designed and constructed by **Conley Major***
And presented to Judy Sundayo in honor of her community service
*By the **Pan African Association of America;** Photo by Judy Sundayo*
http://www.panafricanassociation.org/

Roll Call

(In honor of those not mentioned elsewhere in this book, who have made contributions to the San Diego African American community. This is not a complete listing. Apologies to those we are not able to honor due to space limitations.)

Roll call
Name the names!
Who's doing what?
Who's bringing 'bout change?
Roll Call
The community is made
Of a whole lot of folks who are not afraid
To do what's necessary and take a stand
We honor you all, each woman and man . . .

Rahmo Abdi
Advocate for voiceless young girls in the community
Sahra Abdi
Winner of 2006 California Peace Prize; SDSU (class of 2002); immigrant from Somalia; avid community organizer
Hodari Abdul-Ali
A native San Diegan, after studying at SDSU, transferred to Howard University in Washington, D.C. where he graduated magna cum laude; in 1981, founded Pyramid Books in Washington, D.C.; later opened a store in San Diego, where his mother Barbara Brown was the proprietor; Pyramid Books was the first Black-owned bookstore chain in the country*
Anthony "Tony" and Marlene Ackee
Longtime community supporters; Committed to helping youth via music and the arts

357

Greg Akili
Activist; Helped organize the United Domestic Workers Association; Photo courtesy G. Akili

Dr. Vangie Akridge
Licensed Clinical Psychologist; Community Activist; Veterans advocate

Hakim Alaji
With wife Khalada Salaam-Alaji, operated the Community Preparatory School; Teacher & role model; Member, Encanto Neighborhoods Community Planning Group

Adisa A. Alkebulan
Professor, Africana Studies, SDSU, History & in Pan-African languages in the Caribbean; Editorial Board, Journal of Black Studies*

Damon Allen
Born in San Diego; Attended Lincoln High School; Former Canadian Football League (CFL) quarterback (1985-2007); CFL All-Star, 2005; Canadian Hall of Fame, 2012

Dennis Volyer Allen *(1883-1967)*
Early Black San Diego resident, 1912; Mailman; Founder & President, San Diego Race Relations Society to stop employment discrimination; 1920 advocated to get Blacks hired in SD Fire Department; One of the Founding Members of the SD Chapter of the NAACP, where he served as President, 1924-1929; During his term, had officials remove signs barring Blacks from stores, theatres & restaurants, in San Diego & Tijuana; Board of Directors, Bethel A.M.E. Church; First Chair, Calif. Human Rights Commission, 1938; Dennis V. Allen Park named in his honor

Marcus Allen
Former football player Lincoln High School, at University of Southern California (USC), won Heisman Trophy, Maxwell Award & Walter Camp Award; Pro football career, spanning 15 years; Inducted into College Football Hall of Fame, 2000 & Pro Football Hall of Fame, 2003; San Diego Hall of Champions, 1999

Montez Al'Uqdah
Retired from AT& T; Long-time Community Activist and Supporter

Kevin L. Alston
SDSU grad, former Tokyo talk show host; journalist, actor, comedian and Professor of Business, San Diego Miramar College

Roll Call *(continued)*

Barbara Louise Anderson

SDSU grad (class of 1954); certified librarian at age of 20; first person of color in California to head a county library system; first African American Director of San Bernadino County Library until 1994*

Del Marie Neely Anderson

SDSU grad (class of 1965; 67); Ebony Fashion Fair Model; On cover of Jet Magazine, 1961; President, San Jose City College; Chancellor, City Colleges of SF (1995-1998)*

Doris Anderson

Executive Director, the Elementary Institute of Science

Edward W. Anderson

Early African American entrepreneur in San Diego; ran IXL Laundry 1897-1909, a hog farm, Coronado, a garbage service and a mortuary; with wife, Mary won a judgment against Fisher Opera House, 1897 for refusing to seat them in orchestra after having purchased orchestra seating; significant anti-discrimination case; after his death, his wife sold the Anderson Mortuary to Hartwell W. Ragsdale, and it became the Anderson-Ragsdale Mortuary; Former President, SD Chapter, NAACP

Ernest Frederick Anderson

SDSU grad (class of 1967); taught at SDSU starting in 1973; became Associate Dean, College of Health & Human Services*

Katye Anderson

SDSU grad (class of 1964); Professor at Mesa College where she founded the Black Studies Department & chaired it for 22 years before her passing; beloved by students and colleagues alike*

Salimu Anderson

Community Activist; supporter of African American Arts & Culture

Mariea Antoinette

Classically trained harpist with a fresh smooth jazz, rhythm & blues style; Photo by J. Sundayo

Rulette Villarante Armstead

First woman to reach Captain in San Diego Police; SDSU grad (class of 1974. 88); Assistant Chief of Police, 1992; Woman Police Officer of the Year, 1989; San Diego Woman's Hall of Fame Inductee, 2004*

Roll Call *(continued)*

Donna Arnold
Dean, School of Arts & Communication, Southwestern College, Chula Vista

Issac Atkinson
Early African American resident, San Diego; owned a bakery in Julian; started the first Black newspaper in San Diego, "The Colonizer," 1892

K.D. Aubert
Played on SDSU Aztec Softball team; became fashion model and actress; appeared on TV, in music videos and in 9 movies including "Turning Point"*

James Avery
Seasoned Hollywood Actor, Starred as Will Smith's father on "Fresh Prince of Bel-Air;" Mentored by Dr. Floyd Gaffney at Southeastern Community Theatre, San Diego

Dr. Edward A. Bailey *(1884-1963)*
Former President, San Diego Chapter, NAACP

Willie Banks
Attended Oceanside High School; Track & Field Athlete; Set World Record of 58 ft. 11.5 inches at national championships in Indianapolis; 2nd in NCAA Championships, 1977 & 1978; J.D. from UCLA; member of Olympic teams in 1980, 1984 & 1988; Olympic Committee Athlete of the Year, 1985; Chair, Athletes Advisory Committee; Oldest American to clear 6 ft. in High Jump at age of 56: President of US Olympians Association, 2005-2008; SD Hall of Champions, 1988

Karen Ruth Bass;
Attended SDSU, 1971-73, majoring in philosophy; elected to California State Assembly, 2004, representing 47th District; speaker of Assembly 2008-10; sponsored 17 bills which became law; U.S. House of Representatives, 2010, California's 33rd Congressional District; Co-Chair, Obama's California Presidential Campaign

Rev. Wendell Bass, Sr.
Minister of Christian Education, New Creation Church of San Diego

Dr. Georgetta Katye Bartley
SDSU grad (class of 1975); configuration manager, SPAWAR

Lillian Kennedy Beam
SDSU grad (class of 1968); Director, Education Cultural Complex (ECC) in 1980's; Vice Chancellor of the United States International University, Director of East Africa Coalition for International Trade, Tanzania

Dr. Charles Bernard Bell, Jr. *(1928-2010)*
After earning Ph.D. in Mathematics at Notre Dame University, 1953, became San Diego State University's second African American faculty member, 1958; Brilliant mathematician, publishing over 39 mathematical papers

Charles Edward Bell, Jr., J.D.
President, Earl B. Gilliam Bar Association, 2014-15; Deputy City Attorney

Claude Bell
Vice President, ACB Communications, Telecommunications Expert

Mayte Benitez
Born & Raised in San Diego; Graduated Morse H.S & SDSU; Youth Program Coordinator, Urban Collaborative Project

Nechel Best
Voice Talent/Audio Producer; Freelance Broadcast Media; thebestvoicechoice.com

Roll Call *(continued)*

Dr. Willie P. Blair
President/Chair, Black American Political Association of California, S.D. Chapter

Carroll Parrott Blue
*Award-winning documentary filmmaker; Professor, Communications Dept. SDSU, Film, "Conversations with Roy DeCarav" won Blue Ribbon, American Film Festival, 1984; Jury Award, Sundance Film Festival,2004; Produced PBS segment of "Eyes on the Prize"; Author, The Dawn at My Back: Memoir of a Black Texas Upbringing; ** *

Priese Printz Lamont Board
*Grammy-nominated songwriter& producer; helped launch the Black Eyed Peas Hip Hop Group, where he served as music director and keyboard player**

Steven Clete Bradford
*Attended SDSU; IBM Marketing rep; L.A. Conservation Corps Coordinator; First African American to serve on City Council, Gardena, California**

Trey Brady
Proprietor of "The Juke Joint," a premier jazz restaurant, SD Gaslamp District, 1990's

Dr. Andre J. Branch
President, San Diego Branch, NAACP, 2015-16

Theodore Moses Brinson *(1877-1957)*
Prior Army veteran; Musician; Postal Clerk; mail carrier; Member, Bethel A.M.E. Church; Former President, San Diego Chapter, NAACP,

Debra Brooks
Program Director, California Black Health Network

Dr. Harold K. Brown
*First African American Administrator, SDSU; SDSU grad (class of 1959); President, Kappa Alpha Psi Fraternity; star basketball player; Led Congress of Racial Equality (CORE), 1960's; Supervised Afro-American Studies Program, SDSU; Director Community Economic Development (CED) in the SDSU College of Business**

Henry H. Brown
Early African American resident, San Diego; Proprietor of a successful saloon, 1890's

James Brown
Early African American resident of San Diego County, late 1800's; farmer

Dr. Kristian L. Brown
*Winner, Thomas E. Carew Prize for Cardiovascular Research; published in American J. Physiology & Heart Circulation Physiology, as well as the J. of Burn Care & Research; Obtained both MD degree & Ph.D. in biomedical engineering**

Linda Brown
President, Black Storytellers of San Diego

Betty and Roosevelt Brown
Roosevelt is fondly known as "The Bookman;" Together with his wife Betty, they give away thousands of books annually to San Diego children to support the Reading Literacy Learning Program; they have given away over one million books

Michaelanthony Brown-Cheatom
Author, "The Rorschach Mutuality of Autonomy Scale in the Assessment of Black Father-Absent Male Children," in the J. Personality Assessment, 1993

Dr. Aaron Bruce
*Chief Diversity Officer, San Diego State University**

Michael Brunker
Executive Director, Jackie Robinson Family YMCA

Dr. Cedric Gael Bryant
Lectured at SDSU, 1973-83, African American Literature; Maine Professor of the Year, 1996, Carnegie Foundation*

Dr. Jonathan T. Buchanan
First Black man to graduate from San Diego State in 1936, majoring in zoology; later became an optometrist practicing in Los Angeles*

Willie Buchanon
All American; Aztec football 1970-71; Pro Football Career; President, Aztec Athletic Foundation.; Real Estate Broker; Inducted into San Diego Hall of Champions, 1994*

Petrina Branch Burnham, J.D.
Athlete lettered in lacrosse; Admitted to California Bar, 2009; Former NAACP President; Served on police chief's Community Advisory Board on Racial Profiling; Past President, Earl B. Gilliam Bar Association; Owner, P.B. Designs, markets handmade cloth Afrocentric themed dolls

Reginald Alfred "Reggie" Bush, Jr.
Born in Spring Valley; Played football, Helix H.S.; Won Silver Pigskin Trophy; Still 2nd all-time for 100 meter dash all-time list for San Diego; Played in U. S. Army All-American Bowl, 2003; No. 1 Running Back U.S. in 2003; 2 time All American, University of Southern California (USC); Doak Walker & Walter Camp Awards, 2005; Pro football; Super Bowl Team, 2010;

Roland Wentworth Boniface Bullen
SDSU grad (class of 1971); Deputy Executive Director, Bureau of Western Hemisphere Affairs (WHA), U.S. Dept. of State; U.S. Ambassador to Guyana; Deputy Chief of Mission, U. S. Embassy, Dominican Republic*

Dr. Burney
Early Black resident, San Diego; retired professional; owned a ranch, 1890's

Michael Jerome Cage
SDSU basketball player; drafted by L.A. Clippers 1984, NBA rebounding champ, 1988

Bishop Annie B. Campbell
Doctorate in Divinity; Active in Community & Church Service; Recipient of Sojourner Truth Award of Excellence by Professional Women's Association; Founder, Giving and Living for Others Ministries; Member SD Urban League; Boy Scouts & Parent Teachers Association

Julius T. Campbell *(1933-1985)*
SDSU grad (class of 1956); the proud paraplegic President of Kappa Alpha Psi, the first Black Fraternity at SDSU; President of Associated Men Students and as such, the first African American president of predominantly white campus group*

Milton Gray Campbell *(1933-2012)*
First African American to win the gold medal in the decathlon of the Summer Olympic Games, 1956; Drafted by Cleveland Browns Football Team, 1957; Released by Browns owner, Paul Brown for marrying a white woman; played in Canadian Football league till end of career, 1964; Doctor of Public Service conferred by Monmouth University, N.J., 2008; New Jersey Hall of Fame, 2012

Tyler Christian Campbell
Diagnosis of Muscular Sclerosis dashed his football dreams, but not his spirit; completed degree in Business Management, SDSU; became an Ambassador and spokesperson for the National MS Society*

Roll Call *(continued)*

Derek Cannon
SDSU (class of 1989); Jazz Trumpeter, played with Natalie Cole, the Four Tops & the Temptations; directed Jazz/Afro-Cuban Studies, Grossmont College; recorded "Free Your Mind" with Walter Beasly*

Nicholas Scott "Nick" Cannon
Born in San Diego; Attended Monte Vista H.S.; Nickelodeon Comedian; Started rap group "Da G4 Dope Bomb Squad;" Formed own label, Can-I-Ball Records; Actor; NAACP Image Awards, 2012

Kern Carson
SDSU standout Aztec football player; later played pro ball for Baltimore; Coordinated community services for UCSD; manager of Ebony Inn*

Clara Carter
Founder, Multi-Cultural Convention Services Network & Destination Elite, San Diego's Online Travel Magazine, Formerly S.D. Regional Chamber of Commerce

August L. Castille
SDSU grad (class of 1954); Principal, Penn Elementary School; Principal, Fulton Elementary School; Owner & Travel Agent, Easter's Park Travels*

Francheska Ahmed Cawthorne
SDSU (class of 1986) author Sista, Girlfren' Breaks It Down When Mom's Not Around

Dr. Herb Cawthorne
Former President Urban League of San Diego & Reporter, Channel 10 news

Dr. Eric J. Chambers
Award-winning TV producer, editor and commentator; four-time Emmy and five-time Golden Mike Award Winner; worked for KGTV and CBS; author of Dining with the Ancestors: When Heroes Come to Dinner

Lonnie Chappel
Co-Founder, Community Actor's Theatre

"RuPaul" Andre Charles
Born in San Diego, His Louisianan mother named him "Ru" from roux, the base of GUMBO; Entertainer; First Drag Queen Supermodel; wrote autobiography, Lettin' It All Hang Out; Hosted the RuPaul Show, 1996; Released several successful albums; Appeared in numerous movies; Won TV.com's Best of 2012 & 2013 Awards

Photo Courtesy of Carlos LeGarrrette, circa 1970's

Cesar Chavez *(1927-1993)*
World Renowned Civil Rights Activist and Labor Leader; Together with Dolores Huerta founded the National Farm Workers Association, which later became the United Farm Workers Union; His non-violent and grassroots labor organizing strategies became the foundation for organized labor nationally and internationally

Marc Cherry
Administrator, San Diego Public Library, San Diego

Dr. Dennis R. Childs
Associate Professor of African American Literature, UCSD, Affiliated Faculty, Department of Ethnic Studies; Faculty Advisor, Students Against Mass Incarceration; UCSD Black Student Union Outstanding Faculty Award; UCSD Hellman Fellow: Recipient, UCSD Chancellor's Associates Faculty Excellence Award; author, <u>Slaves of the State: Black Incarceration from the Chain Gang to the Penitentiary</u>, 2015

Benjamin Wallace Cloud
Attended SDSU, 1949-1952; Won first prize in annual engineering essay contest; cut education short to serve in WWII, as Navy pilot; Earned the Air Medal & the Distinguished Flying Cross; First Black to serve as White House military social aide, 1966; First Black Executive Officer of the Kitty Hawk, 1972; averted racial violence onboard; Served as Board Member, SD Air & Space Museum; Son of John Cloud*

Joel J. Cloud
Heavy equipment operator, manager, 1950's; Business owner/partner in C&H Construction & Demolition, 1965; Owner Hester's Granite Quarry, 1978-1993; Founded J. Cloud, Inc., 1993 the first recycle operation in San Diego County to have recycled rock approved for use by Cities of San Diego, Chula Vista & La Mesa; a materials aggregate producer, General Contractor; son of John Cloud; married Rita

Rita Cloud
Helped to establish Friends of the El Cajon Library; Married Joel J. Cloud; active with NAACP, USO & the Chamber of Commerce

Sergeant John Cloud
First African American Police Supervisor in San Diego; Owned a ranch, El Cajon

Bessie Alberta Cobb
SDSU class of 1939; English major; member, College YWCA, Gamma Psi l Literary Honor Society, Amotl (future librarians), Foreign Language Honor Society & Woodsonians; wrote poem, "Change" underscoring if she could choose to be anyone, she would still choose to be herself; published in poetry anthology, <u>Negro Voices</u>, which included Langston Hughes' works*

Rev. T. E. Cobb
Former President, San Diego Chapter, NAACP

Myrtle Cole
First African American woman elected to the San Diego City Council, 2013, representing District 4; re-elected to a four-year term in 2014; Former Regional Coordinator, the United Domestic Workers Local 3930

A.E. "Frederick" Coleman
A man who was formerly enslaved, was first person to find gold in Julian, California; elected as town's Recorder; first Black elected in any office in San Diego County; Coleman Rd. & Coleman Creek named in his honor

LeShae Collins
District Director for Assembly-member, Honorable Dr. Shirley Weber

Steven C. Collins *(1954-2008)*
Former President, Southeast Rotary; Board of Neighborhood House Association, S.D. Police Citizen's Review Board & member, City of San Diego Salary-Setting Commission; SDSU Manager of Government & Community Relations; Winner, Black History Local Heroes Award, 2008*

Orlando Coons, Sr. *(1915-1998)*
First African American to successfully compete as a gymnast at the national level; enrolled SDSU, 1936; all round champion gymnast 1939 & 1940, California College Athletic Association Championships; first Black Gymnastics Coach at a predominantly white college/university, when hired by San Diego State University*

Steven L. Coons *(1947-2008)*
SDSU grad (class of 1973); son of Orlando Coons, Sr.; Professor, Black Studies, Political Science, Miramar College; launched United Nations & Amnesty International clubs on campus*

Sidney Cooper, Jr.
Carries on the work of his father to celebrate annual Juneteenth Celebration in San Diego through the Cooper Family Foundation; author, novels, Black Street & Black Street II: Wall Street Raider

Sidney Cooper, Sr.
In 1961, began the free community celebration of "Black Independence Day" June 19th Juneteenth, the day Blacks learned about Emancipation Proclamation

Derek W. Cotton
Won Southern California Collegiate Fencing League Competition, 1986

Robert L. "Bob" Countryman
Former Forensic Chemist, U.S. Department of Justice; Founded Coalition of Black Organizations in San Diego

Mary E. Cox
SDSU grad (class of 1970); State Coordinator, Jesse Jackson Presidential Campaign, 1988; Candidate for Mayor of Washington, D.C. 1990*

Rebecca and John Craft
Early Black San Diego residents, 1910; fought against racial discrimination on the police force & in schools; Rebecca was a teacher, but could not get hired in that profession in SD; founded Women's Civic League, 1934; Active with Parent Teachers Association, with youth programs at Bethel Baptist Church; Former President, SD Chapter, NAACP; John, a Court House janitor, started his own cleaning business, Crafty Cleaning Company; Former President, SD Chapter, NAACP

Dwayne Crenshaw
CEO RISE San Diego, aimed at elevating urban leadership through dialogue-based civic engagement, non-profit partnerships & trainings toward community change

David Lee Crippens
SDSU grad with master's degree (class of 1968); First President of the SDSU Black Student Council*

Clarence Stanley Crocket
Outspoken lecturer SDSU's English Department, 1964-67; criticized discriminatory practices of SDSU fraternities & sororities*

Roll Call *(continued)*

Isaac Curtis
Former SDSU student, played for Cincinnati Bengals, 1973-1984; maintains that teams career receiving record of 7,101 yards*

Marvin Vernell Curtis
First Black commissioned to compose music for President's Inaugural Choir; Directed President Clintons Inaugural Choir; Directed SDSU's Black Gospel Choir

Chida R. Darby
Managing Editor/CAO San Diego Voice & Viewpoint Newspaper;

Alyce L. Davis
The first Black librarian at SDSU, 1959

Dr. Harold Davis
Author, public speaker, transformational life coach, entrepreneur;

Jasper Davis
Only the second Black to be hired on the San Diego Police force, 1931, after years of protest; despite overt prejudice from colleagues, he worked on the force 23 years

Terrell Lamar Davis
NFL Running Back for Denver Broncos (1995-2001); The Broncos all-time leading rusher; Attended Lincoln HS; Inducted into SD Hall of Champions, 2006

Trimaine Davis
Outreach, Recruitment & Admissions Officer, EOP Program, SDSU*

Walter Davis
President, Walter Davis Enterprises; Activist for Social Justice; Executive Producer, Marketing Strategies of California; Columnist & T.V. Producer

Terri Davis-Cole
Community Relations Officer, SD Police Department

Dennis W. Dawson
President of the Earl B. Gilliam Bar Association, 2015

Dr. Sylvia Gayle Dayton-Jones
SDSU grad (class of 1979); business woman, Washington, D.C*

Gail Devers
Grew up in National City & attended Sweetwater HS; Sweetwater H. S. later named their football & track stadium in her honor; Won Silver Medal in 100 meter hurdles, 1991 World Championships; Won her 3rd Olympic Medal at 4 X 100 meter relay team; Inducted into National Track & Field Hall of Fame, 2011; U. S. Olympic Hall of Fame, 2012; NCAA Silver Anniversary Award, 2013; SD Hall of Champions, 2006

Rufus DeWitt
Co-Founded Southeastern Community Theatre (Later renamed Common Ground Theatre) along with Dr. Robert Matthews, 1963

Kendrick Dial
Trainer Consultant, National Conflict Resolution Center; Member of "Lyrical Groove" for spoken word artistry; Author, Da JOurneY NoT withstanding

Charles H. Dodge *(1868-1942)*
Cashier, Southern Trust & Commerce Bank (which later merged with Bank of Italy and renamed, Bank of America), 1912; Advanced to position of currency counter, the highest position held by an African American in a white-controlled financial institution in America, 1930's; Former President, San Diego Chapter, NAACP

Roll Call *(continued)*

Sandra Dryden
Volunteer Organizer, Common Ground Theatre

Dr. Peter Alfred Dual
The first African American full-time Dean at SDSU when hired to serve as the Dean of the College of Health & Human Services, 1983-1993*

Dr. Kora Louise H. Dunbar
Retired school principle, San Diego Unified School Board; Student Learning Outcomes/Program Review/Accreditation Coordinator

Michele Jacques Early
SDSU grad (class of 1978) Public administration, minor in Afro-American Studies; Director of DeWitt Proctor School of Theology's D. Min Program*

Nathan Harrell East
Internationally known jazz, R&B, and rock bass player & vocalist; Graduated B.A. Music, UCSD; Founding member of jazz quartet, Fourplay; recorded & played with Eric Clapton, Herbie Hancock & others

Omo Awo "Jahsun" Olumfemi Ifokolade Edmonds
Poet; Founder, NOMMO Collective and WRITERZBLOCK workshops; Martial arts & Capoeira instructor*

Sam Edmonds
First African American Motorcycle Police Officer in San Diego, 1963

Herman Edwards
SDSU grad (class of 1971); played Aztec football; Philadelphia Eagles; assistant coach under Tony Dungy; Head Coach New York Jets, & Kansas City Chiefs; ESPN Sports Analyst; author You Play to Win the Game*

Arthur Leon Ellis
Taught in SDSU's Social Work Department, 1978; Chairman, Police Review Board; Member, California State Task Force on Mental Health & Juvenile Delinquency; San Diego Human Relations Commission*

Louis Elloie, Jr.
Professor, Psychology Department, SD Mesa College, Former President, Black Faculty Association

Carl Evans, Jr. *(1955-2008)*
Noted Keyboardist for Fattburger, which he Co-founded, 1984; Talented Musician & Composer

Dr. Nora Marcella Faine-Sykes
Appointed to San Diego Foundation Board of Governors, 2002; Vice President & Chief Medical Officer of Sharp Health Plan; volunteer for Palavra Tree, Children Having Children & the S.D. HIV Council*

Earl Faison
American Football League player (19960-1966); AFL Champion, 1963; SD Chargers Hall of Fame; SD Chargers 50th Anniversary Team; Head Coach & Principal, Lincoln HS; SD Hall of Champions 1997

Marshall Faulk
SDSU Aztec offensive running back, 1992; Professional football;, NFL Offensive Rookie of the Year, 1994; St. Louis Rams, NFC Champion, 1999; NFL Offensive Player of the Year/Super Bowl Champion, 2000; NFL Offensive Player of Year, 2001; Retired, 2006; NFL Network Analyst; Inducted into Hall of Fame, 2011

367

Roll Call *(continued)*

Rhonda Felder
Executive Board, San Diego Association of Black Social Workers

Robert Fikes, Jr.
Editor, Newsletter of the California Black Faculty & Staff Association; SDSU Africana Studies Unsung Hero Award; Earl B. Gilliam Bar Association Community Service Award; NAACP Dubois Scholarship Award*

Cheryl Alyece Williams Fisher
SDSU grad (class of 1971); Former Director, SDSU's Office of Diversity & Equity; Board Member, Neighborhood House Association; authored, <u>To Mrs. O With Love</u>*

Deborah Fitch
Trainer & Curriculum Specialist, SDSU's Academy for Professional Excellence; Board, Harmonious Solutions

Dr. Edward Sidney Fletcher
SDSU grad (class of 1953); worked 36 years SD public schools; retired as Assistant Superintendent, San Diego City Schools; Education Director, SD Urban League; President SDSU Veterans Alumni*

Kim Folsom
Founder/CEO, Showuhow, Inc., specializing in video-based support tools for tech companies; advised Consumer Electronic Assoc., SDSU Entrepreneur Mgmt. Center, Sheppard Venture & Qualcomm Stadium *

Dr. Suzanne Forbes-Vierling
Department Chair, College of Behavioral Sciences & Psychology, Argosy University; Instructor, Tribal Energy Cardio, San Diego

Frances Smith Foster
Assistant professor, Afro-American Studies, SDSU, 1971; Professor, English; Assistant Dean, Student Affairs, College of Arts & Letters; authority on American slave narratives; author of 6 books; First Black woman to receive Modern Language Association's Jay B Hubbell Medal, 2010 for lifetime achievement in literary studies*

Marne Foster
President San Diego Unified School District Board of Trustees; San Diego Community College District, Continuing Education

Sandra Foster-King
Historical figure in dance & choreography; Taught at San Diego School of Creative & Performing Arts; Lecturer, Dance Department, UCSD; Recipient "Outstanding Faculty Award" Josephine Baker's "Choreographer's Award, 1983; San Diego Dance Alliance Award "Outstanding Contributor to Dance," 1997; "Dance Educator of the Year," 1999; Member International Association of Blacks in Dance; Attended Alvin Ailey's Summer Intensive, 2010; SD Women's Hall of Fame

Romell Foster-Owens
The first Black chosen as Miss San Diego, 1972; among 10 finalists for Miss California, same year; Owner of Jowharah Films; Two films she produced, "Native New Yorker" & "Pins & Needles" selected for Cannes Film Festival, 2008; Emmy Award winning producer, director & writer; NAACP Image Award winner; Black Filmmakers Hall of Fame Award*

Hozell C. Francis
SDSU grad (class of 1977); wrote <u>Church Planting in the African American Context</u>*

Lloyd Francis
Owner of the Francis Tang Soo Do Martial Arts Studio*

Roll Call *(continued)*

Norvell Freeman Sr.
SDSU grad (class of 1957); worked at General Dynamics for 33 years; Retired as Director of Industrial Relations; Served as San Diego Grand Juror

Daniel Fry
Early African American resident, San Diego; Operated blacksmith shop, 1890's

April Gabrielle
Family mediator; Small Business Owner of "Put in on Paper Publishing;" author, The Myth of the Broken Home

Charles Gadson
Owned and operated a Baker's Confectionary Shop on Market Street; 1920-1938; the Charles Gadson residence still stands at 470 17th Street in San Diego

Dr. Floyd Gaffney
Former Professor, University of California, San Diego; Co-founded Department of Drama & Dance, UCSD; 36 year-tenure as a Director, Developer and Artistic Director, Southeastern Community Theatre; He renamed it Common Ground Theatre, 2003

David "Smokey" Gaines
First of two Black head basketball coaches at SDSU; produced 5 winning teams, 1979-1987; Western Athletic Conference Coach of Year, 1985; owned 5 restaurants*

Nasara Gargonnu
Personal Trainer, Fit With Jenny; Vemma Affiliate at Vemma; Health Minister at Total Deliverance Worship Center: Fitness Trainer, Jackie Robinson YMCA

Cameron Gary
SDSU alumna (class of 1984), Police officer; 3rd degree Aikido Black Belt; trained for SD Police Academy

Dr. Phillip Timothy Gay
Ph.D., Harvard University; Hired at SDSU in 1976; Chair of Sociology Department; Published Modern South Africa; Film & stage actor; wrote TV screenplay & novel*

Thomas "Tomas" L. Gayton
Retired Civil Rights Attorney; Published Poet: Author, Yazoo City Blues & Sojourn on the Bohemian Highway

Elijah J. Gentry *(1877-1968)*
Shoe-shiner, early 1900's; Choir Director, First Baptist Church; President, SD, NAACP, 1923

Hollis Gentry, III *(1955-2006)*
Graduated, MA Music, UCSD, 1980; Noted local jazz saxophonist; Protégé of Cannonball Adderley; Co-founded, local band, Fattburger; Founded his own band, Neon; Toured nationally and abroad with Larry Carlton & David Benoit; One of first musicians to earn UCSD'S Outstanding Alumni Award, 1991;

Dennis T. Gibson
Ballpark Administrator, City of San Diego; CFO/Business Operations Manager, City Water Dept.; Financial Analyst & Policy Advisor to the Mayor; County Assistant Tax Collector

Florence Gilkesson
First tenure-track faculty person in Afro-American Studies at SDSU, 1972*

Earl B. Gilliam, J.D.
SDSU grad (class of 1953); First African American U.S. District Court Judge for the Southern District of California, appointed by President Jimmy Carter; First African American to serve as a San Diego County Superior Court Judge; the S.D. Black Lawyer's Association was re-named in his honor

369

Roll Call *(continued)*

Tanya Gentry
President, Sickle Cell Disease Association of America, San Diego Chapter

John M. Gissendanner
Taught in Afro-American Studies at SDSU & English at Towson University*

Doris F. Givens
SDSU grad (class of 1977, '78); taught Black Studies at SD City College; First Black President Kansas City CC*

Perette Godwin
SDSU grad (class of 1985); TV News Anchor & Reporter, KYMA-TV, Yuma, KSWB-TV and Fox News in San Diego; publicist; freelance reporter, XETV*

Linda Gooden
Executive VP Information Systems & Global Services, President IT, Lockheed Martin; SDSU grad*

Henrietta Goodwin
First Black graduate San Diego State University, January 30, 1913, when called SD Normal School*

Ruby Berkley Goodwin
Completed teaching certification, San Diego State Teachers College, 1922; authored autobiography, It's Good to Be Black which won gold medal from Commonwealth Club for best nonfiction book by a California author in 1953; Personal Secretary & Publicist for actress Hattie McDaniel; Grandmother of Leah Goodwin*

Terry James Gordy
Terry James Gordy, SDSU grad (class of 1979), son of Motown Records Mogul, Berry Gordy; married, Desiree D'Laura Thomas (class of 1978); their lavish Bel-Air Wedding, 1979 was attended by Marvin Gaye, Diana Ross, Lionel Richie, Smokey Robinson & Alex Haley*

Dr. Arthur Joseph Graham
SDSU grad (class of 1967); Playwright, "Daddy was a Welfare Check;" Co-founded SDSU ASU w/ Nap Jones*

Dr. Frank Harris, III
Associate Professor Post-secondary Education, SDSU; Co-Director, Minority Male Community College Collaborative (M2C3)*

Dr. Sharon Grant-Henry
Professor Counseling and School Psychology, SDSU's College of Education; At 14 years of age, the youngest member of CORE marching with parents to protest racial discrimination, 1964*

Dr. Louis Cleveland Green
SDSU Professor, Economics, 1976-2003, Specialization: International Trade*

Ruth A. Green
Former President, San Diego Chapter, NAACP

Dr. Tonika Duren Green
Associate Professor, Director, S. D. State University's School of Psychology

Bryan Greene
Black Artist; graduate of SDSU; famous print entitled, "Story Time Woman*"

Mamie Louise Greene *(1939-2007)*
Employment Specialist, California Employment Development Department; Board Member, Black Federation, San Diego County Board of Health & the Educational Cultural Complex; V.P. Black Advocates in State Services; Secretary, SD Chapter, National Council of Negro Women: Former President, San Diego Chapter, NAACP

Anthony "Tony" Gwynn *(1960-2014)*
Star athlete at SDSU in late 1970's for basketball and baseball; drafted by San Diego Padres to play pro baseball, 1981; retired in 2001; inducted into the Baseball Hall of Fame, 2007; SDSU named their Stadium, Tony Gwynn Stadium in his honor; only athlete in WAC history to be honored as all-conference performer in two sports*

Anthony "Tony" Gwynn, Jr.
Son of Baseball Hall of Famer, Tony Gwynn; played outfielder on 3 pro baseball teams; Mt. West Conference All-Star team, 2003*

Christopher Karlton Gwynn
Played for SDSU; later 1984 Olympic Baseball team; pro-ball, San Diego Padres; Director, Player Personnel, Padres; Director; brother of Tony Gwynn*

Judge Alfred Haines *(1845-1934)*
Only Caucasian Branch President, SD NAACP, serving 3 yrs.; re-wrote & expanded State's Civil Rights Law; former Assistant District Attorney; only the 2nd President of the California Bar Association; Superior Court Judge; Historical Haines Houses are in Golden Hills & Chula Vista

Earl Hamilton, Jr.
President, Board of Directors, Community Actor's Theatre

James Hamilton
Early African American resident of San Diego County, late 1800's; farmer

Jennie L. Hamilton
Director, Community Actors Theatre (CAT); Retired teacher, SD City Schools

Marvell Hamilton
Co-Founder, Community Actor's Theatre

Ashanti Hands
Dean of Student Affairs, San Diego Mesa Community College*

Kasimu Harley
Co-founder of African American History Society at Bell Junior High School; Student advocate; Community activist; Marriage & Family Therapist; Writer and poet*

Kathleen E. Harmon
Double masters degrees from SDSU (1978); nurse at Mercy Hospital; Social Worker, House of Hope; Former Vice Chair County Democratic Central Committee; California Delegate to Democratic Conventions; Vice-Chair, Black Political Action Committee; President, San Diego Peace Coalition, Inc.*

Angela Harris
Owner, Community Engagement Firm specializing in community outreach; Board Member Urban Collaborative Project

Roll Call *(continued)*

Dr. Olita Elizabeth Dargan Harris
SDSU Social Work professor, 1979; Assoc. Dean, College Health & Human Services*

Nathaniel Harrison
Formerly enslaved; First recorded permanent Black resident, San Diego, 1848; built a cabin on 160-acre farm, Palomar Mt; Nathaniel Harrison Grade, in Pauma Valley named in his honor

Dr. Ernest Eugene Hartzog
SDSU grad (class of 1955; 1962); SD County's first Black HS Principal, Lincoln HS, 1970; President, National Alliance, Black School Educators, 1979*

Dr. Marilyn Harvey
Director, Transfer Career Center, San Diego City College; Board of Directors, Harmonious Solutions

Patricia A. Harvard-Hinchberger
SDSU grad, masters Educational Technology, 1977; registered nurse; research faculty member, King Faisal Specialist Hospital in Saudi Arabia; Assistant Professor, Nursing, CSDH; National Black Nurses Association Institute of Excellence*

Walter S. Hawkins
Master's in Social Work, SDSU (class of 1972); Community activist; Director of Research & Policy Analysis, CSU, San Bernadino*

Elvin Hayes
Center/Power Forward for NBA; first Pro team: San Diego Rockets (1968-1984), Inducted into San Diego Hall of Champions, 2003

Andre Henderson *(1945-2010)*
SDSU grad; Successful businessman; owned 13 Taco Bells; Pastor of San Diego's Highland Park Church; taught business & leadership in Africa*

Wallace "Wally" Henry
Born in San Diego; Attended Lincoln HS; Played football at UCLA; Played pro football as a wide receiver & punt returner; ranks 76th NFL All-Time Punt Returns List (148)

William T. Hendrey *(1873-1962)*
Barber & deliveryman; First President, SD Chapter, NAACP, serving from Jan – Nov in 1919

Harold T. Henson
SDSU grad (class of 1950); First African American to compete at the national level, 1949 NCAA Wrestling Championships; earned Bronze Star for military service in Korea; retired from military with Legion of Merit Medal; Deputy Director of Public Works in Washington, D.C.*

Dr. Alison M. Henson, Jr.
SDSU Wrestling Team, 1940's; served with distinction in 3 wars; achieved rank of Army colonel before retiring from military service in 1970, having earned both the Purple Heart and the Bronze Star; later became a Doctor of Chiropractic Medicine*

Peter H. Henson
Retired Air Force, Lt. Colonel; son of distinguished SDSU athlete, Harold T. Henson, and nephew of Alison M. Henson, graduated SDSU, 1976; after retirement, 2003, worked as pastor, Eagle's Nest Worship Center, NE*

"Dub" Hicks
Co-Founder, Community Actor's Theatre

Rev. J. Lee Hill, Jr.
Senior Pastor, Christian Fellowship Congregational Church; Serves on the Interfaith Committee for Worker Justice, San Diego & the SD Regional Interfaith Collaborative

372

Roll Call *(continued)*

Richard Arnold Hill
SDSU Head Track Coach in 1972; led track team to first WAC Championship, 1980; became Athletic Director at Massachusetts Institute of Technology (MIT)*

Todd Hitchcock
Senior Pastor, Bethel Baptist Church, San Diego

Jini Hogg-Bornes
SDSU All-American 400 meters sprinter; Employed in EOP office SDSU*

Dr. Jarita Charmain Holbrook
SDSU grad (class of 1992); Only the 6th Black woman to earn doctorate in astronomy & astrophysics (UCSC, 1997); Taught at UCLA; Asst. Research Scientist, Univ. of Arizona; Principal Editor, African Cultural Astronomy: Research in Africa, 2008*

Aisha Lastar Hollins
Communications Field Consultant; Former Associate Director, Community Resources, University of California, San Diego

Khaleedah "Ishe" Hollins
Singer; Songwriter; Author, Sol the Super Hairo, celebrating natural African hair

Sherehe Yamaisha Roze Hollins
Educator; Consultant; Artist; Visual Storyteller; Poet; Author, Heart Love Messages of the Soul, awarded San Diego Book Award for Best Poetry Book of the Year, 2002

Rev. Clovis Honore
Community Organizer, San Diego Black Health Associates, Alliance for African Assistance, and the S.D. Congregations for Change

Dr. Rodney Hood
Practices Internal Medicine at the Care View Medical Group in San Diego

Dr. Willie Edward Hopkins
SDSU grad (class of 1977; '79); author, Aligning Organizational Subcultures for Competitive Advantage & Ethical Dimensions of Diversity*

Willie J. Horton, Jr.
Lifelong San Diegan, teacher, SD City Schools; Principal; Boards for SD Zoological Society, Youth Symphony, Urban League, SDSU Alumni; Outstanding Achievement in Education Award from National University*

Dr. Ticey L. Hosley
Professor, Counseling Department, Miramar College; Lincoln HS Alumni Association*

Dr. Raymond Crump Howard
Professor in Counseling Education, SDSU, 1974-1989; highly regarded for his work in SDSU's Community Based Block Program (CBB)*

Traci D. Howard
Dir., Admissions, Cal Western School of Law, SD; Law School Admissions Council*

William Tayari Howard
Amassed over 10,000 broadcast hours Radio/Television over 39 year career; raised $1.7 million for charities/non-profits; accumulated over 100,000 community service hours; Lifetime Achievement Award by President Barack Obama, 2011

Ruby L. & Clarice Hubert
*Sisters graduating from San Diego State University in 1942 in Elementary Education; co-authored
A Century of Black Princes: A Family Tree**

373

Roll Call *(continued)*

Amos Hudgins
A homeowner and Barber Shop owner, Coronado, early 1900's

Delores Huerta
World Renowned Civil Rights Activist and Labor Leader; Together with Cesar Chavez founded the National Farm Workers Association, which later became the United Farm Workers Union; her non-violent and grassroots labor organizing strategies became the foundation for organized labor nationally and internationally

Dr. Marvalene Hughes
SDSU professor & counselor, 1972-1986; Director of Counseling & Career Placement; President CSU, Stanislaus, 1994; First woman president of Dillard University*

Dr. George Hutchinson
U. S. Navy Captain; Professor of Recreation & Leisure Studies, SDSU, 1973*

Bryce Jackson
Retired Basketball Coach; Co-Founder, LADR, alternative economic system; mentor

Francis K. Jackson
Entrepreneur; Owner & CEO of Nefran Real Estate/Ameriwest Mortgage

Dr. Maurice Jackson
SDSU assistant professor of sociology, 1962-65; taught at U.C. Riverside; Chaired UCR Ethnic Studies Department*

Nancy Johnson
Community Service Officer, San Diego Police Department

Precious Jackson
Volunteer extraordinaire; Recipient of Equal Opportunity Youth Award, 1999, from SD Urban League for work with Project New Village; mentor; tutor; member Urban League's Thurgood Marshall Achiever's Society

Thomas Jackson
Early African American resident of San Diego County, late 1800's; farmer

Dr. Ambrose Jacobs
SDSU football player, 1967; Lt. Colonel, US Army; Taught at West Point; was American Defense Attaché to the Republic of the Congo; Professor, Bennett College*

Dr. Adam Jeffers
SDSU Career Counselor; Adjunct Assistant Professor, Multicultural Counseling; Community activist and leader; Presenter on the history of Islam in regard to African Americans*

Fahari Jeffers, J.D.
Co-Founder with Ken Seaton Msemaji, of the United Domestic Workers Association; Community activist; Lawyer; SDSU grad (class of 1975); Chair of the Board of the San Diego Convention Center, 2000; Along with Ken, adoptive parent to 16 children*

Amos Johnson, Jr.
SDSU grad (class of 1959); Former pastor, New Creation Baptist Church

Charles E. Johnson
Former President, San Diego Chapter, NAACP

Claudette Johnson
SDSU grad; Cover girl for Jet Magazine, 1963; Ebony Fashion Fair Model

Gary "Big Hands" Johnson
NFL Defensive Tackle, majority of career (1975-1985) with San Diego Chargers; Inducted into San Diego Hall of Champions, 2007

Roll Call *(continued)*

Helga Johnson
First African American woman to become a police officer in San Diego

Herb Johnson
President & CEO, San Diego Rescue Mission, MBA, Harvard Business School

Dr. John Johnson
Former President, Urban League of San Diego; Former Deputy City Manager; Served on the Board of Directors, San Diego Chamber of Commerce

Dr. Lorraine R. Johnson
Licensed Clinical Social Worker (LCSW); distinguished psychotherapist; National speaker; Appointed by Mayor as Human Relations Commissioner, City of San Diego

Rudolph "Rudy" Allister Johnson, III
President/CEO, Neighborhood House Association; former General Manager, San Diego Convention Center; co-authored, <u>Cracking Up: The True Story of One Family's Recovery from the Devastation of Crack Cocaine</u>*"

Solomon Johnson
Founder, Bethel A.M.E. Church, first Black church in SD; Helped establish NAACP in San Diego

Terry Warren Johnson
Elected as the first African American Mayor of Oceanside, 2000

Tom Johnson
Former President, San Diego Chapter, NAACP

Vallera Johnson
SDSU grad (class of 1971); recipient of Jurist of the Year Award by the Women's Law Division of the National Bar Association*

Dr. Wayman H.D. Johnson
SDSU grad (class of 1969); Professor, Computer & Information Sciences, Mesa College; Headed Black Faculty Assoc.; Retired Dean, Learning Resources & Instructional Support*

Charlie Joiner
Pro Football Player (1969-1986); SD Chargers Hall of Fame; Pro Football Hall of Fame, 1996; Retired as oldest wide receiver (39) at that time; Coached Chargers 1987-1991 & 2008-2012; SD Hall of Champions, 1986

Claude D. Jolly
Former President, San Diego Chapter, NAACP

Napoleon A. Jones, J.D. *(1940-2009)*
SDSU grad (class of 1962); law degree, University of San Diego; Federal Judge, U.S. District Court, Southern California District, appointed by President Bill Clinton 1994; Staunch advocate for the African American community*

Otis L. Jones, J.D.
SDSU grad; law degree University of San Diego; worked for Legal Aid; Deputy District Attorney, real estate broker; business law professor; President, California Association of Black Lawyers; President, Association of Black Attorneys, SD County*

Roll Call *(continued)*

Dr. Steven Jones
CEO, Jones & Associates, Consulting; one of America's top experts on diversity; Dynamic keynote speaker, facilitator, organizational effectiveness consultant

Willie Jones
Beloved local Lincoln HS student, class president, star of school wrestling team, outstanding scholar; had been awarded a $98,000 scholarship to Cornell University, with no gang affiliation, was killed by gang violence when leaving a graduation party; Willie Jones Ave in San Diego was named in his honor

Woodrow Jones, Jr.
Taught in Political Science Department, SDSU, 1974-1991; Dean of College of Liberal Arts at Texas A & M*

Zoneice Jones
Co-Founder and President, Pazzaz Educational Enrichment Center

Frank R. Jordan
Worked in TV & Radio Production; Former President, San Diego Chapter, NAACP, 1992-1995; Former President California State Conference of NAACP

Lorrie Jordan
SDSU grad (class of 1996); Reporter & Weather Anchor, WCBD-TV Channel 2; Weathercaster, KNSD, SD*

Florence Griffith Joyner
"Flo-Jo" (1959-1998)
3 Time Olympic Gold Medalist in Track & Field; Holds world record in 100 & 200 meter events; Considered the fastest woman runner of all time; Founded the Florence Griffith Joyner Youth Foundation, San Diego, 1992

Shirley Junior
Former Professor, Child Development Dept., SD Mesa; Volunteer, Campfire Boys & Girls; Recipient, Channel 10 Leadership Award; Created Rites of Passage for Young Black men

Maisha Kadumu
Co-Founder with Walter Kadumu, Center for Parent Involvement in Education, CPIE; Community Activist; Original elder, Rites of Passage Program for African American Girls, SD

Walter Kadumu *(1948-2008)*
Co-Founder with Maisha Kadumu, Center for Parent Involvement in Education, CPIE; Former member US cultural group; Founded Black Men United; Nationally recognized for volunteer work; Among first to celebrate Kwanzaa in San Diego*

Dr. Samuel Kinde Kassegne
Associate Professor, SDSU, 2010; Co-founder, American-based, Ethiopian Computing & Information Technology Association*

Aster Keleta
Employee, San Diego Community College District; Entrepreneur

Benjamin Kelso
President, San Diego Black Police Officers Association, 2014-15

Ethan Neil Kendricks
Freelance writer; Film curator, San Diego Museum of Contemporary Art; Cannes Film Festival Videographer; teaches screenwriting, SDSU

Dr. James Nwannukwu Kerri
Afro-American Studies Professor SDSU, 1977-1983; Chair of Afro-American Studies Department; Board Trustee, Project Change International*

376

Roll Call *(continued)*

Dr. Jack Kimbrough *(1908-1992)*

One of San Diego's first Black Dentists; degree in Chemistry, UC Berkeley; doctor of dental surgery, UC San Francisco; with physician, Dr. Antonio DaCosta founded first African American Dental and Medical Facility in San Diego, 1940; First African American President, San Diego Dental Society, 1934; organized sit-ins to de-segregate hotels & restaurants in San Diego, 1948; helped organize first chapters of Urban League & National Association for the Advancement of Colored People (NAACP); served as presidents of both organizations; 15 years active with Flying Samaritans, assisting poor in Baja California; avid scholar & researcher, African Art & Culture; Donated extensive African Art Collection for all San Diegans to enjoy

Clarence Hilyer King, Jr. *(1915-1996)*

Graduated San Diego State University in 1935; became an engineer and served as International President, Association for Systems Management*

Ray King

CEO, Urban League of San Diego, 2014-15

Gloria Ann Knight

Co-Founder, Community Actor's Theatre

Ernest "Ernie" Ladd

Professional Football Player & a Professional Wrestler; Nicknamed, "The Big Cat;" NFL career (1961-1968) starting w/ SD Chargers; San Diego Hall of Champions, 2005

Dr. Walter Lam

Founder and Chief Executive Officer of the Alliance for African Assistance

Rickey T. Laster

Pastor, New Assurance Baptist Church, San Diego

Dr. Jacqueline D. Leak

Cultural psychologist; College Lecturer in Psychology & Women's Studies; Life Coach

Che Che LeSeur

Licensed Clinical Social Worker, SD County, Health & Human Services, Juv. Forensics

Julius Lester

Author of over 25 books of fiction, non-fiction, children's books, and poetry; Studied at SDSU (1959) as exchange student from Fisk; His letter to Aztec editor complained about white fraternity performing in blackface; helping to bring about an end to this practice on campus*

Ananda Lewis

Television personality, Talk Show Host, Social Activist, Born in San Diego

Charles L. Lewis III *(1966-2004)*

Elected to the San Diego City Council, representing District 4, 2002, till death, 2004

John G. Lewis

*SDSU alumna (class of 1991); Professional Interpreter in American Sign Language (AMSL), spoken English & spoken French; VSR Manager, Gallaudet University Interpreting Services (GIS);
helped found National Alliance of Black Interpreters**

Rev. John J. Lewis

Former President, San Diego Chapter, NAACP

Phillip Liburd

Education Chair, Black American Political Action Committee, San Diego Chapter

Ira H. Lipscomb

SDSU Graduate; Editor 1940-41 Student Handbook; Associate Editor of El Palenque *

Roll Call *(continued)*

Olin Lipscomb
SDSU student; Staff Sergeant Crew Chief servicing aircraft, Tuskegee Airmen WW II*

Dr. Wendell Lipscomb
SDSU student; Tuskegee airman; instructor for Tuskegee airmen worked with Daniel "Chappie" James who would become nation's first Black 4-star general; Graduated UC Berkley, Doctor of Psychiatry; First Black intern at Kaiser Permanente, San Francisco*

Yayesh Lisssane
SDSU (class of 1984); President Ethiopian Community of San Diego, assisting refugees adjust to life in U.S.*

Cleavon Jake Little *(1939-1992)*
SDSU grad (class of 1965); raised in Linda Vista's Navy housing; Hollywood comedian & actor; best known for role in movie "Blazing Saddles;" Tony Award for stage role, "Purlie Victorious." starred in movies, e.g. "Cotton Comes To Harlem," Mentored by Dr. Floyd Gaffney, Southeastern Community Theatre in San Diego*

David Lloyd
Founder, CEO, Bay City Marine Shipbuilding, Co., San Diego; Philanthropist

Pamela Lloyd-Ogoke
Deaf since her youth, completed post-MA Deafness Rehabilitation Administration, SDSU (1990); Serves on Gallaudet University Board of Trustees; Past President, National Black Deaf Advocates*

Loren Sharice Lott
Talented Singer & Actor on Stage & Screen; American Idol XIV Finalist, Born & Raised in San Diego; Attended High Tech HS; Graduated Clark-Atlanta University: Granddaughter of Drs. Carl and Dorothy Smith of SD

Thomas E. Logans
SDSU grad (class of 1965); Former President of Oceotl, a predominantly white service fraternity on campus; Former President of Kappa Alpha Psi fraternity*

Dr. Marlene Elizabeth Long
SDSU grad (class of 1959); Howard University Medical School grad; Missionary nun, New Guinea & in Africa, with African Medical & Research Foundation*

Robert Lowe
Early African American entrepreneur; built the "Creole Palace" 1924, a nightclub in San Diego's Hotel Douglas, along with George Ramsey

Reuben MacCalla
San Diego native; Singer, Songwriter, Performer, Livin Out Loud, a Los Angeles-based group

Sylvia MacCalla
San Diego native; Renowned Actress, Singer, Livin Out Loud, a Los Angeles-based group

Thomas MacCalla, Jr.
San Diego native; Executive Producer Kin Productions, CEO Visions in Motion; Executive Producer, Livin Out Loud, a Los Angeles-based group

Roll Call (continued)

April Mahoney
Author, Poet, Producer, Radio Personality

Wanda Clay Majors
Co-founded, Golden ANKH Association; Active, YMCA & Community Economic Development Corporation (CEDA); Directed SOAR & EOP mentoring, SDSU*

Kamau Makesi-Tehuti
Member, Association for Advanced Study of Classical African Civilizations (ASCAC); Afrikan Traditional Spiritual Healing Circle; author, How to Make a Negro Christian

Dr. Cleo Malone *(1933-2008)*
Community Activist, Counselor & Director, The Palavra Tree, Substance Abuse Prevention, Treatment & Resource Center in San Diego for over 25 years

Dennis Malone
Director, Community Concerns Ministry; Former Facilitator, Project New Start

Henry G. Manley Sr.
Graduated from San Diego State University in 1937; a Major in the U.S. Army; President of San Diego Track & Field Officials Association*

Rev. Willie Evet Manley
Founded Greater Life Baptist Church, 1990; Head Metropolitan Fellowship Foundation; Recipient Ambassador of Peace Award, United Nations, 2003; Former President, SD NAACP

Beatrice Green Markey
First Black faculty member at San Diego State University in 1956; assistant professor, political science; taught at University of Hawaii at Hilo*

R. C. Marshall
Early African American resident, San Diego, Grand Master of California's Prince Hall Masons, late 1890's; resided in Coronado, California

Tilisha Tionette Martin
SDSU alum (class of 1997); dependency attorney, county Public Defender's Office representing minors who suffer abuse; Lectured SDSU's Graduate Program Social Work; trained Legal Aid workers; Supervising Attorney, Minors Counsel Office *

Ollie Genoa Matson, II *(1930-2011)*
Second Black coach, SDSU, 1971-75; Won the Bronze Medal in the 400 meter and the Silver Medal in the 4X400 meter relay in the 1952 Summer Olympics in Helsinki; played pro-football; Inducted into Pro Football Hall of Fame, 1972*

Ardelle Matthews
Teacher & Community Activist; Co-Founder, with husband Robert of African American Educators Association; Active organizer/supporters of many organizations & boards, including RADY Children's Hospital Auxiliary; Kids News Day, Encanto Planning Commission, Jack & Jill Women Inc., Tema Ghana Sister Society; Elementary Institute of Science; SD Human Relations Commission; Chair Annual MLK "King & Queen" Pageant; Presbyterian Church Elder

Dr. Robert Matthews
Teacher & Principal, San Diego Unified School District; President, Education Cultural Complex; Principal, Mt. Erie Christian Academy; Co-founded Southeast Community Theatre (renamed Common Ground Theatre) with Rufus Dewitt, 1963; Co-Founder, with wife, Ardelle, African American Educators Assoc.; Community Activist; Chair Annual MLK, Jr. Parade; Board Market Creek Plaza; Presbyterian Church Elder

379

Roll Call *(continued)*

Dr. Horace Mays
SDSU grad (class of 1937); Executive Director, L. A. Council of Churches*

Robert Andrew "Bobby" Meacham
SDSU student, 1979-81, playing Aztec baseball; Played 6 seasons pro-baseball; San Diego Padres first base coach; Managed two minor league teams*

James McCann
Former President, San Diego Chapter, NAACP

Frank McCarter
First African American police officer in San Diego, 1909

Henry McClarran
Co-Founder, Community Actor's Theatre

Lloyd W. McCloy
Pastor, Logan Heights Chapel A.M. E. Zion Church, 1931; Former President, SD NAACP, 1937

Roland McFarland
SDSU grad (class of 1964); performed at Old Globe Theatre; former VP Broadcast Standards & Practices, Fox Broadcasting & MyNetworkTV; active in Beverly Hills/Hollywood NAACP*

S. A. McFarland
Early African American resident, San Diego; Federal Government Clerk, late 1890's

Thomas O. McJunkins *(1919-1977)*
The third Black faculty member at SDSU; assistant professor, sociology, 1959; Associate Superintendent, San Diego Unified School District, 1970's*

Barbara J. McKinney
Wife of Bishop George D. McKinney & First Lady, St. Stephens CCOGC

Pastor George A. McKinney
Executive Pastor, St. Stephen's Cathedral Church of God in Christ

Bishop George Dallas McKinney
Co-founder, St. Stephen's Church of God in Christ, 1962; Senior Pastor; Author of 8 books, including African American Devotional Bible; Received numerous honors including Racial Reconciliation Man of the Year Award, and the Peace Maker Award;

Glen McKinney
Youth Pastor, St. Stephen's Cathedral Church of God in Christ

Wendy McKinney
Wife of Pastor George A. McKinney and Administrator, St. Stephens CCOGC

Greg Anthony McKinney
Patented inventor for life-saving technology for swimmers and divers

Jean McKinney *(1935-2004)*
Co-founder, St. Stephen's Church of God in Christ in 1962; Co-pastor, writer, poet, helped establish Half-Way House, Christian K-12 grade school, & AIDS/HIV residential facility

Dr. Taylor A. McKenzie
SDSU grad (class of 1969; 1971); professor in speech department at Grossmont College; senior minister at Church of Christ in San Diego*

Theodore William McNeal *(1904-1992)*
Veteran civil rights leader; Labor activist; Helped organize "Bottle & Cork Club" in Chicago, forerunner to Jesse Jackson's "Operation Breadbasket" In retirement, moved to San Diego; Advertising Manager, Voice & Viewpoint Newspaper; Labor Council volunteer; Former President, San Diego Chapter, NAACP

380

Roll Call *(continued)*

Ferman David McPhatter

SDSU grad (class of 1952); played on 1950 championship football team; team captain, 1951; Teacher, SD School District 1953-1982; retired as principal, Woodrow Wilson HS; McPhatter Summit School named in his honor, 1990; paralyzed in auto accident; participated in National Veterans Wheelchair Games for 10 years*

Michael McPherson

Professor, Psychology Dept. San Diego Miramar College

Miles McPherson

Pastor, the Rock Church, San Diego; Community Activist

Dr. Eddie Spencer Meadows

Taught in Music & Africana Studies Departments, SDSU; Published widely on jazz & African American music; Fulbright fellowship to Ghana; lectured UCLA & UCB*

Walter W. Meadows

Early African American resident, San Diego; only Black jeweler, 1890's

Keith Mikell

Well-respected artist: attended SDSU, late 1970's; his works have been exhibited at the Agora Gallery and the Lucy Florence Gallery in Los Angeles, as well as seen on TV on the sets of sitcoms*

E. Walter "Wally" Miles

Only Black professor oat SDSU at hire in 1967; Chairman of Board, SD Urban League; Chairman, SD Chapter, American Civil Liberties Union (ACLU); ACLU National Board; Chairman, Commission on Status of Blacks in American Political Science Association; Associate Editor, Western Political Science Quarterly; Commendable performance, local TV, 1985 debating on affirmative action with Clarence Pendleton, President Reagan's conservative Black appointee, heading the U.S. Civil Rights Commission*

George Millen

Early African American resident, operated blacksmith shops, 1890's

Jane B. Milligan

SDSU alumna (class of 1987); Co-founder, African American Writers & Artists Association; Poet; HS teacher*

Claudie Minor

SDSU Aztec Hall of Fame football player, played for Denver Broncos

Ralph Edward "Mitch" Mitchell

Degreed in Television, Film & Educational Tech., worked for KFMB; Public Affairs Manager, Hewlett-Packard

Abdi Mohamoud

Executive Director, Horn of Africa; Chosen by SD Metro Magazine as top business leaders under 40, 2004*

Derrick Monroe

SDSU grad (class of 1986); Community Center Manager, City of Encinitas

Archibald Lee Wright "Archie Moore" *(1916-1998)*

Professional Boxer, rated at Middleweight, Light Heavyweight and Heavyweight; Fought in 219 fights in his career, winning 185; Longest reigning Light Heavyweight World Champion of all time (1952-1962); holds record for the most career knockouts (131); Ranks #4 on the Ring's list of 100 greatest punchers of all time; His boxing career spanned 4 decades; Trained Muhammad Ali, George Foreman & James Tillis; Actor in TV & Film; Lived in San Diego, where he was given Key to City in1965; Inducted into SD Hall of Champions, 1956

Roll Call *(continued)*

Chantè Torrane Moore
Raised in San Diego; Top R& B performer having worked with El DeBarge & Kenny Lattimore; First Album, entitled, "Precious"

Dr. R. Vernon Moore
Past President, Association of African American Educators, San Diego

Pamela Moorehead
Former Teacher, County Office of Education's Juvenile Court & Community Schools; 2007 Teacher of the Year

Ernest Morgan
Early African American resident of San Diego County; with Elvira Price operated the Bon Ton Restaurant, only Black owned business of its kind at the time

Curtis Moring, Jr.
President and CEO, Curtis Moring Insurance Agency; Community Activist; Former President, San Diego Chapter, NAACP

Dr. Willie Morrow
Pioneering barber & entrepreneur; Discovered methods for African American hair to be processed in healthier ways; Authority on Black hair care; Taught on 4 continents & received more patents related to hair care than any other hair stylist in history; Authored <u>400 Years without a Comb</u>; Established first Black radio station in SD; Founded Black History Museum of Black Hair Care Industry; Civil rights activist;

Haven Moses
SDSU's most valuable player (MVP) on 1967 football team; First Aztec to be chosen Division I, All American; first round draft pick, Buffalo Bills; played for Denver; Inducted into SD Hall of Champions, 1993*

Diane Moss
Founder of Children Having Children; Founder of Project New Village, a grassroots organization geared toward food justice; Runs Annual Fannie Lou Hamer Fundraiser

Martin Moss
Professor, Counseling Department, San Diego Miramar College; former Head football Coach, Mesa College

Robert Clinton Moss *(1914-2008)*
First Black student to play on SDSU sports team; played football; twice all conference lead scorer in basketball; on same team with Art Linkletter, (who would become a star in Hollywood); First Black U S. Postal Supervisor in San Diego, 1940's*

Robert C. Moss, Jr.
SDSU grad (class of 1961); played on Aztec football & baseball teams; Teacher & counselor for San Diego Unified School District; Faculty, UC San Diego until he retired in 1992; published author on sports*

Roll Call *(continued)*

Farahi Jeffers and *Ken Seaton Msemaji*, Founders of The United Domestic Workers Association, walking with renowned leader of the United Farm Workers Association, *Cesar Chavez*; Photo Courtesy of Carlos LeGarrrette, circa 1970's

Ken Seaton Msemaji
Co-founder & First President, United Domestic Workers Association, 1977-2005; Political Director, Sheet Metal Workers, Local 206, San Diego

Jared Moten
Executive Director, New Hope Unlimited

Abdur-Rasheed Muhammad
SDSU grad student, Anthropology; First Muslim Imam in U.S. military, 2004-05*

Amos Muhammad
Opened Mosque No. 8 in San Diego, respected as one of the most educated mosques in the nation; Served as Imam; Advocated for social change & equality in San Diego

Bernard Muhammad
Artist; Painter, Owner, Kensington Urban Artist

Hugh Muhammad
Student Minister of Muhammad Mosque No. 8; Author; Advocate for social justice

Dr. Raquel Ann Lovings Muhammad
Founded first Black SD private school, Nation of Islam School; Designed curriculum for Nation of Islam schools throughout U.S.; Wife of Imam Amos Muhammad

Dr. Edward L. Murray, III
Psychologist; SD BAPAC Excellence Award; Author of <u>When Push Comes to Shove</u>

Dr. Yvonette Murrell-Powell
Lecturer, USC's School of Social Work; Education Management; Member, Black Social Workers of San Diego

Ellen D. Nash
SDSU grad (class of 1979); Manager SDSU Human Resources; Dedicated community work with United Front for Academic Achievement of African American Children*

Tamiko Nash
SDSU grad; First Runner-up, Miss California, 2005; Wife of NFL player, Terrell Davis*

Charles Neal
Former Extended Opportunity Program (EOP) Counselor, SDSU; helped start the SDSU African American Scholarship Fund

383

Roll Call *(continued)*

Johnnierenee Nia Nelson
Poet-in-Residence at the Worldbeat Center in San Diego; Author of 5 books of Kwanzaa Poems, including "Classic Kwanzaa Poems"

America Newton
One of the earliest Black women to establish residency in SD County; Worked as a laundress in Julian, 1872; America Grade trail near Julian named in her honor

Fred Norfleet
SDSU grad (class of 1973); former Channel 10 (KGTV) "Spectrum" talk-show host; owner Norfleet Video Productions*

Kenneth "Ken" Howard Norton, Sr. *(1943-2013)*
Heavyweight Boxing Champion; Won bout with Muhammad Ali at the San Diego Sports Arena in front of 12,000 spectators, the most memorable athletic event to happen in San Diego, March 31, 1973; He broke Ali's jaw during the 12-round fight; it was first of 3 fights with Ali; Inducted into San Diego Hall of Champions, 2001

Mshinda Nyofu
SDSU grad (class of 1985), community activist; active in the US Cultural Organization and the Black American Political Association of California (BAPAC);

Vernon Oaks
Chair, Afro-American Studies Department, 1973; Administrator Howard U*

Dr. Clyde W. Oden
Attended SDSU; Received his Doctor of Optometry degree from U.C. Berkeley; President & CEO, UHP Healthcare, Inc., Los Angeles*

Douglas Alphonsa Oden, J.D.
Born in San Diego; Graduated Western State Univ. College of Law; Former President Earl B. Gilliam Bar Assoc. & California Assoc. of Black Lawyers; Board member, former President of Reach One Teach One Inc.,

Tayo Peter Olafioye *(1937-2012)*
Taught in SDSU's English Department, 1974-1976; authored 18 books of fiction, poetry and criticism;

Willie Eldon O'Ree
Canadian-born Professional Hockey Player; First Black in National Hockey League (NHL); Los Angeles Blades & SD Gulls; Jersey displayed SD Sports Arena; SD Hall of Champions, 2008

Robert Osby
Fire Chief, San Diego, 1992, supervise 1,300 firemen & lifeguards; Fire Chief, Oceanside; retired, 2005; Chair, Intn'l Assoc. Metro. Fire Chiefs; Founder SD Chapter, Intn'l Assoc. Black Prof. Fire Fighters*

Jerri Parker
Developed & implemented Rites of Passage Program for Girls, 7th Day Adventist Church, 31st St., San Diego

Caryn Pass
SDSU grad; Former President, SDSU Black Alumni Association

Gwendolyn Patrick-Buie
Library assistant, SDSU, 1967; vice-president, California State Employees Association (CSEA) 1996; co-chair Study Commission on Black Affairs (SCOBA), early 1990's*

Fannie Lois Jeffries Payne *(1915-2008)*
SDSU grad (class of 1964); Delta Sigma Theta Sorority, Links, Inc., Talladega Alumni Association, Altrusa Club, Delta Gamma International Society; Woman of Dedication Award*

Roll Call *(continued)*

William Payne

Second Black teacher to be hired by San Diego Board of Education at Pacific Beach Jr. High, where white parents tried to have him removed, to no avail; 25 yr. career in education, ending as lecturer and Admissions Director SDSU's College of Education*

George W. Pearson

Former SDSU student killed in action in Vietnam while attempting to save fellow servicemen; 1st African American listed on the SDSU War Memorial*

Clarence M. Pendleton, Jr. *(1930-1988)*

Politically Conservative Chair, U.S. Commission on Civil Rights, 1981-1988 appointed by President Ronald Reagan; Engendered significant opposition as Congressional funding was reduced to the Commission under "Penny," & his outspoken criticisms embittered him to women and minorities; Prior to that he had headed the Model Cities Program in San Diego & directed SD Branch of the Urban League

Dr. Nolan Penn

Retired Professor of Psychiatry and Associate Chancellor for the University of California, San Diego, School of Medicine; Noted Clinical Psychologist

Wilhelmina Elaine Perry

Professor, Social Work, SDSU (1968-1978); With her partner, SDSU professor Antonia Pantoja, co-founded the Graduate School for Urban Resources and Social Policy, Inc. & the Latino Educational Media Center*

Rev. Grandison Madison Phelps, Jr.

First African American to run for public office in SD, but defeated in bid for City Council seat, 1961; Pastored St. Paul's United Methodist Church, 1955-1992; helped start S.E. Interdenominational Ministry Alliance*

Cheryl Alethia Phelps

Policy Analyst; Social Entrepreneur; Philanthropist

John W. Porter

Former President, San Diego Chapter, NAACP, 1938

Dr. Wally J. Porter *(1927-2001)*

Renowned San Diego Educator; Graduated Memorial Junior HS in SD, & HS in Kansas; Attended L.A. City College where he met Clint Eastwood; Served in Army as a Medic & in the Finance Corps; Owned janitorial service; Nightclub MC opening for Sam Cooke, Redd Foxx, Little Richard & others; Graduate degrees from SDSU; Former Dean, Student Services, Educational Cultural Complex & Mid-City Continuing Education Center; Former President, San Diego Chapter, NAACP; SD elementary schools named in his honor; Father of Yvette

Yvette Porter-Moore

Writer, Educator, Publisher at Footprint Expressions; Genealogist & Family Historian at Root Digger Genealogy Research Service

Arthur "Art" Louis Powell *(1937-2015)*

Played football, San Diego HS; Played in Canadian Football League, 1957-58; 9 year NFL Career (1959-1968); Ranks 18th all-time in career touchdown receptions; Inducted into San Diego Hall of Champions, 1992

Charlie Powell *(1932-2014)*

Grew up in Logan Height; Starred in football, basketball, track and baseball, San Diego HS; California HS Football Player of the Year, 1950; Turned down offer by Harlem Globetrotters; Played minor league baseball, 1952; Youngest player to sign with NFL in their history at 19; Played Pro football, 7 years; 4th-ranked heavyweight Boxer in the world, early 1960's; San Diego Hall of Champions, 1995

Elizabeth "Liz" Quinnett

Program Manager, Public Child Welfare Training Academy, SDSU; Board of Directors, Harmonious Solutions

Dr. LaVerne E. Ragster

SDSU grad M.S. Biology (class of 1975); returned home to teach at University of the Virgin Islands; President of that institution; UCSD Professional Achievement Award*

Hartwell W. Ragsdale, II *(1925-2004)*

Purchased Mortuary from Edward Anderson's widow, Mary,1955 to form the Anderson-Ragsdale Mortuary, one of the oldest funeral & mortuary businesses in SD; Community activist; President, SD NAACP, 1964

Hartwell W. "Skipper" Ragsdale, III

President & CEO, Anderson-Ragsdale Mortuary, Inc.; President, California Funeral Directors Association

Cynthia Raimo

Served the SD community for years as an Accountant & trusted Business Advisor; Regional V.P., Primerica, Inc.; Investments, Savings & Life Insurance Consultant

George A. Ramsey

Early African American entrepreneur; managed Creole Café, AKA Creole Palace in downtown SD; Built Hotel Douglas in Gaslamp Quarter, SD, 1924; Known as unofficial mayor of "Darktown" as the Black Community was known in early 1900's

Dr. Janaha A. Ransome

Community Leader; Youth Advocate

Ruby Raphael

Born 1899 in GA; Operated Beauty Shop in downtown San Diego, early to mid' 1900's

Mercer Z. Ray

Former President, San Diego Chapter, NAACP

Charles E. Reid *(1938-2004)*

Former Marine; Mathematics major; Programmer; Design Specialist; Aerospace Engineer; Manager, General Dynamics; Human Resources, County of SD; President, SD Community College Board of Trustees; President, National Association of Community Colleges; Chair, SD Economic Opportunities Commission; Former President, SD Chapter, NAACP; Wife is Sonja

Sonja Reynolds Reid

Management of Ebony Fashion Fair; Active with San Diego Historical Sites Board & Las Munecas Auxiliary to Children's Home Society; NAACP Fundraiser: As NAACP President, coordinated "Operation Sweep" to raise more funds & increase membership; President, National Coalition of 100 Black Women; Trustee of SD Community College District; V.P. Advisory Council, Educational Cultural Complex; Wife of Charles

Alton L. Reynolds

SDSU grad (class of 1977); manager local TV, channel 69; U.S. Air Force cryptographer during Vietnam War; taught accounting at SD Mesa College*

Gloria Lockman Rhodes

SDSU's Outreach Librarian; former Chair, Racial & Ethnic Diversity Committee of the Association of College & Research Librarians*

Elizabeth Riggs, J.D.

First African American woman judge in SD County, 1979; only Black woman judge in County for 20 years; Founder, Black Attorney's Association of San Diego, later renamed, The Earl B. Gilliam Bar Association, President; Honored by SD Women's Hall of Fame, 2008*

Roll Call *(continued)*

John Ritchey

Only Black player on the SDSU Aztec baseball team in 1946, ignored by pro-scouts due to race, led the Negro American League (NAL) batting .369 in 1947; signed with San Diego Padres in 1948, breaking the color-barrier in the Pacific Coast League; his bronze bust is displayed at Petco Park*

Mercedes H. Richey

SDSU grad (class of 1963); Principal of Lincoln High School, 1971-74*

Doris C. Ringgold

Founder of House of Metamorphosis (HOM) a Residential Drug Treatment Facility, 1976, which has served over 6,000 individuals with alcohol & other drug addictions

D.Ann "Debra" Roberson

Career Counselor; Educator; Faculty, San Diego Community College District, Owner, College-Bound Baby, S.D.

Arnie Paul Robinson, Jr.

SDSU grad (class of 2003); 2nd Aztec to win Olympic Gold Medal for long jump, 1976 Olympics, Montreal; won Bronze Medal Munich, 1972; seven national AAU titles, 1971 Pan American Games Championship; Professor, Physical Education Dept. San Diego Mesa College until retirement; Inducted into San Diego Hall of Champions, 1985*

Chris Robinson

Formerly Oprah Winfrey's personal trainer; former SDSU track & field star; appeared on "CBS Early Show" and "Martha Stewart Morning Show" authored, <u>The Core Connection: Go From Fat to Flat by Using Your Abs for a Total Body Workout</u>, 2008*

Floyd Andrew Robinson

Pro-Baseball player for Chicago White Sox, Cincinnati Reds, Oakland Athletics and Boston Red Sox; inducted by San Diego Hall of Champions, 2009

Margaret & Albert Robinson

Founded the Julian Hotel in 1887 (as Hotel Robinson) and operated it for 28 years; Albert was from Missouri, was formerly enslaved; Margaret was the daughter of a Mr. Tull, the first African American man called to serve as a juror in San Diego County; The Julian Hotel, located in Julian, California is the oldest, continuously operated hotel in Southern California, as per the National Registry of Historic Places

John Edgar Roundtree, J. D. *(1880-1961)*

The only Black attorney in the United States in 1932; Former President, San Diego Chapter of the NAACP, 1933-1935;

Charles Dee Rucker

SDSU grad (class of 1975); Police officer 17 years; Taught Criminal Justice Administration, Southwestern College, 20 years; best known for his paintings of African American life, which have been exhibited in galleries around the world & locally at the Charles Rucker Gallery in San Diego*

Harold V. Rucker

SDSU grad (class of 1971); Administrative Law Judge on California Unemployment Appeals Board; Former Deputy District Attorney; President, Administrative Law Judges Association (ALJA), 94-95, Judge Pro Tem, Superior Court, 1981-85*

Rashaan Salaam

Born and raised in San Diego; All American high school running back, La Jolla Country Day School; Inducted into Athletic Hall of Fame; played in NFL 4 seasons; Winner Heisman Trophy, 1994; Youngest player in NFL history to rush for 1000 yards, when he was 21; Son of Khalada Salaam

Roll Call *(continued)*

Khalada Salaam-Alaji
Former Principal & teacher, Community Preparatory School, private school in SD African American community with excellent academic ratings; Member, Encanto Neighborhood Community Planning Group

Joseph Maurice Samuels
SDSU Professor, 1972-1982; SDSU's first affirmative action officer*

Dee Sanford
Internationally Acclaimed Speaker, TV & Radio Host; Business Consultant & Trainer

Theresa Saunders
One of the original members of the first mosques in San Diego; Current Member Mohammed Mosque No. 8; active & dedicated community volunteer

Dr. Danny Lyon Scarborough
Founded SDSU Black Repertory Total Theatrical Experience; taught in Afro-American Studies Department, 1977; his SDSU Dance Troupe won an Emmy, 1979*

Dr. Errol Roy Seaton
Academic Advising, SDSU; taught British & American Literature, Western Washington University; reviewed 20 books, S. D. Union & S.D. Tribune*

Tiaina Baul "Junior" Seau, Jr. *(1969-2012)*
Played basketball, Oceanside HS; CIF Player of Year in Basketball & Football; Outstanding pro ball career as a linebacker; 13seasons, SD Chargers; Restaurateur; Diagnosed Chronic Traumatic Encephalopathy (CTE), brain trauma common to football players, which some feel led to his suicide; Posthumous election to Pro Football Hall of Fame, 2015

Prince Sewood
Retired after working for State of California, Department of Corrections

Lynn Sharp-Underwood
Executive Director, City of SD Commission on Gang Prevention & Intervention; Implemented Safe Passage Program & Compassion Project: Board Member, Urban Collaborative Project

LaTanya M. Sheffield
Former SDSU student (class of 1986); won 400 meter hurdles in 1988 NCAA; 1988 Olympic finalist in the 400 meter hurdles

Sean Sheppard
SDSU grad; former SDSU strength/conditioning coach; started Sheppard Community Scholarship, SDSU; established non-profit, "EMBRACE" for needy veterans & youth*

Dr. Maxine Sherard
Former Member California State Assembly, District 78

Charles Clifford Shockley
First African American corporate Pilot in United States; former President, local chapter, Tuskegee Airmen; headed Minority Business Development Center & Defense Conversion Center, SDSU

Donald Frederick Shy
Standout Aztec football player; world-class hurdler; played pro football; Owner, Papa Shy's Gourmet Barbecue, Oceanside*

Willie "Ezell" Singleton, Jr. *(1941-2012)*
Outstanding HS quarterback & All-American athlete; played for San Diego HS, 1959; started on basketball team & played baseball; Appeared on Ed Sullivan Show, 1958; Played football & baseball at UCLA, only the 2nd Black quarterback to play for the Bruins; SD Section Hall of Fame at Market Creek Plaza; went Ordained minister

Lena Nozizwe Siwundlhla

TV News Correspondent, Channel 8 KFMB-TV; Emmy & Golden Mike Awards; correspondent on "America's Most Wanted" SDSU grad (class of 1980); authored, Starring in Your Own Life

Webster Slaughter

Played pro-football for the Cleveland Browns as a wide receiver; played pro-ball for 13 years, with 5 teams*

Ella Fay Sloan

Professor of Cosmetology at San Diego City College; initiated the W.E.B. DuBois Leadership Institute for Young Scholars; Arranged student travel to Africa to bring school supplies to underprivileged children in Ghana

Tony Smalls

Owner of Cane Patch Pies, and proponent of community-based gardens

Gloria Jean Smith

SDSU grad; helped establish Black Student Union in 1970's; Activist for change on campus and in the community; Owner, Gloria's Elegant Fashions, San Diego

Hollis Smith

SDSU student, 1963; worked in aerospace industry 18 years; CEO of Green Power Foundation; founding president of the Southern California Minority Business Development Council*

Dr. Jesse Owens Smith

Taught in Afro-American Studies at SDSU in late 1970's; president of California Black Faculty & Staff Association; professor CSU Fullerton*

Lionel & Edith Smith

Community Activists; Advocates for the Rights of Students and Parents through Leadership and Relationship Building

Delicia Turner Sonnenberg

Artistic Director, Moxie Theatre

Clarence Earl Stanfield

SDSU grad (class of 1958); counselor and administrator, San Diego Community College District; leadership roles for the Salvation Army, California Council of Adult Education & Association of S.D. Community College Administrators; Plaque honors him, S.D. City College*

Dr. E. Percil Stanford

SDSU professor, Gerontology; Director, Center on Aging; became Western Regional Director of the American Association of Retired Persons (AARP), 2011; President of KIND Corporation, an organization which finds housing for elderly in San Diego who are low-income*

Willie Samuel Steele

SDSU student receiving two NCAA titles in 1947 & 1948 in track; won three national AAU championships in long jump; won Olympic Gold Medal, London, 1948 with jump of 7.82 meters; first-ever Olympic Medal for Aztec athlete; SDSU Blue Key fraternity removed race restrictions to make Steele a member; elected to Hall of Champions, Balboa Park, 1958

William and Maxcine Stephens

Active in supporting community events that promote cultural pride, harmony and community building, including neighborhood clean-up programs & their Neighborhood Council; Elementary Institute of Science Leadership Team

Dr. Cecil Steppe

Former Director, San Diego County Department of Social Services; Former Chief Probation Officer; CEO Urban League of San Diego; nephew of Rebecca Craft

Roll Call *(continued)*

Rev. George M. Stevens *(1932-2006)*

SDSU grad (class of 1958); accompanied Rev. Martin Luther King, Jr. on historic march from Selma to Montgomery, 1965; Led Congress on Racial Equality (CORE) in San Diego, 1967-69; Board member, NAACP; Elected to San Diego City Council, representing the 4th District, 1991; Associate Minister, Mt. Erie Baptist Church; the George L. Stevens Senior Center, in San Diego dedicated in his honor in 2006*

Joseph H. Steward

Early African American resident, San Diego; first African American admitted to the San Diego Bar, 1891

Vernon Sukumu

Community activist; Entrepreneur; Supporter of African American Art & Culture; Former head of the Black Federation; Director of the Welfare Rights Organization, which founded the city's first homeless and women's shelters; Active Leadership in the NIA Cultural Organization

Harold Surratt

SDSU Telecommunications major, 1978; Hollywood actor in such movies as, "the Pelican Brief" & "the Devil's Advocate" as well as on T.V. including "ER," "The Practice," "Fringe" and "Orange is the New Black"*

Renee Swindle

Creative writer; graduate writing instructor; authored novel, <u>Please, Please, Please,</u> 1999, a featured selection of the Literary Guild*

Steve Tadlock

Member, Past President, Montgomery Lions Club; MAAC Board of Directors

Robert Tambuzi

Community Activist & Supporter; Advocates for Youth & Family Development through his work with Project New Village; Involved with resolving gang conflicts; Recipient of San Diego Peacemakers Award from the San Diego Mediation Center; Active in helping to organize annual Cesar Chavez Walk, Kwanzaa Celebrations; a Farmer's Market & Food Co-op for Seniors; Founder, Central Regional Alliance Committee for Accessible & Affordable Housing; Past President, African American Writers and Artists Association; Executive Director, United African American Ministerial Action Council

Sylvia Cameron Telafaro

Award-winning fiction writer, poet, story teller and activist; President American Academy of Women Artists; President African American Writers & Artists

Stacie Terry

Head Coach, SDSU Women's Basketball Team, 2013

Amanda Jeremiah Thomas

SDSU alumna (class of 197) in Aerospace Engineering; worked at JPL; worked on Mars "Curiosity" project which landed a rover on Mars; Awarded the Alumni Monty in 2013; supervisor at NASA's Deep Space Network in the Mojave Desert*

Roll Call *(continued)*

Dr. Charles W. Thomas II *(1926-1990)*

Professor of Urban Studies and Planning, at the University of California, San Diego, Author, Community activist; Former President, San Diego Chapter, NAACP; Licensed Psychologist; Founding Chairperson of the Association of Black Psychologists; tragically slain in 1990; fondly remembered as the Father of Black Psychology

Dr. Shirley Wade Thomas

Professor in Afro-American Studies Department, SDSU, 1972-1988; Community advocate; expert in Black Child Development*

LaDanian "L.T." Tomlinson

NFL running back, 11-year history; played for San Diego Chargers for 9 seasons; 5 Pro-Bowls; NFL record, most single-season touchdowns (31), most single-season rushing touchdowns (28); Associated Press (AP) NFL Most Valuable Player (MVP), 2006; AP NFL Offensive player of the Year, 2006; Best NFL Player ESPY Award, 2007; Dennis Byrd Most Inspirational Player Award, 2010; 10,000 Yards Rushing Team; SD Chargers 50th Anniversary Team; His Jersey No. 21 retired by the San Diego Chargers, 2012; Ranked 5th in NFL history in career rushing yards (13,684), 2nd rushing touchdowns (145) and 3rd in total touchdowns (162);

Thelma Gorham Thompson

SDSU grad (class of 1937); talented speaker; Chief of U.S. Department of Health & Human Resources Children's Bureau, Region V; honored for organizing adoptions for children of color; Co-authored, "Adoptive Resources for Negro Children"*

Richard Thompson

Associate Professor, Music, SDSU; Performer & Composer; Jazz Group, Mirage released CD, "Swing Low, Sweet Chariot;" Recipient of First Individual Artist Award Brooklyn Arts Council for his classical music composition "Legend of the Moors.*"

Sylvia M'Lafi Thompson

Well-respected member of the San Diego Theatre community; performed in Athol Fugard's "Boesman and Lena;" performed in "Othello," for San Diego Women's Rep, "Raisin in the Sun," and "The Trip to Bountiful"

Dr. Charles Phillip Toombs

Africana Studies Professor, SDSU; Calif. Faculty Assoc. Chapter President; President, campus chapter, Amer. Assoc. of University Professors*

Reginald S. Townsend

San Diego Police Departments first African American Detective, 1915

Randa McDaniel Trapp, J.D.

Born in San Diego; Graduate of Lincoln High School; Superior Court Judge; Past President, Earl B. Gilliam Bar Association; Former Regional Director, California Women Lawyers; Board Member, A=California Association of Black Lawyers & Southeast Economic Development Corporation; Former President, S.D. Chapter, NAACP, 1996; Named 79th Assembly District's Women of the Year, 2004

W. Harold Tuck
SDSU grad (class of 1999); Chief Information Officer, SD County, 1986-2012

Nina Tucker
SDSU grad (class of 1973 & 1989); Assistant Professor Social Work, Oral Roberts University*

Jesse Tull
Early African American resident in San Diego County, late 1800's; farmer

Beulah G. Underwood
Former Business Professor, San Diego Mesa College; author of <u>A Paycheck Away from Poverty,</u> 1985

Dorothy L. Vails-Weber
Counselor, SDSU, 1970; retired 1998; active in San Diego's African Methodist Episcopal Church, Co-founded Savant Development Inc. 2002*

Blossom Lorraine Van Lowe-Gholston
Founder of Woodsonians, a group of Black students at SDSU in 1930's named after Black Historian, Carter G. Woodson; 1st full-time Black school teacher in SD, 1942*

Gloria Verdieu
Community organizer & activist; Leader in Friends of Malcolm X Library, San Diego

Joshua Von Wolfolk *(on right) with Nnamdi (left)*
Longstanding community activist and advocate for social justice; active in pressing for social change & equality in San Diego

Dr. Cheryl James-Ward
Assistant Professor, Educational Leadership, SDSU; Director, Chinese & American Educational Leadership Symposium; author, <u>Using Data to Focus Instructional Improvement,</u> 2013*

Geraldine Adams Warren *(1947-2009)*
Field Representative, State Senator James Mills; Former President, San Diego Chapter, NAACP, 1979; Wife of John Warren, Publisher of the Voice & Viewpoint Newspaper; Board Member Human Relation Commission, Boy Scouts of America, United Way; Executive V.P. Washington, D.C. Chamber of Commerce; Managing Editor, San Diego Voice & Viewpoint Newspaper; Co-founded Eagle's Nest Christian Center; Founded & was President, county's first Black Chamber of Commerce; Coordinated the annual Gold Coast Classic Football Game at Qualcomm Stadium

Roll Call *(continued)*

John Warren, J. D.
Publisher and Editor of the San Diego Voice & Viewpoint Newspaper, a national award-winning publication and San Diego's largest newspaper reporting news from an African American Perspective, with a readership of over 90,000 people

Malaika Washington
Early childhood educator; Owner and operator, Baby Geniuses Daycare, San Diego;

Medicus Washington
Long-time Community Activist & Proponent of positive social change

Dr. Patricia Ann Washington
Educator; Lecturer, UCSD;; Former Assistant Professor, SDSU Women's Studies Dept. President's Award for Community Service, SD Chapter NAACP; Special Congressional Recognition Outstanding Community Service Award; Political Activist;

Russ Washington
Offensive & Defensive Lineman, San Diego Chargers (1968-1982); Inducted into San Diego Hall of Champions, 2002

Tom Watts
Elementary school teacher; founded Elementary Institute of Science, 1964

Judge Daniel Webber, J.D. *(1942-2002)*
President, Black Graduate Student Association at UCLA, where he graduated with his law degree; Helped found California Association of Black Lawyers; Served as President of the Earl B. Gilliam Bar Association & the NAACP in San Diego; Administrative Judge, California Unemployment Insurance Appeals Board, 1992; Challenged Police Dept. to acknowledge police misconduct in Black community like controversial case of police shooting of Tommy DuBose; Advocated institution of a Police Review Board; Former chair, Black American Political Association of California

Carl Weathers
SDSU grad (class of 1970); theatre major; Hollywood actor; starred opposite Sylvester Stallone in "Rocky" in 1976; linebacker for Oakland Raiders; starred in many other films for big screen and TV, including "Fortune Dane," "Action Jackson," and "Hurricane Smith"*

DeEtta M. West
Music major at SDSU; sister of Hollywood actor/comedian, Cleavon Little; she worked as an actress; singer, talk show host; licensed minister; works for the Gospel Music Channel*

Rodney West
Center Administrator, San Diego Unified School District; Community Activist

Derrick White
Executive Director, San Diego Youth Action Board

Rev. Leslie R. White, Sr.
Pastor, Bethel African Methodist Episcopal (A.M.E.) Church, San Diego

Roll Call *(continued)*

Dr. Sheryl White
Cultural psychologist & member of the San Diego Delta Foundation Board

Rosemary White-Pope
Dedicated to serving the senior community in San Diego; Director of Fourth District Seniors' Resource Center; Senior Nutrition Site Manager, Martin Luther King Community Park & Recreation Center; Board Member, ElderHelp of San Diego; Member of Mayor's Senior Citizen Advisory Board

Candice Wiggins
Played basketball guard for La Jolla Country Day High School; Played college ball at Stanford University, where she was all-time leading scorer in Stanford & Pac-10 women's basketball history; Played for Women's National Basketball Association (WNBA) since 2008; WNBA Sixth Women of the Year Award, 2008; Helped Minnesota win championship, 2011; Represented US in team competitions, Puerto Rico, 2004, Tunisia, 2005 & Brazil, 2007; Speaks to raise awareness about AIDS through the non-profit, Until There's a Cure (UTAC)

Daneen Wilburn
Talented local vocalist, performing gospel, jazz as well as rhythm & blues

Doug Wilkerson
NFL Offensive Lineman w/ SD Chargers (1971-1984); Inducted into San Diego Hall of Champions, 2005

Johnnie Lee Williams *(1925-2010)*
Born & raised in southeast San Diego; attended San Diego City College 7 SDSU; enjoyed a 26-year career with the City Police Department, advanced to Homicide Detective; managed a coin laundry and rental properties*

Leon L. Williams
SDSU grad (class of 1950); First African American elected to the San Diego City Council, 1969, District 4; first Black elected to San Diego County Board of Supervisors, 1983; first Black Chairman; 2011; the SDSU Trolley Station was dedicated in his honor*

P. Frank Williams
Emmy Award-winning television producer, writer & commentator; SDSU alum; produced & wrote for BET Hip Hop Music Awards, NAACP Image Awards, VIBE Awards & 2004 Olympics*

Reuben Williams
Tour guide, early 1900's, San Diego, "Reuben the Guide" gave guided tours by mule of San Diego & Tijuana

Sherley Anne Williams
Former Professor, Literature, UCSD; passed away in 1999; Pulitzer Prize & National Book Award Nominee for book of poems, The Peacock Poems; Emmy Award Winner for TV performance of poetry book, Someone Sweet Angel Chile; National Book Award Nominee for Novel Dessa Rose; Caldecott & Corretta Scott King Awards for book, Working Cotton.

Darlene V. Willis
SDSU Dean of Students, 2005; Co-founded Concerned Parents Alliance*

Emma Wilson
San Diego Community College District Continuing Education Center instructor

Lei-Chala Indee Wilson, J. D.
SDSU alumna (class of 1985); Former Public Defender; Former President, Earl B. Gilliam Bar Association; Former President, California Association of Black Lawyers; Former President, SD NAACP; Former President National Council of Negro Women, SD; On Boards, National Bar Association, American Civil Liberties Union; SD Mediation Center & SD Public Library System

Roll Call *(continued)*

Maxine Wilson
Served as Chair, Memorial Recreation Council, Logan Heights Community Council & President of Kiwanis of Southeastern San Diego; Member, Park & Recreation Council, Boys & Girls Club, NAACP & Southeastern San Diego Planning Committee; Feeds hundreds during the holidays

Dave Winfield
Major League Baseball Player, 1973-1995; 12 time All Star; World Series Champion, 1992; 7 times Gold Glove Award; 6 time Silver Slugger Award; AL Comeback Player of the Year; Executive Vice President/Senior Advisor to San Diego Padres, ESPN, FOX Sports commentary; Advisor to Executive Director, Major League Baseball Players Association; Baseball Analyst, ESPN Baseball Tonight & Sports Center; International Trustee for American Academy of Hospitality Sciences; Businessman; Inducted into San Diego Hall of Champions, 1998

Kellen Winslow
Professional NFL football player, SD Chargers, 8 years; 5 Pro Bowls, 3 First-team All-Pro; NFL 75th Anniversary All-Time Team; NFL Leader in Receptions, 1980 & 1981; NFL All-Decades Team, 1980's, SD Chargers Hall of Fame; Pro Football Hall of Fame, 1995; Inducted into San Diego Hall of Champions, 1995

Dr. Akunna Winston
Professor, Business Department, San Diego Mesa College; Corporate Executive; Mission Africa Board of Trustees; annually coordinates the collection of books and school supplies to send to libraries for students in Africa

Dr. Jonathan Luke Wood
Founder & Past Editor, Journal of African American Males in Education; co-authored two textbooks: Assistant Professor, Dept. of Administration, Rehabilitation & Postsecondary Education, SDSU; recipient, Barbara Townsend Emerging Scholar Award, 2013*

Robert Lee Wood
SDSU grad (class of 1973) with degree in accounting; became financial consultant; opened real estate brokerage firm in Georgia*

George Washington Woodbey
Outspoken orator and political activist in early 1900's San Diego; formerly enslaved, authored, <u>What to Do and How to Do it: Socialism vs. Capitalism</u>

Issac Wooden
Homeowner, City Employee, Logan Heights, early 1900's

Dr. Wilma Wooten
Chief Medical Information Officer, San Diego County

Patricia Delores W. Oyeshiku Worthy
Graduated with Masters in Education, SDSU (class of 1971); became Peace Corps volunteer in Brazil; taught at Morse High School, San Diego; received the honor of California State Teacher of the Year, 1981 and was a finalist for the National Teacher of the Year Award*

Felicia Yearwood, J.D.
Civil Rights Attorney, working on social justice issues; Board Member, Urban Collaborative Project; Board Member, BAPAC; Chair, Social Justice Ministry, Christian Fellowship Congregational Church; Co-created the Black Agenda Project

Tony Young
Served as San Diego City Council member, 2005-2013, from District 4, including service as City Council President; CEO SD Chapter, American Red Cross, 2013-2014; President, RISE San Diego aimed at elevating urban leadership through dialogue-based civic engagement & non-profit partnerships toward community change

Roll call
One by one
Our Community honors each
And every one
We celebrate your successes
We champion your cause
Your dedication has gives us pause
To remember with gratitude
Your sacrifice
You had the right attitude
You paid the price
To made a difference
To pass the test
We'll never forget you
You're the best of our best!

~Judy Sundayo

Rev. Alyce Smith Cooper and Dr. Carrol Waymon,
Awash Ethiopian Restaurant, San Diego, 2014

*Information replicated from, The Black in Crimson and Black: A History and Profiles of African Americans at SDSU, by Robert Fikes, Jr.

Jaime V. Jones' paternal family, Arkansas, circa 1940's

What I Think

I have repeatedly heard some say,
"As soon as I hit the lotto. . .
Retire, get a man, finish college, get married,
Get divorced. . . Then I will write."
I think to myself, yeah, sure, right!
As soon as life and passion get hold of you,
Fills you up, you will write day and night!
I sometimes like to think as soon as I feel like it
Oh, then I will clean up my little house,
But this I admit. . .
At the moment, I would rather sit like some misfit!
Think and write than my house to clean, mend or fix
So, here I sit; I sit; daily writing, writing, thinking

(Continued)

397

What I think (continued)

Like some dang lunatic
I've heard plenty say,
"As soon as I get around to it. . .
This relationship, enabling, overeating, smoking,
Drinking, drugs, I'm going to quit!"
Here is what I think: what is eating at you
Honestly. . . Admit; then look to improve
Your one on one personal relationship
Go get help if you need it; Get help quick!
Before me and your creativity
Pack up and then split!

~Jaime V. Jones

*Jaime V. Jones, Awash Ethiopian Restaurant,
San Diego, California, 2014*

Judy Sundayo's friends, **Dr. Charlotte Houston,** *Licensed Clinical Psychologist, her husband, the* **Honorable John Houston,** *U. S. District Court Judge, and their son,* **John Allen Clarke Houston, M.D.,** *graduate of* **Harvard University Medical School,** *San Diego, California, circa 2000's*

Truth, Justice & Righteousness

Truth, Justice and Righteousness
Yes, the principle of MAAT
Guides the heart to virtue
And the mind to be taught
For all is recorded in the Akashic hall
By thought, word & deed are we held to judgment's call
And on that day of decision there is nowhere to hide
We all know somewhere deep inside
At the center-point of our being is Truth
Then good old Justice follows forsooth
And last but not least, it's
Righteousness, which seals the deal
These are the spokes
Of our life's oldest wheel
And so, my soul, you lack nothing
You want for nothing; you are all
Lighter than the feather of MAAT you call
To love, honor and integrity
Though weightless, you ground us
For eternity!

~Judy Sundayo

Take Your Medicine

Take your medicine
Eat your greens
Say your prayers
Patch your jeans

God is watching
From inside
Do what's right
'Cause you can't hide

Not from yourself
Or God or man
Conscience dictates
Take a stand

Heal yourself
Then help your brother
Save the earth
There is no other

You were born for Glory's crown
See yourself
Look around
Then, look within until you see
That Love has crowned you
And you're free

Take your medicine
Open wide
God is watching
From inside

~Judy Sundayo

Ujamaa

Cooperation for success is the best

Ujamaa is the name

So, let's confess

That the best business is

The business that

Works for the good of all

And, if we listen carefully,

We can hear our ancestors call

Harambee! Harambee! Harambee!

Let's pull together

Pool our resources; gather our treasure

In our own banks!

And by the way, our own industries,

Thanks!

(continued)

Ujamaa *(continued)*

Prosperity is divine
If we could only find
The time to reach up and grab hold
We'd know our blessings
Accrue like gold!
We'd see how much we've already been given
Then, perhaps we'd be a little more driven
To find more ways to share
Let's show each other that we really care

And pool our knowledge and our stuff
If only some of us prosper
It's not enough
I AM because WE ARE!
So, it will take UJAMAA
For us to go far!

~Judy Sundayo

*Jerry Robinson, Chief Executive Officer (CEO), The Central **San Diego Black
Chamber of Commerce**; long time San Diego resident; dedicated community
activist; small business advocate; the vision of the **Black Chamber of Commerce** is
"to promote the growth of each of our members through cooperative economics."*
http://www.csdbcc.com/index.php

Judy Sundayo with friend and jegna (teacher & guide), **Dr. Carl Clark,**
Clinical psychologist and former president of the San Diego Chapter of the
Association of Black Psychologists, San Diego, California; Author, **Children Crying**
in the Night *(on Child Abuse); Multimodal psychotherapeutic treatment including*
Neuro-feedback, Anxiety, Post Traumatic Stress Disorder, Attention Disorders,
Depression, Substance Abuse & Relationship issues; practicing with wife and
partner, **Evangeline Clark,** *Marriage, Family, Child Therapist; Photo courtesy of*
Judy Sundayo, 2009;
http://clarkscenter.com/

Respect

There's something about respect

That's brilliant like polished steel

A strength of heart and resoluteness

One can feel. . .

I think it resembles honor

I know it cuts through pride

It's a dignified adoration

One cannot hide!

~Judy Sundayo

Outdistanced by a Dream

I stop and pant in scant remembrance
Of my former self
Breathless beliefs long forgotten
What race is this I run?
Was it once fun?
And do I near the finish?
Mental palpitations notwithstanding
I resume
Mind over matter-of-fact illusions
One step at a time
One leap saves nine
And keep on trucking
In sad requiem
I run . . . and I run . . .
Outdistanced by a dream

~Judy Sundayo

*Judy Sundayo in Havana (La Habana), **Cuba** (Republic of Cuba),*
The 3rd largest city in the Caribbean, which sees over 1 million
Visitors per year; Cuba is the only remaining communist country with a "very high"
human development index (HDI) by the United Nations; in 2014
President Obama began efforts to have the U.S. Embargo against Cuba lifted;
Photo taken circa 2000's; for more information go to
http://www.whitehouse.gov/the-press-office
And search for "Fact Sheet: Charting a New Course on Cuba"

This photo taken in the Giza Plateau in Kemet (Egypt) in 2010 by
Judy Sundayo, showing Pyramid of Pharaoh Khafra and his likeness
Likely guarding his burial place and temple; this so-called Sphinx is the largest
Monolith statue and the oldest known monumental sculpture in the world; in
Egypt, Muslims make up 90% of the population; article 45 of the Egyptian
Constitution affords religious freedom to not only Muslims, but also to Christians
and Jews; to study about Muslim Alliances with Christians and Jews, see
http://www.islamic-study.org/muslim_alliance_with_christians_and_jews.htm

God and Allah Part I: At the Mall

God and Allah

Frontin' at the mall

Allah said, "God, you 'bout to fall!"

God said, "I ain't quitting, Allah,

You got a lot a gall!"

Soon throngs of people gathered

Crowdin' 'round to see

Which one was gonna win?

Who the champion would be?

By the time the clock struck 6 a.m.

The crowd let out a WAIL!

There was God and Allah. . .

Both first in line for the sale!

(continued)

*Nefertari's Temple of Hathor at Abu Simbel, in Aswan area of
Kemet (Egypt), built by Pharaoh Ramesses II, 13th century, B.C.,
Adjacent to his own larger temple at Abu Simbel, Photo by Judy Sundayo, 2010; Of
all the fantastically engineered and beautiful artworks ever created, we humans
are the most precious; we must find a way to preserve and protect this most
valuable treasure from our own hatred and ignorance; for a history of Jewish-
Muslim Relations, see this website chronicling a Collaboration between the Duke
University Islamic Studies Center, the Carolina Center for the Study of the Middle
East and Muslim Civilizations and the Oxford Center for Islamic Studies,
all made possible by the Transcultural Islam Project,
funded by a Grant from the Carnegie Corporation
http://islamicstudies.duke.edu/disc-initiatives/transcultural-islam-project*

God and Allah Part II: Talkin' Smack

God and Allah walkin' down the street

Talkin' 'bout what time they gone meet

Allah said three, and God agreed

Then Allah said, "God, if you don't bring it,

I'm a have you on your knees!"

God said, "Oh, you **know** I'm a bring it,

Allah please!"

Well, we rushed there all nervous,

Expecting bloodied troops!!!

There was God and Allah. . .

Shootin' hoops!

(continued)

406

The Pyramid of Pharaoh Djoser, located in Saqqara, Kemet (Egypt), built in 2611 B.C., the largest structure ever built until that time; designed by Imhotep, Master architect, physician, healer and priest; photo by Judy Sundayo, 2010; as This temple has persisted, so does the hope for understanding between people; To explore Issues in Christian-Muslim Relations: Ecumenical Considerations see World Council of Churches website below and search Christian-Muslim Relations http://www.oikoumene.org/en

God and Allah Part III: Face-Off

God and Allah

Walkin' down the street.

Curbing their dogs, nice and neat

Well, God's Rottweiler got up in

Allah's Pitt Bull's face

I thought there was gone be blood

All over the place!

Well, before it was over

With all the downs and ups!

There was God and Allah. . .

Sharing Pittweiler pups!

(continued)

Ivory's Rock Conference Center, in Ipswitch, Australia,
Fondly named "Amaroo" (The Beautiful Place") by locals;
Photo taken by Judy Sundayo, circa 2000's; A reminder that when we are at Peace
within ourselves, it is easier to see peace and beauty outside of ourselves; For
information on learning more about Islam from a Christian perspective, see,
http://christiananswers.net/islam.html

God and Allah Part IV: The Great Divide

God and Allah

Walkin' down the street.

Surprised, I asked,

"How'd the two of you meet?"

Well God looked at Allah

and Allah looked back.

Then they both started laughing

so hard it was wack!

"We've never met, child!

We are one and the same!

It's you our creation,

who've divided us by name!"

(continued)

*Photo taken from inside the Temple at Edfu in Kemet (Egypt) by Judy Sundayo
2010; A reminder, we gain greater perspective by first going within ourselves
before looking outside at others or at outside circumstances; to consider,
"Can Muslims & Christians Work Together for Good?" see*
http://whoonew.com/2014/02/interfaith-discussion-st-norbert/

God and Allah Part V: Meet Up

God and Allah

Walking down the street

What's gonna happen when they meet?

Tempers gonna flare?

Sparks gonna fly?

Somebody gonna give somebody a black eye?

Oh, oh, look out!

They're about to pass!!!

B – A – M

One image in the looking glass!

~Judy Sundayo

When My Beauty Fades

When my fast graying hair
Begins to thin
And once luminous eyes
Need highlighting
When my natural look is
Taking longer and longer
To achieve
In the second half of my life,
Lord, please
Let me find a space
I can share with grace
The things I've learned with those in need

Let me share myself with joy
And a sense of peaceful accomplishment
Paradoxically, I note
With the efforts spent to share,
To give
My light isn't as dim
As once I thought
In fact, more clearly now,
I see myself as once I thought I'd be
A lovely woman
Sharing my life with my community
With a flow within
My beauty isn't fading- - -
It is blooming in another light.

~Alyce Smith Cooper

*Friend of the authors' **Leah Goodwin**, President and CEO,*
***Leah Goodwin Creations**, management of special occasions,*
Art exhibits cultural events custom poetry; grant writing;
http://leahscreations.com/

Gathering of the Women Who Write

What a special gathering of wise,
Wonderful women-friends
No pretense, none necessary
Each one brilliant in her own way
Teachers, healers all
Beauty abounds inside core
And outer trappings too!

Wisdom, compassion adorn inner compartments
Sparkling eyes glimmering smiles
Arms opened wide to embrace all who are in need. . .
After prayer, washing, peaceful meditation
Sacrament of laughter
(Oh, how we laugh our healing!)

(continued)

411

Gathering of the Women Who Write *(continued)*

Pain and confusion ebb
Powerful confidence arises
Bread broken *(gluten-free);*
Healthy food and drink;
Consumed; seasoned wisely with gratitude;
More laughter, *don't you think?*

Movements in consciousness spiral through
These living pools. . .
Paused to refresh, these women live to catch the Golden
Rings of Righteousness
As they spin up life's spiral in syncopated blues
Jazz-exaggerated beat
Cooking up a Gumbo Pot of guiding light
Have some on your plate tonight!

~Alyce Smith Cooper

Friend of the authors' **Jan Carpenter Tucker,**
Creative Director and Graphic Designer, Owner of **J.L. Carpenter Design,**
specializing in print and web design, branding, marketing, & communications;
Collaborative member of Leah Goodwin Creations, San Diego, California
www.jlcarpenterdesign.com

*Jaime Jones' niece and nephew, **Marie Watson***
*And **Derek Jason Watson**, San Diego, California*

Love Holds a Spot for You

Loving, laughing, learning and growing through life
Love steps in and holds for you
A prepared precious place polite
A perfect place for us to grow into
To step into
Navigating naughty or nice
Love always saves for you a secure spot
Just for you ready and right
Once someone asked me, "If what they did seemed so wrong,
why was I still there
Trying /working to get along?"
Love would be my answer
Because of love I am super seriously strong
Stronger than any evil, mean spiritedness or pain;
See, to God I boldly belong
No need to fret, to waste or worry or
Feel something is wrong

(continued)

Love Holds a Spot for You *(continued)*

Love and life will take hold of you and
Before too long
Filled up, whole, complete, lacking nothing
Sing this song
Stop,
Sit and stay right here you definitely belong
See love, love holds for you
This sweet spot strong
Signed and sealed for you,
No way this is wrong

~Jaime V. Jones

*Judy Sundayo's daughter, **Aurora**, with **Jaime V. Jones**, La Jolla, California*

*Judy Sundayo's friend and graduate school advisor, **Dr. Tom MacCalla,** Educator, University Administrator, Author of **"Rhythm & Muse"** and **"Artistry in Word Music"** Photo courtesy of Judy Sundayo, taken at Dr. MacCalla's birthday celebration, Half Moon Bay, California; Judy has been honored to know Dr. Tom MacCalla and his wife, Dr. Jackie Caesar and their family since 1974*

Dr. MacCalla

I remember when I met Dr. MacCalla
He asked if I wanted to become a fella
Of a university program called CEM
With a group of grad students, some 12 of them
Well, at first I thought it was out of my range
But Doc said I'd become an agent of change
Since I was majoring in psychology
I almost gave Doc my apology
'Cause if I changed my major
Wasn't sure what would happen
But then Doc said, I would receive a stipend
So for $206 of monthly cash
I changed my major extremely fast
And Dr. Mac showed me what to do
To get my money from U.S. I "OWE" U
It's true that Doc was the best exec
But even Doc rushed to cash his check!

(continued)

415

Dr. MacCalla *(continued)*

Yes, those were the days and that's how things went
For Community Environmental Management
Then came a day that was hardly funny
Word was, the School was going to take our money
Well, Dr. Mac wasn't having that
So, outside the president's office we sat
A sit-in for justice . . . for what was right!
Black, white and Latino looking for a fight
But Dr. Mac could talk a good game
And he resolved everything all the same
Without a scuffle or a curse
We were glad he'd defended our meager purse!
The CEM fellows were definitely back
With good-time Gene and Dr. Mac!
Now, we had a lot of adventures with CEM
And Doc had instigated most of them!
He's pretty persuasive, shrewd and smart
How else did he convince Jackie to share her heart?
And they have been blessed with love and glee
And a pretty extraordinary family
Years later, when I got grad school tired
It was Dr. Mac who got me hired to work for IIUHD
A Tom and Jackie Agency
Along with Dr. David Brinks
They helped establish community links
Into Headstart and Daycare, Doc went without fear
And everything worked 'cause he worked his idea
Of all the things I've learned from him
This has been the best . . .
Work hard, believe, go for the gold
And God will do the rest . . .
So, now I'm proud to celebrate
YOU, Dr. Mac . . . I think you're great!!!

~Judy Sundayo

416

Judy Sundayo's brother of another mother, Dr. Herb Martin (left),
Clinical and Sports Psychologist, CEO, Peak Performance Consultants;
http://peakperformanceconsultinggroup.com/
encouraging Judy Sundayo's son, Hasar; photo taken by Judy in San Diego,
California at an open House Celebrating the success of Park Dental Arts, the Dental
Practice of Herb's Wife, Dr. Peggy Curtis Martin & Dr. Hilda Meza-Thompson
http://www.parkdentalarts.com/

Close to Excellent

When people ask me, "How's your day?"
"Close to excellent!" I say
I'm blessed beyond any measure I set
And hands down, my attitude is my best asset
A positive outlook and a giving heart
Changes the game and sets you apart
There were those who helped me
Get my life together
So, by helping others, I give back, whether
Or not there's any return
If there's anything worthy for someone to learn
It's that excellence comes not in what you receive
But in helping others to achieve!

~Judy Sundayo

417

Just An Observation

I have noticed that the Universe
Keeps giving, giving and giving
Unlike me
And many of the loving living

Without blaming, shaming, guilt or doubt
And without fearing
Without judging, criticizing, nagging
Whining or complaining

No animosity
Yet with great generosity, the Universe
Keeps forgiving
Making the Universe infinitely powerful
And loving
Lord, today help me be more like the Universe
Giving and forgiving!

~ Jaime V. Jones

Jaime V. Jones and Judy Sundayo, La Jolla California, 2013

*The authors' friend **Professor T. Ford, J.D.**, Counseling Faculty, Grossmont College; Black Studies Faculty, Mesa College; Lifelong supporter of the arts, Including music, art, drama, literature, & storytelling; Photo by Stephen Harvey; San Diego,*

Be Thankful

Be thankful for what you got
And your health is the first
Whatever the condition, you're a live spirit-burst!
Be thankful for your family
Ain't perfect . . . never is
But they've still been created, remember, they're His!
Be thankful for the Earth
She's birthed us all
Recycle your trash; can't you hear your Mama call?
Be thankful for your friends
Cause they got your back
Take a risk to share your secrets and
Ask for what you lack
Be thankful for this life
It's a blessing of grace
Be thankful for the love that fills this place
Be thankful! Be thankful!
And happy be your mood
So your blessings will reflect your gratitude!

~Judy Sundayo

Do it Today

Whatever you can do today, do it fast

For the richness of this moment will not last

Know that yesterday is a cancelled check

Tomorrow's a promissory note, at best!

That you spend your time wisely is what I pray

For the only hard cash you have is today!

~Judy Sundayo

*Judy Sundayo, her brothers **Granville** and **Kelvin** bearing gifts for their cousin,*
Resheata (Ray) Springs, *for her birthday party, Washington, D.C., circa, 1960's*

Alyce Smith Cooper, San Diego California

Life Issues

All the experiences bundled
Into one rag tag package
Someone entitled, the bundle . . . life
The comings, the goings in and about
The curious happenings of the journey
Most of the happy experiences are celebrated
Some of the major ones like surgeries,
Wisdom teeth extractions,
Taxes, divorce or job loss are tolerated
Or prayed through
Some experiences are mourned but
Not planned for or discussed
I take issue with the lack of conversation
About the end of life
As we currently experience the journey,
Every story has a beginning, an in-between, and an end
Why no discussion as we approach the final bend?
(continued)

421

Life Issues *(continued)*

Simply put . . .
I want no heroic efforts made to keep me alive
I did not come to stay
But only to shine my light as I could in any meaningful way
When my time is up, my cup drained dry,
Let not an abundance of tears flood your eyes
Play gospel music by James Cleveland
Jazz by Ella, Sarah, Miles
Don't leave out Stevie Wonder and Ray Charles
African Drum call to honor the ancestors
Whose lives I hold in high esteem
Show pictures of my life if my service you appreciate
Then over the eulogy
Let Rev. Father Charles O. Brown officiate
Feed the folks well who come to shoulder the weight
Of a light transformed
Please commit my ashes into the sea on a calm sunny day
To be one with the waves playing upon the shores
Free at last
To swim as I please

I am alive today
With a charge to keep,
A GOD TO GLORIFY
As Matriarch to those who chose my line
See the LIGHT
BE the LIGHT
Experience the LOVE
If you can follow the WAY
We will find each other again in that final day

~Alyce Smith Cooper

*Alyce Smith Cooper's great, granddaughter, **Lyric Adriana**,*
Wise beyond her years, San Diego, California

Sassy Old Lady

I hope when I'm old - - really old
White hair and cane old
I'll be a sassy old lady
With a gamey cackle for a laugh, a straight back
A bun at the nape of my neck
Twinkles for eyes
I'll have stories to tell the children
What it was like in my day
What it will be like in theirs

(continued)

423

Sassy Old Lady *(continued)*

For the young men, I'll have a cup of tea
And a listening ear
A word of encouragement

For the young women, my heart will go out
For I remember those days
I know their pain and hunger for understanding
Won't take no foolishness from any of them,
No need to. . .

Have earned the right to speak my p-e-a-c-e
With all that said and done,
I'll rise from my rocking chair,
Summon my cat and together with cat and cane,
I'll retreat to my quarters
(and the arms of my husband!)
~Alyce Smith Cooper

Alyce Smith Cooper, after church, San Diego, California

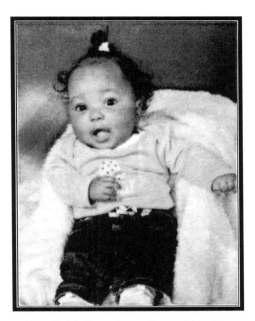

Alyce Smith Cooper's great, granddaughter,
Lisa Jada

Bits and Pieces

Attracted by soul's starry light
Minute particles coalesce
Surrounding innermost core
Long forgotten dream pieces
Sparkling unborn hopes iridescently brilliant
At midpoint
On the upward path
Long sought-after bits and pieces
Flesh soul blood and bone
Begin an undulating arabesque
Creating a being of light

(continued)

Bits and Pieces *(continued)*

From a body
Filled with doubts and tears
Forging from vacillating uncertainty
A willing compassionate warrior
Seasoned, well-ripened, prepared
Bits and pieces of finely drawn
Well-tempered, exquisitely wrought
Soul material comes together
Dons fine apparel
To prepare for the debut
~Alyce Smith Cooper

Alyce Smith Cooper, San Diego, California

Jaime V. Jones and Alyce Smith Cooper, La Jolla, California, 2012

Harvest What You Say

We all get, we harvest exactly what we say
Good or bad, we are created powerful that way
Careful what comes out of your mouth
Each and everyday
Like it or not words spoken, you order, you pay
So, think before you speak; you harvest what you say
Swiftly spoken words become your reality someday
Doom, devastation, destruction or delicious
Decadent, delight either way
No one can fix this, but you, so do not delay
Your words prophesy all of your tomorrows today
Speak what you want in your life;
Words spoken out loud
Don't play
God a negative thought?
Do not speak it out loud no way
Careful what you speak about;

(continued)

427

Harvest What You Say *(continued)*

What you don't like today
Those words will return to you
Like left over verbal vomit in a few days
Eventually, no one will want to ask you
To come over to stay
If you with stinky, smelly statements
everyone you spray
Be aware of each and every word you speak, I pray
I have heard others repeatedly respond in this way
That is just not something I would ever say."
While you stood looking in their mouth
When they said it yesterday
Not even listening to themselves? What the hay!
Mouth open, mouth on automatic,
Mind on vacation far away
Others have to remind them
Of all the negative they say
Reminder, speak only words that honor,
Help and heal everyday
Not up to thinking before you speak today?
Close your mouth, put your lips together and
Leave them that way
Until you are ready to be refreshed and
Responsible for what you say
Words spoken, harvested and ordered
You personally pay
Words planted, watered, harvested
Ordered then one day
Dear you harvest exactly what you repeatedly say

~Jaime V. Jones

428

*Judy Sundayo, **Yiriba Bernard Thomas**, Lead Drummer for
Teye Sa Thiosanne West African Drum & Dance Troupe, Dr. Carrol Waymon,
Retired Professor, San Diego Community College District, Community Activist and
Advocate for Social Justice; and
Alyce Smith Cooper; in front of San Diego's Malcolm X Library, the first Public
library in the country to be named after Malcolm X, California, 2012*

History

Every person and every community
Everywhere has a history
And it's no mystery that it matters
For history is the foundation
On which our future house will stand
For good or ill it dictates
What our destinies will command
Will it be shaky or will it be strong?
If the foundation is weak
The whole house will be wrong
Lopsided, ready for collapse
It will certainly become
A potential deathtrap
And so history becomes
A foundational mission

(continued)

History *(continued)*

To dig down deep past all the derision
And onto firm ground set your stakes
Beginning with the cornerstones
Of civilization
It was God, knowledge, family and health
That built a nation
With purpose and service as central themes
We must build our future based
Not on mere dreams, but on the real
A mighty foundation of concrete and steel
Every person and every community
Everywhere has a history
And it's no mystery
That this is the key
A forever and unchangeable foundation
Laid for our destiny
If you seek to know anything
Know your history!

~Judy Sundayo

Longtime friend of the authors'
***Barbara Brown**, proprietor of **Pyramid Bookstore** in*
San Diego, a bookstore that specialized in books by and
About African Americans; A kind and generous individual, educator and social
activist until her passing; Photo taken circa 1990's, courtesy of Dr. Asha Bell

Jaime Jones and Judy Sundayo, La Jolla, California
Circa 2013

Jaime Jones

A card comes and the return reveals
It's from you, my friend, Jaime Jones
My spirit is lifted for you are gifted
In sharing such joy from above
And sure enough, the card is signed with
"Three hundred and sixty degrees of love"

Your gifts inspire
And so I conspire to share my love with you
For your giving heart and your words of truth
And the many kind things that you do

You remember every birthday
And every anniversary too
You send me Easter wishes
And a 4th of July Whoop-de-do!

(continued)

431

Jaime Jones *(continued)*

Thanksgiving comes and you remember
To thank me for being me
And right on time for Christmas
Your card arrives happily

But your kindness doesn't need an occasion
Your gifts flow in every season
I thank you for all your love and support
Love doesn't need a reason

So, Jaime Jones, you're wonderful
I find myself asking you please
Stay just as full of love as you are
That's 360 degrees!

~Judy Sundayo

*Jaime Jones in preparation for performance at Awash
Ethiopian Restaurant, circa 2014*

Judy Sundayo's daughter by another mother,
***Heaven Leigh Johnson**, at the time of her graduation*
from Syracuse University, Syracuse, NY 2011

The Magical Life

Born with a spark that lights the fire
Of happiness, that true desire
Born with a smile that warms the soul
A heart that sings; a spirit bold

These are the signs of a magical life
Problems are passages!
No worries! No strife!

All is ADVENTURE!
A stroll through the maze!
A search for new facets of laughter
Or praise

When Grace is your Master
Then Trust is the air
That you breathe as you fashion
Your next word of prayer
(continued)

433

The Magical Life *(continued)*

For guidance and joy. . .
For acceptance and love. . .
For forgiveness, integrity,
Strength from above. . .

But, the thing about magic is. . .
There's no explanation!
Like life, it's a gift
Of divine innervation!

One only must **think** it, **speak** it and
B-R-E-A-T-H-E
Dream it and **live** it!
Nurture!
B-E-L-I-E-V-E!
For the Magical Life is a blessing from God
A gift of great measure,
As he gives you the nod!

~Judy Sundayo

Heaven Leigh Johnson

*Judy Sundayo (far left) with friend, the late **Wendy Warfield** (center), Wendy's mother, **Dr. Grace J. Warfield** (right) member of the Gray Panthers, and Wendy's children, **Jojo** and **Hadiya** (second and third from left respectively) Minnesota, circa 1980's*

Erasing Isms

It's time to erase all the isms
To finally face our fear
Racism, sexism, ageism. . .
To make them disappear

No more prejudice 'bout the color of our skin
No more insults 'bout the bodies we're in
No more decisions pushing elders aside
No more assumptions that the poor have no pride

I erase all corporate policies
That won't let a Black man advance
I erase all tenets of business
That won't give a woman a chance

I erase all attacks against gays
These cause irreparable harm
I erase all hatred and malice
Against those who practice Islam

(continued)

435

Erasing Isms *(continued)*

I erase any kind of intolerance
Against Lesbians loving the same
I erase all manner of ignorance
Against those choosing gender change

Some may ask, "Are we ready?"
"Are we made of the right stuff?"
Others may think, "Is there such a thing
As an eraser that's big enough?"

Believe it, 'cause if you've been watching
We've erased "Don't ask, don't tell!"
So keep on watching as we damn
Marriage inequality to hell!

My answer is, "Yes! It's time,
Past time, to get things done!"
And our eraser is gigantic!
It's our LOVE for everyone!

So, let's join in solidarity
That peace will rule the day
Let's daily use our erasers of Love
To erase these isms away!

~Judy Sundayo

*Judy Sundayo with fiancé, **Al Washington**
and son, **Hasar**, Coronado, California 2014*

436

Dr. Constance Carroll was appointed *Chancellor of the San Diego Community College District* in 2004 after serving as President of Mesa College for 11 years. During her tenure, enrollment increased each year; she led the successful, statewide effort to obtain legislative approval for community colleges to offer bachelor's degrees; She was *appointed by President Barack Obama to the National Council on the Humanities*; and she brought the District's bond measures to $1.6 billion, with over 40 new buildings for the campuses. For more information about the San Diego Community College District, go to
www.sdccd.edu

Community: It Takes a Crew

It takes a crew
To do what we do
From our temples and mosques
To our churches too
From our pre-schools and high schools
And libraries
To our colleges and universities
From our museums and theatres and civic halls
To our orchestras, symphonies and masquerade balls
From our beaches and bays to our
Snow-capped mountains
From our parks and our flowers
To our water fountains
(continued)

Community: It Takes a Crew *(continued)*

From our streets and highways and airports and roads
To our shipping industry with lots of loads
From our doctors and dentists and nurses and those Who
help to keep us on our toes
To our police and lawyers and judges and courts
Who keep the order, the law and torts
From our business people in sales and trade
To all the consumers who buy what's made
From our parents and families and childcare saints
Who're designing our future with love and paints
From those who clean and pick up trash
To the bankers who broker in stocks and cash
From our builders, bricklayers, masons and such
Who build our structures; thanks so much
To our social workers and psychologists
Who help us heal when problems persist
From our writers and poets and singers of songs
To our artists and sculptors who labor long
From our drummers and dancers
Who stay on the beat
To all who make our city complete
It takes a crew
Willing to work in unity
To make a successful community!

~Judy Sundayo

Mesa College Facilities Crew: The Best, Hands Down!

438

*Authors' friend, **Trish Weir**, Co-Founder of the first National African American Woman's Conference; Founder and Director of **The San Diego Ambassador Program**, a Rites of Passage Program for Boys & Girls aimed at helping them to become first-class citizens and global leaders through self-directed experiences Providing life-long and service learning skills;*
For more information or to volunteer, contact Trish Weir at
trish.weir@hotmail.com

Passage Rites

Let the little ones come
To claim their rights
To know their history
To set their sights

On a future of infinite possibilities
Let the little ones come
Let them come, please
And we will nurture
And teach and guide
Them to their power deep inside

Then they will finally realize
Why we must keep our eye on the prize

(continued)

Passage Rites *(continued)*

Then every thought and word and deed
Will build their pathway to succeed
Their leadership and service
Will surely follow
But for now we must only
Prepare for tomorrow

Let the little ones come
For each is a gem
And our fate and our future
Belong to them

~Judy Sundayo

Friend of the authors' **Neferka Ra Ankh**, *an original (baby) Elder in*
The Rites of Passage Program for African American Girls *in*
San Diego County; believes age is a state of mind; she makes
Time daily for spiritual practice, prayer, meditation and exercise;
African and Line Dancing enthusiast; Proponent of health and happiness;
QueenNeferka@gmail.com

440

Judy Sundayo with her niece, **Nxyi Ires***,*
Billings, Montana, 2013

There is a Place
There is a place
A blue and green and yellow place
A soft and calming peaceful place
That goes where I go
That flows where I flow
And listens to my soul when it cries for a place to rest

There is a time
A naturally quiet time
A mellow and soothingly secret time
That opens the world's cage
That doesn't age
And whispers to my heart
That the beginning and the ending are one

(continued)

There is a Place *(continued)*

There is a meaning
An unspoken word giving happiness and peace
A language of its own
A brightly lit star
That touches my love
That comes from above
And lights my way to God
When I'm lost and wandering

There is a place
A blue and green and yellow place
A soft and calming peaceful place
A place where I love to go
That flows where I flow
And listens to my soul when it cries to return home

~Judy Sundayo

*Judy's friend and colleague, **Jackie Szitta**, an avid traveler and*
*Judy's fiancé **Al Washington**, and daughter, **Aurora**,*
Photograph taken by Judy Sundayo, in China, 2007

The Nile River in Kemet (Egypt) on the African continent, circa 2010
Photo taken by Judy Sundayo

Grandmother Africa

GRANDMOTHER AFRICA birthed suckled reared
Her brilliant children
Was able to keep some by her side
To keep the home fires burning
Many were stolen sailed away from her arms richly black
To form the fortunes of the earth
Build empires give birth to cultures diasporic

Centers to give honor to African Genius
In Moscow, Paris, Jakarta, L.A., New York, N.Y.,
Peoria, Ill., San Diego, C.A., Tokyo
Cultural food cooked up like collard greens
Okra, yams, Fufu, Bar-B-Q, sweet potato pie, fried chicken,
Red soda water tasted to the tune of the blues
Jazz hummed/moaned/shouted gospel style
(continued)

443

Grandmother Africa *(continued)*

Celebrating the science of the peanut, the pyramid
The cotton gin, the traffic light
Blood plasma and so very much more
Broad noses, sparkling eyes, full luscious lips
Hair with that familiar kink
GOD'S light shining from the souls of Black Folk
Sent from Sirius to this experiment called earth
Together we stand/forward we move
Boldly facing century 21
Lifting high our faithful hopes
In the sound of the dance
The words of the symphony
The rhythm of the breath of the poet
In the latent artist which sleeps
In the breast of so many of your children
GRANDMOTHER AFRICA
Sweetly solemnly respectfully we salute you
Embrace you and our relatives flung to the four winds

Your children from all corners of the universe
Are coming together to know and care for you
In your elder song breathe deeply knowing
Your family loves you and will continue
Creating worlds upon worlds
Remembering our Heroes/Sheroes
Kings/Queens/High Priests all your blood
And never forgetting YOU

~Alyce Smith Cooper

Friend of the authors' Maria Dowd, renowned motivational speaker,
*Author of "**Journey to Empowerment**"; Founder of **African-American Women on***
***Tour** (AAWOT), 1991, held in over 40 cities in the U.S, Caribbean and France; top*
*Producer at **Warm Spirit**, a company dedicated to quality skin care and wellness;*
http://www1.solcitybeauty.com/?kw=beauty+products

Black Woman: We Can Do Anything!

From the bedroom to the boardroom
We've done it all
After all for over three hundred years
We were bred for strength and endurance
And often for beauty
So now, we just need to get up off
That big, bodacious booty
And realize that our stage
Has been set for success
There's nothing we *can't* do
Once we decide to be the best
And continue to tighten up on a few things
Like diet and lifestyle
You know, keep the collard greens and cornbread
(NON-GMO of course!)
Lose the fried ANYTHING!
Keep the gumbo, stews and chicken soups
Lose the smoking ANYTHING! *(OOPS!)*

(continued)

Black Women: We Can Do Anything! *(continued)*

Keep the food that's live and organic
And lose the microwave, but don't panic
If it takes a few more minutes, just relax and de-stress
Get your pressure down, meditate and stretch
Keep the meals we make from scratch
And lose all the prepackaged crap
I mean, come on, even Aunt Jemima *didn't*
Make no pancakes outta a box!
At least in terms of self-care, we're losing the perms
And keeping the locks!
We're beginning to see that natural is best
From what we eat to how we dress
Our hair and bodies and minds for that matter
Avoiding a lot of mental chatter
And that includes gossip and negativity
Let's tighten that up so we can see
What we really want our lives to be
After all, *Control of Thought* is the first of the
Ten Cardinal Virtues taught in ancient Kemet
Let's bring *that* forward from our past
And give our minds a sweet repast
And challenge us to explore
Our talents like the women who've gone before
'Cause if we want to, we know we can . . .
Express ourselves through writing like Phyllis Wheatley, or
Like Gwendolyn Brooks, *the 1st African American woman to*
win the Nobel Prize for Literature,
Or like Rita Dove, Toni Morrison, Alice Walker,
Octavia Butler, Maya Angelou
We can become a television talk show host like
Oprah Winfrey, *who hosted the most highly rated talk show in*
history for 25 years!,
Or like Tyra Banks or Wendy on the Wendy Williams Show

(continued)

Black Women: We Can Do Anything! *(continued)*

We can sing to our hearts content, like Marian Anderson,
Leontyne Price, Ella Fitzgerald, Aretha Franklin,
And Whitney Houston
We can perform dramatic roles on stage or screen, like
Hattie McDaniel, Dorothy Dandridge, Whoopi Goldberg &
Hallie Berry
We can excel in sports like Althea Gipson, Alice Coachman,
Wilma Rudolph, Serena Williams & Venus Williams
We can master science and mathematics like . . .
Euphemia Lofton Haynes, *the first African American woman
to obtain her Ph.D. in mathematics*, Mae C. Jemison, Rebecca
Lee Crumpler, Evelyn Boyd Granville, & Kate Okikiolu
We can excel in education like Mary Jane Patterson,
Autherine Lucy, Ruth Simmons & Dr. Anna Julia Cooper
We can excel in business like Madame C. J. Walker,
Oprah Winfrey, *the first African American woman billionaire*,
Ursula M. Burns, Rosalind G. Brewer, Lisa Price,
Edith W. Cooper and Kawanna Brown
We can excel in government and politics like . . .
Shirley Chisholm, *the first African American woman elected to
Congress and Later the first African American woman to run
for President of the U.S.*, Ruby Bridges, Patricia Roberts Harris,
Amelia Boynton, Condolezza Rice & Constance Baker Motley
Yes, as African American women, we've done it all
And now is NOT the time to fall back
Let's strengthen our talents and add what we lack
Remembering we have the genetic disposition
To be in the best physical, mental and spiritual condition
Our ancestors are guiding us; our talents are strong
Let's go for the gold!
There's nothing wrong with wanting the best
It is coming to fruition now what God has blessed!
~Judy Sundayo

447

Alyce Smith Cooper with long-time friend, *Ken Howard*,
Photographer for the New York Metropolitan Opera, 2015

Marks Along the Way

There is a pathway made by thousands who trod life's
journey into eternity
In your wisdom you may try going your own way by yourself
on uncharted trails
But even then if your senses are keen
You will experience a token mark left by a previous traveler,
you must be keenly observant
For It could be a dried tear in the dust
The wafting scent of frankincense
or the lingering moan of a chant
It could be a tassel from a threadbare prayer shawl
or the cold embers of sacrificial fires long ago extinguished
Most assuredly no path is totally unique
It is only we who imagine ourselves separate from the
WHOLE, when our loved ones go on ahead
Catapult into dimensions unseen beyond tactile embrace
we taste the bitter spit of loss
Scorching pain, which sears from within
Serves to remind us, we are but travelers on a journey
To meet our completed souls
What mark will you leave for the weary ones
who will find their way someday?

~Alyce Smith Cooper

448

*Friends of the authors' **Elder Nnamdi Sikumbuzo***
*And his wife, **Syvera Hardy,** both strong community supporters,*
Nnamdi through his work over the years with the Boyhood to Manhood
Program and the Pan African Association of America and Syvera with
*Her active leadership roles with the **San Diego Black Nurses Association***
www.sdblacknurses.org/

Our Elders

Strong, resolute of spirit
Purposeful
Our elders are . . .
Masters of knowledge and wisdom
May the ancestors guide
And God protect
For we see you with pride
And you've earned our respect
You, our elders remind us
Of times long past
When character counted
And our word would last
A lifetime
Strong, resolute of spirit
Purposeful
(continued)

449

Our Elders *(continued)*

Our elders . . .
With an ankh in the right hand
And Sankofa bird in the other
A sign that it's never too late to recover
Our history
And so let's follow, as our elders gather
For its they who remind us
That Black lives matter!

~Judy Sundayo

*Long-time friends of the authors' **Eusi Kwayana,** prolific writer, editor, activist and proponent of peace; General Secretary, the People's National Congress, 1961, Guyana; Chairman, Guyana Marketing Corporation; Founder and Member, Working People's Alliance, 1974; President and Founder, African Society for Cultural Relations with Independent Africa, (ASCRIA); and his wife, **Tchaiko Kwayana**, tenacious advocate for students and parents; Professor, San Diego Mesa College, Teacher, San Diego City Schools;*
Both Dedicated Educators, Writers, Activists for Social Justice and early members of the Pan African Association of America in San Diego;
Photo taken by Judy Sundayo, Eusi's 90th birthday celebration, Malcolm X Library, San Diego, 2015

Alyce Smith Cooper's hard-fought-for family store, California, circa 1950's

The Real Story

It is coming to an end
This age in which we currently live
We have suffered, we bleed, have bled
Marched sat in prayed seen some changes
Saw a Black man placed into presidency
Cashed in on the bounty that has come
Bought the real estate clothing cars jewels
Took the cruise vacations played roulette
Won the prizes of flesh revealed
Sensuous encounters till all was depreciated
Everything satisfied all dark passions revealed

Now what?
No more values, no more marriages
No more respect for elders, children women girls or boys
No more respect
Selling our children on street corners
So what do you expect from GOD?
(continued)

The Real Story *(continued)*

Is this the end of the story?
Is this all you want?

Wait ~ I hear someone crying out for mercy
Someone is crying out for healing
For their children
Someone wants his father's memory restored
Someone wants her pain to cease
Is money sex position not enough?
What is the end of the story going to be?

Maybe it is back to the old landmarks
Living for and loving GOD
Living for and loving family
Self-respect
The old landmarks
The value of truth
Rebuilding our communities!
The value of using the gifts to glorify GOD
What is the end of the story to be?

The end is in your heart of hearts
Your mind and in your mouth!
~Alyce Smith Cooper

The family of Alyce Smith Cooper

Maya Angelou – Wisdom Weaver

You wove in wisdom with head held high
An aura of arrogant elegance
Echoed
After the words you spoke
The rough woven fabric of your days
Was what shawled you
Against the biting cold of invisibility
And the bleak prospect of being just another poor
Black girl from the south
Sewn in sad, silent knots and angry tangles
You wove into the fabric of your life
Warmth and friendships and family
Colorful threads of dance and drama and song
Amazingly strong bindings of independence and daring
Deliberately intricate patterns like lace,
Curving here sweetly like your broad, knowing smile
Twisting there like a tentatively raised brow
While your words stitched together an amazing reality
From a plethora of dreams

(continued)

453

Maya Angelou – Wisdom Weaver *(continued)*

You entwined us into a cloth of human culture
In mystical fashion
Who knew the morning even *had* a pulse?
You would weave our path all the way to the well
Where we would find our cool drink of water and
Because of the breadcrumbs you left for us to follow
We would find the pathway home, always
At the center point of our own designs

Ms. Maya, you were the woman weaving wisdom
With phenomenal flair
And in a language our hearts recognized
You were the woman weaving the words
Which sheltered us from ignorance
And on magic carpets
Suspended us high above our own doubts
Transporting us to the magnificence of Love
And self-confidence

No matter they wove cages for us
You wove the key
And now in flight, we sing new songs
Celebrating hope and brotherhood and compassion
And all the possibilities of freedom
For you have woven pride into this
The fabric of our history, and
What you've woven is soul-stunning, and
Strikingly beautiful to our minds eyes
Though gone from view, Ms. Maya
In our hearts
You will always rise!

~Judy Sundayo

President Barack Obama presented Maya **Angelou** with the **Medal of Freedom**, the highest
civilian honor in the United States, on February 15, 2011, in Washington, D.C., 2011

*Oprah Winfrey, talk show host of **The Oprah Winfrey Show**, highest rated talk-show in history, nationally syndicated (1986-2011); Actor, Producer, Philanthropist Recipient of **The Presidential Medal of Freedom**, awarded by President Barack Obama; Considered the most influential woman in the world! Photo by Petr Kratochvil, of artist rendering, publicdomainpictures.net*

Oprah, You Started Something Big

Bold, daring, classy,
Genuine and serene
A multi-talented reporter, commentator
Black queen of airspace

Big sister, little sister,
Mother to us all
You spoke and we listened
For two decades plus
You surprised everybody
With your searing wit and intellect

I don't know why we didn't suspect you had
Talent beyond your years
You knew exactly what to say
And how to say it
What to run and how to play it
Who to interview and what to ask
How to ask it
In order to get the answers
None of us would ever forget

(continued)

455

Orah You Started Something Big *(continued)*

And many who met you became
Close friends and confidants
Some spinning off to shows of their own
Blockbusters all
Oprah, you started something big
Bigger than our own ideas for ourselves
And what we thought we could be
Bigger than the world could see at the time
And you didn't stop there
You continued to challenge us
To read through ignorance and fear
You continued to broadcast
Year after soul-searching year
Lugging heavy wagon-loads of burdensome secrets
You inspired us to shed our shame on a treadmill of self-love
How else could our hearts leap up
And dance on the soft cushions of a hoped-for love
You helped us to remember how to give
And FOR-give
So that we could live our best lives yet
You reminded us and we won't ever forget
That life is much larger than the biggest of our dreams
And it's respect that educates and love that seems
To connect us one to the other
Cross culture, gender and ethnic bounds
The sameness of our life paths as humans
Is what engenders hope!
So, thank you Oprah, you're our best sister-friend!
And we're blessed we still have you
On Oxygen!

~Judy Sundayo

President Barack Hussein Obama became the 44th President of the United States of America in 2008, serving two terms; the first self-described African American to hold that office; President Obama faced unprecedented opposition during his two terms in office to bring about substantive change; Some of his most notable accomplishments while in office were 1) signing into law the American Recovery & Reinvestment Act of 2009 to avert another depression, 2) the Tax Relief, Unemployment Insurance Reauthorization & Job Creation Act of 2010, 3) the Patient Protection & Affordable Care Act "Obamacare," 4) the Dodd-Rank Wall Street Reform and Consumer Protection Act, and the 5) Don't Ask, Don't Tell Repeal Act of 2010; he also ended the U.S. military involvement in the Iraq war and oversaw the military operation which resulted in the death of Osama bin Laden in 2011; Official White House Photo in the Public Domain, taken by White House photographer, Pete Souza, of President Obama in the Oval Office on 12-6-12

Mr. President Obama

My daily prayer for you, Commander In Chief
I pray you know that you are 360 degrees of
Loved beyond belief
That The Obama family
Shows you their love and support
May this run river deep
I pray that you are filled up
With hope, humor and happiness by the heaps
I pray daily you are healed
From the top of your head to the soles of your feet
(continued)

457

Mr. President Obama *(continued)*

I pray as a husband, you deliver to Ms. Michelle
Love, support, humor and heat
I pray as the father, you love each
One of those beautiful babies unique
I pray that the Father, the Son, and the Holy Spirit

I pray you they complete
Keeping you whole, filled up, lacking nothing
And resting in regal relief

I pray that Congress changes, wakes up, matures
Grows up as we speak
I pray God bless them, that so many of them never again
Be this ignorant to cripple weak
I pray for prosperity, wealth, abundance,
Riches, plus money beyond what you seek
I pray that you find ways to get out
And play a couple times each week

Play is a love habit that will serve you well
It is fun and worth a repeat
I was instructed when to you I got to speak to
Inform you God is so proud of you! Good grief!
Cause they have thrown everything at you
Including the kitchen sink!
You are still standing cool
Sometimes you don't even seem to blink
I pray you appreciate daily how God made you
In his image truly unique
Courageous, patient, bold, highly favored
Quick on your feet
Strong, you carry on, unimpressed by petty defeat
I pray you daily *"Do you,"* Commander in Chief
Be determined, tenacious and I pray first God you seek

(continued)

Mr. President Obama *(continued)*

I pray you are mindful
God is in control no matter the climate or heat
I pray that you remember if God is for you
Who cares who is against you, sweet!
Know that nothing you can say or do
Will surprise God, nothing I repeat
Should you find yourself awake

Bothered by something, unable to sleep
Remember God is awake too
And God loves you Commander in Chief
Cast your cares, especially the ones that seem
To make your flesh crawl and creep
I pray that you stay mindful that God
Loves you beyond belief

There is nothing too big or too small,
Nothing should you feel weak
I pray that you know that not time or space
Can stop God; He won't be beat!
I pray you keep close to your heart
That you are God's masterpiece, Commander in Chief
Want or need something?
Open your mouth, ask and speak

God is not limited, not limited by time or space
You are always within God's reach
God will then move heaven then earth to deliver to you His
Promise of personal or professional peace
I pray you recall daily God calls you loved, wise, redeemed,
Powerful, capable and His masterpiece
Remember God loves you every day,
Commander in Chief!

~Jaime V. Jones

Palate Cleanser

Lime

A citrus twang
Of somersaults across the tongue
Fresh and lively
Flavor-flung!
Flitting over memories
Culinary enemies
Of taste
What a waste
To bemoan the past. . .
Serving up a sweet repast
Is lime. . .
Tingling clean. . .
What do you mean
The next course is on the way?
Honey chile, bring on lime
To save the day!

~Judy Sundayo

Part 7 – SPIRITUAL SEASONINGS

Herbs and Spices

Photo by Cristie Guevara: publicdomainImages.net

And I asked the chef,
What's the difference
Between an herb and a spice?
And he looked at me
And smiled real nice
The herbs are the leaves
Of the plant so green
The spices come from stem, root, bark or seeds
I see, said I, that makes it clear
Herbs wear green clothes
Over spicy underwear!
~Judy Sundayo

GUMBO boasts a rich culinary history in which Africans, Spaniards, Native Americans, Arcadians, and the blended Creole and Cajun peoples who ensued from them, used herbs and spices traditionally for medicinal and culinary purposes. Filé an herb used for flavoring *(as well as for thickening)*. Both Creoles and Cajuns use many of the same herbs and spices in their GUMBO. Although salt, black pepper and red pepper are staples for use in most GUMBOs, add your favorite spices to taste!

GUMBO Recipe – Step 7:

Herbs and Spices

What You Need
- Measuring spoons
- Small Bowl & spoon or Plastic Bag

What You Gotta Get *(Most Creole and Cajun recipes have been found to include these ingredients though amounts will vary.)*
- 2 T onion powder
- 2 T garlic powder
- 3 T salt
- 1 T ground black pepper
- 1 T ground white pepper
- 1 T cayenne (red) pepper
- 5 T paprika
- 1 T dried thyme
- 2 T dried oregano
- 2 T dried basil
- 2 T dry mustard
- 2 T cumin or celery seed
- 2 T ground sage
- 2 whole bay leaves

(And additionally)
- 1 T filé powder *(see more about file' in Part 3)*
- ½ cup chopped parsley
- ½ cup chopped scallions/green onions

(And optionally)
- 1 T Slap Ya Mama Original Blend Seasoning, *or*
- 1 T Konriko's Creole Seasoning
- 2 T Tabasco Sauce *(If desired, or to taste)*

What You Do with What You Get

- Combine all ingredients *(except for filé powder, bay leaves, parsley & scallions)* in a bowl & mix well with spoon, or alternatively, combine ingredients in a plastic bag & shake well.
- Add 2 Tablespoons of this mixture to the GUMBO pot after adding the Holy Trinity, meat & poultry.
- Add 2 bay leaves to the pot, but remember to remove them before serving as the texture of the leaves is unappetizingly rough to the palate.
- Let these herbs and spices simmer in the GUMBO pot, allowing the flavors to blend in with the meat, poultry and vegetables.
- Add the chopped the filé powder *(see Part 4),* when you are ready to serve your GUMBO.
- Add parsley and scallions as a garnish just before serving.
- Store remainder of the spice mixture in a jar or in a plastic container with a lid.

What You Bet Not Tell Nobody

- How much seasoning you use is a matter of personal choice. This also depends upon the size of your GUMBO pot. Although most traditional cooks season by taste and don't measure the exact amount of seasoning used, you may want to think in terms of how many quarts of GUMO you have. One Tablespoon (T) of seasoning for every two quarts of liquid in the pot would be wonderfully flavorful and spicy.
- It's best add your herbs and spices to the GUMBO pot after you have added the Holy Trinity to your roux; and then after the roux has been simmered a while with the stock, meat and poultry, do a

taste test and then add more of the seasoning mixture if needed to satisfy your taste.

- Even though what is *called* Cajun cooking today often uses so much pepper and spice that one cannot taste the actual GUMBO ingredients, we recommend you do not fall prey to this. Rather, season your GUMBO enough to "accent" the flavors of the dish, not to mask them.

- If you use filé DO NOT add it until just before serving. If you boil the filé it can ruin your GUMBO by making it stringy. If you'd like more thickening or you just like the flavor of filé you may want to have your family members or guests sprinkle ½ - 1 teaspoon filé to their separate bowls of GUMBO right at the table. That way, if you plan to have GUMBO leftover to serve the next day, you will be able to re-heat it without worry! *(see Part 3 for more information about filé powder)*

- Chopped garlic and tomatoes are also wonderful seasonings for GUMBO *(see Part 4 for information on how to spice up the Holy Trinity by using these ingredients!)*

- If you don't have the time to make the seasoning mixture above, try a pre-made seasoning mixture. Try Slap Ya Mama Original Blend Seasoning, Cajun Injector Cajun Shake Seasoning, Konriko Creole Seasoning or Ragin' Cajun Fixin's Cajun Seasoning.

- For Salt-Free Seasoning, try Benoit's Best Spicy Salt-Free Seasoning.

- For high-end seasonings absent sugar, gluten, MSG or preservatives, try A.A. Borsari's Savory Seasoned Salt *(Sea Salt, garlic, basil, rosemary, thyme, lavender, black pepper, nutmeg)* or Urban Accent's Spanish Smoked Seasoned Salt *(Sea salt, sweet smoked paprika, garlic & chives)*; then improvise your additional seasonings according to your taste!

464

Introduction to Poems Spiritually Seasoned

Herbs and spices add a wonderful kick to GUMBO, bringing out the flavors of everything you have thrown into the pot. Fresh and dried herbs and finely ground spices fine-tune GUMBO, by adhering to all of the other ingredients and helping them to blend together.

In life, we are advantaged if we have something we can rely on to bring out the goodness in ourselves and in others. For many, this is a spiritual experience, a religious belief, a religious experience, faith in God or a higher power or rituals for positive living. The herbs and spices in GUMBO bring out the flavor of the dish in much the same way that the these experiences spice up our lives spiritually. As you read the *Poems Spiritually Seasoned*, we invite you to think about the ways your transcendent or peak experiences, your belief or your faith, bring meaning, balance and flavor to your life.

Judy Sundayo's daughter of another mother,
Heaven Leigh Johnson *at the San Diego Zoo, 2009*

Season Me

Season me happy!
Season me glad!
Season me special!
Not just a fad!

I can be spicy!
I'm a quick study!
A little bit dicey
But no fuddy duddy!

Now, if you want a flavor
That will warm and excite
Hands down, that's me!
Just promise, don't bite!

~Judy Sundayo

Salvation

Salvation is a ladder

With three rungs to climb

From total disbelief to God divine

The first rung is faith

A trust unshakeable

The second is knowledge

An experience unbreakable

The third is transformation

You become the last rung

When you and the Infinite are one

~Judy Sundayo

*Judy Sundayo with granddaughter, **Rachel**,*
Jacksonville, Florida, 2013

Judy Sundayo, at 8 years old, Washington, D.C.

The Question

Little girl ask from where her is
From where the stars? From where the rain?
Little girl ask her mama 'xplain

Mama don't know the answer too
'cept to say from God, from him
Who her can't hear; who her can't see
Who her can't touch; who her can't be
Who her can't never understand
Who ain't a woman or a man

Who her must ask to bless her lunch,
And always everywhere at once

(continued)

The Question *(continued)*

Who live up somewhere in the sky,
And let some in there when they die

Mama say a God like this
Her don't know so little girl miss
Her still don't know from where her is
From where the wind? From where the snow?
From where the place to where they go?
Mama don't know the answer too

So little girl peep the Satguru
And cause her seek and knock that door
Him show her what her lookin for
Within her heart so very deep
Him wake that God who seem be sleep!
And then him speak and then her see!
Him lovin' personality!

This L-I-G-H-T then make her understand
The energy that in a man
That her respect; that everywhere!
That found inside; that always there!
That all is Love; that all is His!
That *L-I-G-H-T*
Is truly what her is!
And when her look inside, her see
From where her is
Is where he be!

~Judy Sundayo
470

Alyce Smith-Cooper, San Diego, California

Wear Your Crown

Let go and let GOD loose in your life
He's crowned you with GLORY over all of Creation!
Like crowing GOOD with WISDOM
A kind of DIVINE Inflation!
Let the gems in your CROWN sparkle
And daily VICTORIES will be thine
For your WILL is the might
That will make those gemstones SHINE!
Wear your crown PROUDLY!
It's a HALO of LIGHT
Then God will BLESS YOU
With HIS LOVE and MIGHT!
Wear your crown of UNDERSTANDING!
Wear your crown of PRAISE!
Wear your crown of COMPASSION
Wear it all of your days!
As it was in the BEGINNING. . .
So it is today
You've been crowned
By the MOST HIGH GOD!
Don't throw your crown away!

~Alyce Smith Cooper & Judy Sundayo

Protection

Protection lives

Shadowed under grace

Only then can we fly

~Alyce Smith Cooper

———

Almost Haiku – Ha, Ha, Ha!

Glorious light

Parting Darkness

Gifted by a smile

~Alyce Smith Cooper

*Alyce Smith Cooper and friend, **E.J. Montgomery**, Washington, D. C., 2012*

Gratitude 101

Thank you my God, our God
for carrying me over the river grief
Thank you for showing me
all the love giving me soothing relief
Thank you for letting me hear encouragement
strengthening my belief
Thank you for my family and friends
elevating me to your reach

Thank you God, my God for this lesson
I now can lovingly teach
That without gratitude I will never experience
your promises sweet
That without gratitude your grace, your favor
never will I meet
To receive what you promised, all I deserve;
practice what I preach

Until gratitude and me become close, tight
I will always believe, that we, you, I, that is right
Do not deserve a single thing; say otherwise,
I'm ready to fight
Thank you my God,
our God because of mature gratitude
I now know better tonight

Thank you my Creator, our Creator
That I stake this stand
Knowing that without gratitude I will daily criticize, judge,
complain, whine and demand;
Thank you for teaching me that each time I do any of the
above first hand
Then gratitude and appreciation I fail to understand

(continued)

Gratitude 101 *(continued)*

Every time I engage by thinking, talking the spirit of doubt,
blame, shame, guilt, and worry; I'm in fear
Yes, I own it, it is me who is afraid right now, right here!
Thinking, speaking and acting this way causes heartbreak,
Disconnect, destruction, many tears
Not to mention by doing so
I give up all my power year after year
Playing chess using this strategy, "check mate!" is all I hear

Starting today, here is what I pray,
That I am grateful, thankful in every way
That I express appreciation each and every day
That I have words of gratitude for everyone,
everything, everywhere along life's ways

Thank you, thank you; thank you is what I want to say
Thank you, that daily I get to be a blessing,
a miracle and a gift
Thank you for success, success, success,
Thank you for success
Thank you for avalanches of abundance,
Thank you for happiness

~Jaime V. Jones

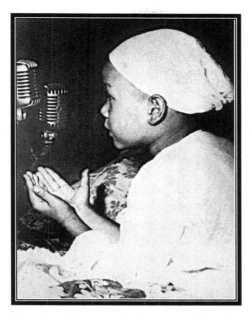

*Judy Sundayo's honorary family member, **Prem Rawat***
Teaching at 8 years old, India, 1965

The Master

Men clamor; he goes
Men call out; he knows
For all the weak and weary,
His feet are traveling in haste
One asks who he is; another thinks he knows
Yet both will miss him as he comes and goes
Love is on his lips; his heart is full of joy
'Mong all life's fine instruction,
His leave the greatest impression
He is the Master; he is!
His eyes know it!
And yours do when they venture deep!

~Judy Sundayo

New Eyes

What air is this I breathe these days
That gives me new eyes
For the bright celestial vistas
Of uncircumscribed capacity
What omnipresent phenomenon is this
My lungs embrace
That leaves my hearing so acute
To heaven's whisper-soft symphony
What minute particles of Love are these
That fill my every inch of feeling
More so than simple joy
More so than seeming satisfaction
What seed is this that has been planted
That begets a fruit so sweet
More so than honey or the finest ambrosia
And what inspired interpretation, that finds this
Life-moving presence within me so sacred
To my heart's most profound understanding
What wind is this that blows my way
That gives me new eyes?
~Judy Sundayo

Judy Sundayo, China, 2007

476

Photograph by Leon O. Allen

A Metronome of Grace

I swim in music
It makes me smile
Waves of rhythm mile after mile
And sometimes I can see a note
Drifting by just like a boat
Like cadence caught her sail to breeze
In waves of calmness, discord flees
I swim and let the rhythm guide
Breath-sequenced to a place inside
Where harmony is what lights my day
It shines upon a sacred bay
And everything is
As it all should be
Melody moving me back to sea
And yet my heart is not the same
Love-drenched, it sings a sweet refrain
And dripping still in time and place
My life is a metronome of Grace.

~Judy Sundayo

Evening Prayer

From the depths of my being
I behold that thou art all there is
Thy magnificence encompasses all I know
The greatness of thee fills me with awe
The brilliance of thy countenance excites me
The steadfastness of thy spirit grounds me
I am thy child, standing before thee bowed and wanting
Embrace me with thy Holy Spirit
Enfold me in thy Love
Permeate me with thy Wisdom
Enable me to do thy Service
Let me behold thy goodness and kindness toward me
This day In all I experience
And the writing of thy hand in all things
Let me now to near thee, Lord
Invoking thee by name

~Judy Sundayo

Sunset over the Pacific Ocean, La Jolla, California,
Photograph by Judy Sundayo

478

*Jaime V. Jones' brother, **Randi Jones**,*
San Diego, California

Don't Know What to Do?

Don't know what to do?
Why let that stop you!
Life is sending a message,
A signal, a clue

Time to pray,
Ask, believe and review
God's gifts, healings, blessings,
Miracles by multitudes
Wow!

Success, victories, avalanches of abundance
Pouring through
Whenever, I am sure I don't know what to do
Mother, Father, God, Holy Spirit,
Help, I need you!
God is here
I feel his spirit presence as it soothes
(continued)

479

Don't Know What to Do? *(continued)*

What is in my heart in my head I daily renew
Who and what I am,
My God, our God to the rescue!
Still don't know what to do?
Honestly share for the moment
You're a bit confused
Remember this is your first clue
Got bills now long past overdue?

Ask, believe, receive
Do your best
Then refuse
To live another day not knowing
What to do!
Because my God, our God
Has big, big, plans for me
For you

Know that if this were not absolutely true
None of these messages, signals
Would get through
So now, the next time that you
Think what to do? What to do?
Ask, believe, receive all your clues

A timely powerful message coming soon
Inhale and exhale the solution then refuse
To live another minute longer
Not knowing exactly what to do
Ask, believe, holy spirit, my God, our God
To the rescue!
~Jaime V. Jones

Alyce Smith Cooper's great, granddaughter,
Lisa Jada

Get Some for Yourself

The Holy Spirit is yours too!
Not for you to speculate on
Watching someone else's praise arise is like
Watching someone else eat ice cream
And you get chill bumps
You missed the core experience!

What we know to be true is this. . .
God abides in us
God loves our praise
Why cheat yourself?
And the God within?

(continued)

481

Get Some for Yourself *(continued)*

Engage in praises with a whole heart
Close your eyes
Breathe deep
Then let the joy thanksgiving erupt
Like geysers propelled by volcano-like thunder
Then you will discover the divine
The holy spirit the everlasting lover
Get some for yourself!
~Alyce Smith Cooper

*Alyce Smith Cooper's great, granddaughter, **Lyric Adriana***

*Jaime Jones with her grandmother, **Susie Jones***
*(center) and her sister **Cookie** (right), San Diego, California*

Bold Believers

Set aside some time for receiving; Set a date
Spend the day looking at all you believe
And receive. . . celebrate!
Celebrations create balance in life so don't wait
Receiving eliminates depression and hot hate
Cheerfully celebrate what is on your life plate

The grass always seems greener on the other side
As we grow up, mature
And become spiritually dignified
The time has come that we, you I
Stop, look, listen receive and recognize
All the multitudes of abundance, blessings, favor,
In our lives

(continued)

483

Bold Believers *(continued)*

Gifts, grace, mercies, miracles multiplied!
No need to listen for success stories;
No need to make up lies
Clearly celebrate what you do have
And a word to the wise
Fill up, be whole, be complete without
Lack in your eyes
Watch how quickly your ABR
(Ask, Believe, Receive) multiples
Say "Thank you. Thank you" and here's why. . .

Gratitude is the best way to fertilize,
Verify and satisfy your ABR
Until they miraculously multiply
Receive it; believe it; you are worthy
Good enough; you deserve blessings and bliss;
You are more than a conqueror,
You are destined and anointed for all of this

Believe it; receive it
And do not be ashamed to admit
Tell others they too are spiritually loaded
Fully equipped!
Being believers we are all heir, wealthy and rich
Shout: God loves me! And God love you!
Believe it!
Receive it; believers, it just doesn't get
Any better than this!

~Jaime V. Jones

*Judy Sundayo's daughter, **Aurora**, 2 years old,*
San Diego, California, 1981

My Earth, My Sky

Lord, you are my earth
In you I have strength
From you I come; from you I grow

My roots ensue from a place
Deep within your heart
With you about them, their grasp is firm
From you I take all nourishment
My food is the love you give

I am the seed of a flower
That will grow in your garden
You are my earth; you are my home

(continued)

My Earth, My Sky *(continued)*

Lord, you are my sky
For you I reach endlessly
Ever feeling you about me even as I do so
You are my purpose; you are the infinite
That the petals on this flower
Will yearn for
You are the peace they will always touch
You are always in me and I in you
Lord, you are my sky; you are my Heaven

In knowing your beauty I find my own
In nourishing myself on your love, I become loving
In growing in your garden I blossom in truth
In finding you, Lord, I find myself
Lord, in this temple, the sky is a limitless sky
Let our earth be one earth; let our sky be one sky

~Judy Sundayo

Ivory's Rock Conference Center, Ipswitch,
Australia, 2009, Photograph by Judy Sundayo

Alyce Smith-Cooper, San Diego, California

Alyce

Head Wrapped Tight, White Teeth Glitter
Bigger Than Life, smiling Laughter
Giggles Trinkles Booms Through China Doll Eyes
Flashing Gemstones, dangling Beads
Feathers Drooping
From An Old Straw Hat
Bangles Clinking; Fabric Draping
Clinging To Round Strong Hips
Slipper Shoes Bind Winged Feet
Deep Space Gypsy Like A Sprite
Glides Hither Thither
Praising Creator, healing The Land
Sharing Pain Or Love
Giving Head Wrapped Tight
Bigger Than Life
Always, Always On The Path Of Light

~Alyce Smith Cooper

This Music

This music moves me to the beat of love
For love this music moves me
Till my soul is drenched in kindness
This music tickles
Like the strain of laughter in the distance
A laughter born of knowing
That the fears of life are gone
This music whispers
Like the sound of seashells telling secrets
These secrets speak of Knowledge
And of everlasting peace
This music tingles softly
Like the bells of ancient calling
A calling that I answer
With a silence seeking truth
This music awes my hearing
Like the whistling of a love song
For a love song is this music
As my Lord embraces me
~Judy Sundayo

*Judy Sundayo's long-time friend, **Jani Gray**, talented vocalist*
After her performance at the Northern Rockies Folk Festival,
An annual event; Photo taken In Hailey, Idaho, circa 1990's

Judy Sundayo, expecting any day,
San Diego, California, 1979

Holy Fire

My spirit daily catches fire
Bright flame caught in my heart's thirsty briar
God's love against my own ignites the realm
And spreads along my spine from base to helm

As flames of Grace flicker and vibrate the region
Chasing the dross and hunting down the legion
And then it happens in a flash
My mind's exploded; my thoughts are ash

And I am consumed in an aura of bliss
My doubts and fears have burned to crisps
And cleansed am I in this Holy Fire
Every inch of my being only seeks to conspire

To lay my mind once more on this altar again
That this sacrifice daily will see Love reign
And so I pray in this purged condition
To God be the Glory and the rest to perdition!

~Judy Sundayo

489

Houseguest

I am a guest in this house

Forgive me if my manners are not polished

Your hospitality is enormously gracious

To make me feel at home

I long to extend my gratitude to you

In a way that is worthy of your generosity

But, I continually fall short, so boundless

Is your Grace

Though, I am only a poor child

Your kindness makes my heart rich

And so, will I render you payment~

With love!

~Judy Sundayo

Judy Sundayo, San Diego, California

Jaime Jones' grandfather and grandmother,
Rev. George and *Mrs. Susie Jones*, Arkansas

It's Not Over

I thought it was over

Then love came over

I felt used up

'Till love showed up

I felt I was all out

Until I AM started to shout

Love is all I AM talking about

Today, expect love to show up

And show out!

~Jaime V. Jones

491

The Beatific Vision

The beatific vision awaits within

Age-old

Spectacular

Heart-warming

Set your passport on this destination

Oh, my soul

Snapshot this sight within

And view it daily on the living pages

Of your inner photo album

This image shall forever be

Living and lasting

~Judy Sundayo

Judy Sundayo with long-time friends, Kali Rodriguez and Ann Richmond, Ivory's Rock Conference Center, Ipswitch, Australia, circa 2012

Alyce Smith Cooper, with granddaughter, **Diona**
And mother **Anita Lorraine Smith**

Church Mothers

Holy special breed
Mothers of the church
Mold, shape, raise the children of the flock
Dedicated few faithful till the end
Generations of young souls reared to adulthood
Sometimes eyes don't see the seeds planted
Root, grow, gloom and complete the cycle
Don't miss your chance to kiss a withered cheek
Seek a sparkling eye
To say, "Thank You!"

~Alyce Smith Cooper

Again and Again

I thought this would end
I am hearing it again
I looked around and then
Blessings and love my friend

I don't want it to end
So, here I am again
Favor and friendship I send
Love to you my friend

God is love, amen?
God showed up again
No limitations, no end

Filling us up, whole, complete within
Lacking nothing; without lack,
victorious we win
Keep thinking; then saying this
again and again

~Jaime V. Jones

*Alyce Smith Cooper's great, granddaughter, **Lyric Adriana***

We've Got the Power

We've got the power; we do!
We've got the power to turn the world around
We can do anything but fail
We've got the power to respect our elders
And to raise our babies in the spirit
But we must ***move now***!
We must prepare ourselves to be pilgrims
The world is changing
Preparing ourselves for the lean times to come
Time is now
Meditate and pray!
For that is what gives us the power!

~Alyce Smith Cooper

Let Us Pray

Let us pray with fingers green
Reaching in where God is seen
To that fresh and holy part
We've come to know of as the heart

Let us bow our heads in prayer
That leaves of kindness will be there
To gentle make the words we speak
So blessings through our hands will peak

Let us give thanks for every grace
In every moment's peaceful place
Sustaining breath of love to heal
As we partake this blessed meal

Let us pray with hearts contrite
That we might try with all our might
To be the vision we would see
On earth, as it is heavenly

~Judy Sundayo

__Judy Sundayo__ and __Jane Richmond__, Sister-friends since 1974,
Jane is Co-founder and Proprietor, along with John Finch of the
__Self-Heal School for Herbal Studies__, San Diego, California
http://selfhealschool.com/

Judy Sundayo, Orange County, California, circa 1996

Saved

Saved, Revived
From all the destructiveness of ignorance survived
And that was all there was to say
That told of all the books on all the shelves
It told of all their authors
And it spoke
Of all the words and all the powers
We ourselves could not invoke

Saved, Revived, Renewed
What more could illustrate this Light
The deep blue vale of night?
The bright and blinding vistas of the sun?
My soul silhouetted against my mind's eye?
The long and winding day when it is done?

(continued)

497

Saved *(continued)*

Saved, Revived, Renewed, Rebirthed
Yes, all the goodness in my soul unearthed
And that was all there was to know
That was the essence of every good
That was the shower of Beauty
And of Love
That poured into the hearts of men like rain
And made alive that treasured flower
That we alone could not attain

~Judy Sundayo

*Judy Sundayo with friend, **Dr. Temille Porter**, Clinical Psychologist,*
Manager of the Health, Wellness & Counseling Center, King Abdullah University
***of Science and Technology,** Thuwal, Kingdom of Saudi Arabia, until her untimely*
transition in 2015; Photo taken in Malibu, California, circa 1990's

Photo by Hondo, morguefile.com

What I love about the Bible

It is filled with so many spiritual snacks

Loaded up with love, joy, peace and supernatural acts

Capturing and keeping your attention

Not like some drugs - crack

Feeding and stimulating you intellectually:

The Father, The Son The Holy Spirit pack

Keeping you safe and secure on the right spiritual track

Reminding all believers God's got you front, center and back

Now honestly I had not planned to say all of that

But that is the power of the Bible in me, this is my fact

Yes, the Bible provides me super spiritual snacks

No empty calories

But stories chocked full of courage and brave acts

(continued)

What I love about the Bible *(continued)*

Men and women delivering healing

Delivering glory all the while under attack

Then there is our mighty Lord and Savior

The power Jesus packed!

I am in awe, whenever I think back

To the Garden of Gethsemane, all the soldiers Jesus sacked

Wow! Imagine resurrecting a man out off a tomb

Just by saying that, I AM, I AM!

Try following that act

Jesus came redeemed, restored then he left

The Holy Spirit to comfort us to guide and protect

How great is that? Take some time on this to reflect

I am in love with the Bible and I read it with respect

~Jaime V. Jones

Photo by jclk8888, morguefile.com

Christmas Candle by Ladyheart, morguefile.com

Tiz the Season

Glad tidings of great joy

Ringing in church walls

Handle's Messiah sung

Played with elegance

That masterpiece created to raise money

For the poor and prison bound

While we clutch tightly the innocent children of today

With visions of Jordan Tennis shoes and iPads to receive

While silently the backlash of hatred for one another

Eats away at the heart of OUR CREATOR

The mindless terrorists

Turn their scopes on peaceful demonstrators

(continued)

501

Tiz the Season *(continued)*

Those with authority to bring peace are armed

Poised to fire

Allowed to kill the generations and go unpunished

The blood of the slaughtered flows in our village streets

Tiz the season of the GLORY OF GOD

To ring inside not just church walls

But in the hearts of men and women

Boys and girls

Our Village is under attack

Blinded by the wine of the world have we forgotten?

Under the clouds of self-hatred

Anger turned inward poorly managed grief

Do we forget who we are?

Whose we are?

Tiz the season to turn inward

To grab and hold tightly to the core of our existence

To thaw frozen hearts in the refiner's fire

To call upon the VIOLET FLAME of HOLY SPIRIT

Crying out for MERCY

TRANSFORMATION and then PEACE

Tiz the season

~Alyce Smith Cooper

Alyce Smith Cooper giving libation at Community Event,
San Diego, California

I AM Speaks

Empowerment

Nothing is impossible

Success is in you

Success is within you

Success is who you are

I AM has created you for a purpose

I AM has created you with meaning

I AM has created you for unity

I AM has created you to be authentic

I AM has created you to be your unique self

A light in this world

The LOVE of I AM is who you are

Be the producer of greatness

Be the manifestation of peace

For nothing is impossible

To the I AM GOD

~Alyce Smith Cooper

Grace at the Holy Day

It's a Holy Day and so we pray
We're blessed with holy zeal
And a countenance of compassion
To grace our holy meal

Dearest Father, thank you for this life
For every heartache, every strife
For letting us live a little longer
For making us stronger

Thank you for our family and our friends
For reminding us to make amends
For giving us inner Light
And a peaceful sleep at night

Thank you for our talents and our odd proclivities
May it be your hand that guides us in all activities
Thank you for our future, prosperous and bright
As we continue to grow more beautifully in your sight

It's a Holy Day and so we pray
We're blessed with holy zeal
So welcome all who've come today
To share this holy meal

~Judy Sundayo

*Judy Sundayo's great maternal aunt **Susie Miles**,*
Washington, D.C. circa 1930's

*Judy Sundayo's brother **Leon O. Allen** (right) and his family; wife, **Zelma** (left) and their children, **Christopher** (top center) and **Erin** (bottom center), taken at the Smith Family Reunion, Alexandria, Virginia, 1999*

God, Lord, You The Man

God, Lord, You the man, again
God, Lord, You the man, amen!
God, Lord, yes You the man
God, Lord, yes how blessed I am
God, yes, Lord yes, I do my best
God, yes, Lord yes, You to the rest
God, Lord, You the man, amen!
God, Lord, I know we can
God, my Lord, oh yes, my Lord
You the man again
God, my Lord, oh yes my Lord, You the man
Amen!
God, Lord, You the man
God, Lord, I'm in Your hands
God, Lord, You the man
God, Lord, here I am
Available, use me; I know You can
God, Lord, You the man, Amen!

~Jaime V. Jones

505

Spirit-Ku's: Excerpts to God

I am thy servant
Give me right understanding, Lord
To do what pleases thee!

———

Teach me
By thy all-powerful Light
And in whatever world I be
Guide me
To my perfect home!

———

In all things
Thou art
And thy embrace
And thy caress!

———

If ever there was a Father
You are the Father
If ever there was a lover
You are He
If ever there was a child
I am your daughter
If ever a devotee,
It is me!
~Judy Sundayo

Ceiling of Egyptian Temple;
Photograph by Judy Sundayo

Jean King with friends, **Alyce** & **James Cooper**,
Los Angeles, California, 1971

Bubbling Vessels

Overflow, churning upheaval
Generated from steadfast fire
Heat turned up by circumstances
Passionate outcry soulful yearnings
Places obedience at the forefront
Putting prayer power center front
Casting aside peeling apart past sins
Into the boiling pot of forgiveness
Boiling in the vessels a cleansing balm of Gilead
Washing away sin sickness
Cleansing from fears, creating calmness
From these bubbling vessels
Now flows glowing refreshing
Needs met after the boiling preparation
Victory comes with what
GOD COOKS UP!

~Alyce Smith Cooper

God Peeking Back at Me

See the joy; see the pain
Mama, tuck me in again
A thousand days have passed since I
A child, undaunted, searched the sky
For signs of hope, perhaps a key
Perhaps God peeking back at me
A blessing welled up in my heart
An endless fountain had its start
And there, I quenched my thirst and bathed
Through thorn-rimmed paths
Have come unscathed
And by His blessings and his Grace
Have dared to look upon His face and live
A dream unfurled
Though dead but to this world
And now, I see with eyes of age
The silver chalice and the blade
Determined, once again, I at my best
Embark upon my endless daily quest
For Truth, in Beauty stands above
Denying not my heart or soul or love

~Judy Sundayo

*Judy Sundayo's friends from the left, **Jane Richmond**, Jane's sister,*
***Ann Richmond**, the late **Therezinha da Costa** of Brazil, an original elder in the Rites
of Passage Program for African American Girls, **Judy Sundayo** (standing) and
Sharon Hopper, Photo taken in San Diego, circa 1990's*

508

*Judy Sundayo's long-time friend, **Meera Srivarztava,** Retired businesswoman; Photo taken in Long Beach, California, circa 1990's*

The Song of the Holy Man

Oh wanderer, you play your flute
With such majestic splendor
The squirrels attend you on all sides
And the birds join with your harmony
To make the divine sound of life
Oh Saint, your music is so pleasing
Who is there who can hear your song?
Oh student, with your worldly books
Of many far off places
With plans and formulas and scales
To strike a thousand mental images
And make them soar
Away from you they then take flight
Leaving the infinite boundaries of your soul
Learning only of Truth
Oh Saint, your knowledge is so revealing
Who is there who can see your Light?
Oh mother, channel of a life fresh brought to earth
And draped in innocence
(continued)

509

The Song of the Holy Man *(continued)*

You feed with most abundant purity
You cleanse with but a tender bath of gentle thoughts
That radiate from that most perfect womb
To every child awaiting in humility
And with a guileless heart
Even man full grown draws to your breast
To nurse of the wisdom flowing there
Oh Saint, your bosom is so full of life
Who is there who can taste of your vitality?
Oh Poet, you are but a Word
That speaks to many images though chained
Your poem is but a type of meek response
To conversations with a dream
That one true Word lies only in your soul
It gives a constant testament of love
In most primordial prose
Its rhythm is a peaceful Muse
Who sings of everlasting life
Your poem can be at best a poor translation
Of a language that your heart knows well
Oh Saint, your descriptions are so inspiring
Who is there who can know your Name?
Oh Saint, your mystery is so sublime
You hide yourself 'mid flowers or books stacked high
You surround yourself with the clamor of children
And do all such trivial tasks as the sweeping
Or the cleaning, or putting meaning in a poem
Deeply hidden in such worldliness
There streams the essence of your being, Holy One
At whatever task, I put myself at your feet
Oh Saint, your ways are so perplexing
Who is there who can through myriad illusions
Detect your loving soul?

~Judy Sundayo

510

*A member of Judy Sundayo's honorary family, **Prem Rawat,** travels almost constantly throughout the world to speak about the ability of each individual to find personal peace and fulfillment within; He is a renowned international peacemaker, a husband, father, grandfather, pilot and founder of **The Prem Rawat Foundation,** a non-profit charity addressing the fundamental need of every human being for food, water and peace; Mr. Rawat has been honored with the title "Ambassador of Peace," has received the Distinguished International Humanitarian Award from the President of the National Council of Women, and a Lifetime Achievement Award from the Asia Pacific Brands Foundation having worked tirelessly for over 40 years to bring a Message of peace and hope to everyone throughout the globe; www.wordsofpeace.org*

The Pilot

Through cloudy skies or clear,
He's there
So, welcome aboard; get settled and ready
The flight path is set; the course is steady
The controls are tuned to the highest station
As we move through time to our destination
Love is our constant altitude
The journey within, a certaintude
Of breath and inner memory
Like going home; like being free
So, sit back and relax; enjoy the ride
Our destination?
Of course, the peace inside!

~Judy Sundayo

Amidst the Ten Thousand Things

Amidst the ten thousand things
I am lost
I can never find my way
Without thee
Take my hand, Father
Oh, do not leave me despairing

~Judy Sundayo

*Judy Sundayo's cousin, **Sandra Summers**, her husband, **David Summers**
(top/center); their granddaughter, **Sierra** (Center);
Sandra's niece, **Falilah** (far right); Falilah's children, **Esau** and **Evelyn**;
(far left & bottom left), Lexington Park, Maryland 2006*

Pray for Me Please

Pray with me please
On both your knees
With solemn, heartfelt prayers
Though I've done my best
I'm afraid this test
Has me questioning if God cares

~Judy Sundayo

*Al Washington's sister, **Ann Victorian** with husband **Frank Victorian**, their son **Mason** (far right) and their grandson, **Devin** (2nd from left)*

A Prayer Going Forward

In grace, God gave us breath this day

That we might sing his praise

In love this family came together

And over the course of days

Was blessed

With good company

Good food

A heap of stories

And lots of laughter

And going forward then, let us pray

Our hearts will not forget

That peace and love and grace are what

The love of God begets

(continued)

A Prayer Going Forward *(continued)*

That family is like a kingdom

Where all can live happily

We must just remember that God comes first

And forgiveness is the key!

May the family travel safely

And safely return home

Remembering you are deeply loved

And with God, you are never alone!

~Judy Sundayo

*Judy Sundayo's daughter **Aurora** and Aurora's husband,*
***Richard Chedester**, with their children, **Alex** and **Rachel**,*
Jacksonville, Florida, 2013

Alyce Smith Cooper (top/center) and family

On Winning the Race

No, it is not given to the swift,
The race that is,
It is won by those who last to the end . . .
Make it over the line

Well, how does one win?, you ask
Lots of folks will give you different answers;
Money, dope, sex, power,
But as for me, and my house,
We will serve the Lord,

We will nourish the family unit,
Cherish the elders' wisdom
And the new hope given by the babies,
And we will uphold the values

(continued)

515

On Winning the Race *(continued)*

That have brought us thus far
You know, honoring God, Father and Mother;
Loving self to allow for the energy
As we would have it done to us,
Tithing one-tenth of the first fruits,
And being joyful!

This is the second wind of the runner
Joy is the burst of speed that puts us over the line
That lets us be victorious over all that life may bring
The same joy that lets us know we are
Children of the King, and as such,
Full inheritors of the Kingdom
Bon Voyage!
~Alyce Smith Cooper

Alyce Smith Cooper working with young people at church

Palate Cleanser

Prayer, Patience and Persistence

Sounds like the road to sainthood
Or at the very least to a nunnery or a monastery
Most of us jus' don't have that kinda time!
Now I think we all know we have to pray
For most of us, just to make it through the day
But did you know that making it through each day
Is persistence?
Now, patience . . . well, of that, I ain't so sure
'Cause I have to admit my motives
Ain't always pure
I can throw an bunch of stumbling blocks
In my own self's way
And then, of course, I have to pray

Mother-Father-Spirit-God
Cleanse my life's palate and give me the nod
Prepare me for your next course
I want to be ready!
To taste it and savor it, to be grateful and steady
Cleanse my palate and newly make my heart
That with prayer, patience and persistence
We'll never be apart

Help me pray for patience so I can see
Persistence taking shape as the divine in me
Help me pray for persistence and walk in faith please
For if I pray first, I will surely believe that all I need,
I will abundantly receive
Prayer, patience and persistence are like magic seeds
That grow up and grow out powerfully
For a palate cleansing, super spiritual victory!

~Alyce Smith-Cooper, Judy Sundayo & Jaime V. Jones

Fifth Course

Gumbo Recipes

Alyce's GUMBO Recipe
(As shared by Bea Kemp many years ago!)

What You Need:
10" stainless steel or cast iron frying pan
10-12 quart stainless steel pot with lid

What You Gotta Get *(Serves 25-30)*
6 pounds of chicken thighs
10 pounds of shrimp
6 pounds of crab legs
5 pounds of sausage *(Your favorite Louisiana style)*
1 gallon bottle of *Salsa Fresca (chopped vegetables)*
4-5 bay leaves
1 teaspoon of cumin
1 teaspoon of thyme
2 cups of all-purpose flour
1 stick of butter

What You Do With What You Got
- Wash and clean seafood *(shrimp & crab legs)* separately
- Refrigerate seafood
- Wash chicken thoroughly
- Cook chicken in spring water *(enough to cover)* with bay leaves, garlic & 2 onions cut in quarters *(the bay leaves, garlic & onions will be strained out)*
- Take chicken out when firm, but bones can be easily removed
- Remove bones and skin
- Cut chicken into spoon sized pieces and refrigerate
- Skim fat off top of broth
- Add salsa, more bay leaves, cumin, thyme
- Simmer over med-low heat for 2 hours
- Cut sausage into spoon sized pieces
- Cook sausage in frying pan to release fat

- Spoon sausage into simmering chicken broth mixture
- Simmer 1 hour
- Retrieve crab legs from frig and cut into 3" pieces
- Add crab legs to chicken broth mixture
- Simmer 30 minutes
- While simmering make roux
- In same frying pan in which sausage was cooked, brown 2 cups of flour *(your choice how brown you want the roux to get; some folks like it dark! I do!)*
- When the roux reaches desired color/smell, add melted butter
- Mix melted butter in well and then set roux aside
- To simmering chicken broth pot, add shrimp
- Simmer 10 minutes
- Then, stir in chicken
- Bring entire mixture back to a complete rolling boil
- Now add roux until mixture is as thick as you like *(It will thicken more as it cools)*

Now the fun begins!

Bring in the tasters and their suggestions. You may or may not take the suggestions but the fun is in the tasting and in the opinion giving. Now is when I turn the pot down as low as I can so the wedding dance can take place. I serve my brew over rice. You of course may do as you please. It is your Gumbo Pot to share as you please. *Bon Appetite!*

What You Bet Not Tell Nobody

- Stirring from the bottom up is important unless you want to have bun - bun on the pot bottom. For some that is delicacy for me it is drudgery.
- I rarely add salt as the seafood has a salty flavor. The tomato from the salsa lends some sweetness and there is the flavoring from the sausage, the chicken and the herbs. You be the judge. I'm just saying . . .

Jaime's California GUMBO Recipe
(Basic)

What You Need:
A large 12-quart stainless steel pot

What You Gotta Get: *(Serves 4-6)*
1 small onion peeled and chopped
2 ribs of celery washed and chopped
1 medium bell pepper washed and chopped
1 clove of garlic peeled and minced

16 ounces of string beans *(If canned use French cut.)*
1 medium cabbage, rinsed and cut up
3 - 4 medium zucchini, washed and chopped
1½ cups okra, de-slimed. *(To de-slime, soak 1 hour in 1 quart of water and 1 cup of vinegar.)*

1 teaspoon of basil
1 teaspoon of parsley
½ teaspoon of cilantro, dried
½ teaspoon of black pepper
2 tablespoons of dried onion soup
2 bay leaves

3 teaspoons brown sugar
½ cup butter
1 large bottle of V-8 juice
1 - 3 pounds of chicken
1 cup of sausage *(Add last 30 minutes of cooking.)*

What You Do with What You Get

- Throw all into a pot
- Let cook slow on low heat for 2 - 3 hours until chicken falls off the bones
- You can add all of these as directed or add to taste.
- You can even choose to leave out an item or substitute as you please.
- Serve on your favorite bed of rice.

What You Bet Not Tell Nobody

- If you make this dish without meat it is still delicious!
- You may serve it hot or cold. *Try both!*

Jaime's California Seafood Gumbo

Use basic recipe.
Add:
1 pound fried catfish pieces
1 pound peeled and cleaned shrimp
1 pound crab legs and claws

Jaime's California Combo Gumbo

Use basic recipe.
Add any or all of the following:
16 oz. chicken
16 oz. shrimp
16 oz. sausage
16 oz. crab legs
16 oz. catfish fried

Sixth Course

Digesting Discussions

Study Guide

In writing this book, the authors have intended to spark interest, enthusiasm and critical thinking among readers. Some of the poems in the book contain information that might be considered provocative or disturbing. However, oftentimes thoughts and feelings that are troubling are catalysts for change and greater understanding, either within oneself or between people.

In this Study Guide section, we initiate questions to get readers, particularly students, discussing the issues that are raised in the book, as well as their reactions to them. However, it is hoped that all readers will come up with their own questions and discuss the poems, the photos and the captions freely among their peers and colleagues as well as within their families.

Educators may use the questions provided here following an individual or group assignment for students to read a certain poem or section of the book. Students may also be encouraged to create and answer their own questions. Critical thinking skills will be especially enhanced following discussions between students who hold different opinions. Issues raised in the poems may also be used as topics for research papers, group presentations or an individual presentation of the student's own creativity, whether a poem, a song, a rap or a spoken word presentation.

Some groups, sororities, fraternities, community clubs or organizations may wish to use the recipes for GUMBO and invite their members over to eat and then discuss the book. Discussions always go better on a full stomach. We would also challenge participants to discuss the cross-cultural history of GUMBO, the status of New Orleans and the state of Louisiana since Hurricane Katrina and in what ways the experiences there might be mirrored in similar ways around the country or the world.

As most of the resources highlighted in this book are found in San Diego County, some may ask how this book might be relevant to those living in other parts of the country or the world. We suggest that the location may not be the same, but many of the issues raised in the book will have universal application. We encourage readers, particularly students to take the opportunity to challenge themselves to discover something about their own communities that they had not previously known. In fact, those who do not identify as members of an African American community might take the opportunity to make comparisons with their own families and communities. What are the similarities? What are the differences? How do I feel about what I have read? What can I relate to? What do I have a difficult time understanding? What have I learned? In this way, readers will not only develop their critical thinking skills, but will also lay the groundwork for cross-cultural understanding.

For example, this book presents a poem on African American women and showcases a number of women who live in San Diego who have distinguished themselves in some way or made a contribution to others. Although these particular women might hail from southern California, readers might take it upon themselves to answer the question, who are the women in my locale who have made a difference in my community?

For those readers who are trailblazers or tireless workers in their communities for positive change or social justice, you might consider making yourself available by sitting down and having discussions with others in your community. Young people and elders alike must create more opportunities for dialogue.

This book is an excellent resource to initiate discussions of this type. Whether the topic is sex, sensuality, racism, sexism, homophobia, dating, marriage, children, parenting, the environment, music, dance, art, sculpture, theatre, friendship, government, diversity, cross-cultural unity, health, death, grief, loss, anger, love, values, philosophy or religion—these are all covered in the book. Hopefully, the book will help to initiate many courageous conversations between people of all ages, ethnicities, genders and locales.

The thing that is important in terms of the Study Guide is the same principle involved with GUMBO. It's about using what you possess to feed yourself and others. In the process, you will find you will create a masterful dish and you will have fun in the process.

Finally, for those who have ideas they would like to share or comments they would like to make about the book, feel free visit the website of *The Golden Brown Fairy Godmother* at:

www.alycesmithcooper.com/abfa.html

Study Questions: _____The SALTY Poems

1. Which was your favorite poem in this section? Why?

2. What thoughts came up for you as you read these poems?

3. What feelings came up for you as you read these poems?

4. If you were inspired to do one thing after reading the _Salty Poems,_ what would that be? Why?

5. What's one thing you learned either about yourself, others or the community by reading the poems in this section?

6. What's one thing you already knew or believed, but was affirmed for you by reading the poems in this section?

7. The _Salty Poems_ highlight life experiences having to do especially with sex, sensuality and youth. Which of the _Salty Poems_ reminds you of something you can relate to? Explain.

8. In your opinion, what is the most provocative issue that the _Salty Poems_ raise? Why do you think that?

9. What part of the country do you think the person who is speaking in the poem, _**"Salty"**_ is from? What makes you think that? Do you believe this poem could convey the same thoughts or feelings if written in a different dialect?

10. What do you think the poem _**"Sexy Sally"**_ is about? Why?

11. In the poem, _**"Enter Sobriety"**_ how is this poem a realistic portrayal of drug or alcohol abuse? Of sobriety? Or, what seems unrealistic? Why?

12. What do you believe the poem _**"Fanning That Flame"**_ is about? Why do you think that?

13. Discuss your reactions or your comments regarding the *"Pimp Trilogy"* poems.

14. What do you think the poem *"Reverence to Passion Resurrected"* is about? Why?

15. Discuss your reaction to the *"Sista-Ku Trilogy."*

16. The poem *"Celebrate"* encourages the reader with the line, *"Every chance you get, celebrate."* How do you celebrate? How important are celebrations to you? Do you think young adults celebrate more often than older adults? In what way? What are steps you take to make sure you celebrate safely?

17. In the poem *"My Jeans"* there is a line *"No longer must I hide my true self from myself."* In what ways do we hide from our true selves? What personal experience can you think of where this might have been true for you?

18. In the poem, *"A Sexy Male Moment"* the poet speaks about watching a man as he shaves. What everyday moments in a person's routine have you observed that you might consider sexy? Explain. What do you consider to be the sexiest moments in your daily routine?

Study Questions : _____The BITTER Poems

1. Which was your favorite poem in this section? Why?

2. What thoughts came up for you as you read these poems?

3. What feelings came up for you as you read these poems?

4. If you were inspired to do one thing after reading the *Bitter Poems*, what would that be? Why?

5. What's one thing you learned either about yourself, others or the community by reading the poems in this section?

6. What's one thing you already knew or believed, but was affirmed for you by reading the poems in this section?

7. The *Bitter Poems* highlight life experiences having to do especially with the wake-up calls of life and those who teach us those important early lessons. Which of the *Bitter Poems* reminds you of something you can relate to? Why?

8. In your opinion, what is the most provocative issue that the *Bitter Poems* raise? Why do you think that?

9. In the poem **"Bitter Sweet Savory Season"** it speaks about the different seasons in a person's life. What are the different seasons you have experienced in your life? How are they different? In what season are you currently living?

10. In the poem **"Before Socrates Said It"** the poet speaks about the ancient nation of Kemet. What is the modern name for this nation? Why do you think most western scholars attribute the adage "Know Thyself" to Socrates, rather than to the ancient Kemetic people? What do you think the ancients meant by the axiom, "Know Thyself?" Have you worked toward making this instruction a reality in your own life? If so, how?

531

11. In the poem **"Everybody Listen to African Mother"** each word in the poem begins with a letter that is the first letter of a country on the African continent. How many countries can you name in Africa? What else is this poem about?

12. In the poem **"The N Word is a Dirty Word"** the poet is clearly against the use of the N word. Why? What is the dictionary definition of the N word? How do you feel about this word? Why? How do you feel about the images shown at the bottom of the poem? How do these images relate to the poem?

13. In the poem, **"Survival Gene"** the poet suggests three centuries plus of enslavement have caused African Americans to have the *"genetics of tougher stuff"* due to what they survived. How do you feel about this? What evidence of this have you observed in yourself or in others?

14. Regarding the same poem, **"Survival Gene"** there is a photo above the poem with a picture of Rosa Parks. How would what Rosa Parks did or stood for support or detract from the theory that African Americans have a survival gene?

15. In the poem **"Thomasia"** the poet speaks of her mother as being "soft as cotton yet hard as rocks." In your opinion, is it really possible for a person to be both? In what way? In what ways might you exhibit both of these characteristics?

16. In the poem **"Everything Happens for a Reason"** the poet postulates that there is a purpose for all that happens to us in life. How do you feel about this? What if anything has happened in your life that has convinced you that this is true? Or, do you have a saying that expresses a different belief for yourself?

17. In the poem *"The African American Woman Diaries"* the poet chronicles many different experiences of African American women through the centuries. Which ones were particularly difficult to read about? Which ones made the greatest impression? Which made you the angriest? The most hopeful? What other feelings were generated after reading the poem? What did you learn from the photos and the captions next to the poem? If you could choose one woman whose picture appears with this poem to speak to for inspiration, which one would it be? Why?

18. In the poem *"Orange the New Black"* what do you think the poem is about? What are your thoughts and feelings after reading the poem?

19. In the poem *"Insidious"* what meaning do you extract from the poem? How could you relate this to yourself?

20. The poem *"In Harmony"* speaks about an "Imprint" that *"will never be washed away."* What is something from your own life's experience that has happened to you or made an impression on you that will remain with you forever? Why?

21. In the poem *"I Remember"* the poet speaks about *"The Maafa."* What is "The Maafa?" Given the painful occurrences during the enslavement of Africans in America, why would anyone *want* to remember this tragic time? Do you think the term "Holocaust" is applicable to what happened to Africans in America during enslavement? If so, why? If not, why not?

22. In your opinion, what is the poem *"Code Switch"* about? In what ways do you relate to the messages in the poem? After reading the poem, please explain, what is your gift? How can you move it forward?

23. In the poem *"Lessons"* the poet talks about life being a school. What is one thing you have learned in this school of life? If you were to give yourself a grade on that particular lesson that you learned in the school of life, what would your grade be and why?

24. Regarding the poem *"13 Steps to Survival from a Police Encounter"* which of these steps have you used after being stopped by the police? What other things have you done to keep yourself safe when you are stopped? What if anything do you do to reduce the chances that you will be stopped What else do you do to reduce the odds that the encounter will end badly?

25. In the poem *"That Much Stronger"* the photo and caption show an African American man re-enacting a Buffalo Soldier. Who were the Buffalo Soldiers? How did they acquire that name? Given the genocide that was perpetrated against the Native American Indians in this country, do you think it is appropriate to celebrate or honor the Buffalo Soldier? If so, why? If not, why not? What other circumstances in history have there been when colonizers (or those in power) have used marginalized groups against each other to achieve the colonizer's aims? How does this particular photo relate to the poem? What experiences have made you stronger in your life?

Study Questions: _____The SPICY Poems

1. Which was your favorite poem in this section? Why?

2. What thoughts came up for you as you read these poems?

3. What feelings came up for you as you read these poems?

4. If you were inspired to do one thing after reading the *Spicy Poems* what would that be? Why?

5. What's one thing you learned either about yourself, others or the community by reading the poems in this section?

6. What's one thing you already knew or believed, but was affirmed for you by reading the poems in this section?

7. The *Spicy Poems* highlight life experiences having to do especially with nature, food, health, animals, music, art, talents and abilities, i.e., things, which add spice to life. Which of the *Spicy Poems* reminds you of something you can relate to? Explain.

8. In your opinion, what is the most provocative issue that the *Spicy Poems* raise? Why do you think that?

9. What are the things that the poet mentions in "**Welcome to San Diego"** that you feel are the most attractive things about the city? If you live in San Diego, have you seen all the things the poet speaks about? If not, why not? If you have, what is your favorite thing to do in the city or your favorite attraction? If you do not live in San Diego, and have visited, what was your favorite thing to do while you were here? If you have not visited, would you like to? Why? San Diego has been called, *America's Finest City*? What are your thoughts about this?

10. The poem, *"The Catfish Club,"* speaks about a place where people gather to discuss social and/or political issues affecting the community. Who are some of the people you might expect to see gathering there? Are there other places in your community where you see these types of discussions taking place? If so, where? What do you think you could learn from visiting a place like The Catfish Club? What value could your presence bring to discussions there?

11. What is the theme of the poem *"Ancestral Conversations on Canvas?"* What illustrations have you seen by the brilliant artist, Kadir Nelson? What is it about his work that helps you to recognize his drawings before you even see his name?

12. In the poem, *"Spirit Speak,"* whom is the poet addressing? The photograph next to the poem shows the talented sculptor, Manuelita Brown. Why do you think she sculpts? Of the two pieces of her work that are shown adjacent to the poem, which is your favorite? Why? Why are sculptures important to society?

13. In your opinion, what is the poem *"Cruzin to Santana Beat"* about? How does the poet create visual, kinesthetic and auditory interest with her words?

14. The poem, *"These My Brothers Be"* shows a photo of two men, one white and one Black. What do you think the poet is saying through her poem about her relationship with each of them? Some people believe that all men are brothers regardless of ethnicity. What do you think? Do you have friends of a different ethnicity or culture than yours? Do you consider them close enough to be considered your brother or sister? Please explain why you do or why you do not.

15. What is the author relating to GUMBO in the poem *"California Human Gumbo*?" Why?

16. What are the philosophical issues the author touches on in the poem, "*Coffee and Danish*?" What are your opinions on these issues?

17. What is the poem "*Of Morality*" about? What are your thoughts on the poem? What personal experiences have you had, if any, that you can relate in some way to this poem?

18. In the poem "*One World*," the poet describes a place called the *Worldbeat Center* in San Diego. Based on the description in the poem, what would be the most interesting thing for you about the Worldbeat Center? What if any similarities are there between this place and the Catfish Club? Do you think there is an age difference between people who frequent each place? Why? Does your community have such a place? Why are these places important to a community? Or are they? What are your thoughts?

19. The poem "*Rhythm and Drum*" speaks of a drum and dance troupe in San Diego called *Teye Sa Thiosanne West African Drum and Dance Troupe.* In African history, why is the drum so significant? Why do you think groups like this are important to a community? How can members of the community be supportive?

20. In the poem, "*We Got Talent*," the poet speaks about community theatrical performances. Why is community theatre important? Have you ever been to a theatrical production in your community? Why or why not? If you *have* attended a dramatic performance before, how did you feel afterwards? What is the difference between a

community theatre production and a theatrical production supported by a college, a university or a local city arts council? Are you aware that community theatres usually give discounts to students? How can members of the community support community theatre?

21. What is the poet speaking about in the *"Sista' Ku: Tamayta Haytahs"* poem? What kind of *"Haytahs"* have you experienced in your life? What if anything are these individuals missing?

22. The poem *"Once Upon a Time"* seeks to honor writers and poets. Were you aware of the *African American Writers and Artists Association* or the *Black Storytellers Association*? How are these organizations important to a community? How can members of the community be supportive of these organizations?

23. The poem *"Corn Mother Goddess"* was dedicated to Native Americans and to all who are stewards of the earth. In your opinion, what is the most important advice that Corn Mother gives to the reader? What part of her advice do you personally adhere to in your own life? Why? The photo next to the poem shows a Native American woman. What do you know of the history and the present condition of Native Americans in this country? Are there Native Americans in your family ancestry? What has this lineage taught you? What conflicts are there, if any, for Black Indians? In what ways are you a steward of the earth? Do you think it's important for all of us to be stewards of the earth? Why? What are some ways you do this?

24. Who are the children spoken about in the poem, *"Rainbow Children of Indigo Hue?"* What is the message the author of the poem has for these children? Why is this message important?

25. What were feelings you had after reading the poem, "**Ant**?" What philosophical issues do you think are raised in the poem? Please explain. How might you relate this poem to your own experience?

26. How is transformation illustrated in the poem, "**Name That Tune**?" Give an example of how you transformed an emotion like fear or uncertainty into other feelings like self-assurance or pride? How did you accomplish this?

27. What is the poem "**Ongoing Prophecy**" about? What are your opinions about the so-called "last days" of earth or what some refer to as "doomsday?" Is the foundation of your perspective based more on scientific theories or scriptural writings? How does the poem allude to these issues? What are your thoughts?

28. What do you think is the main purpose behind the poem, "**Telling Our Stories**?" How is the word "stories" being used metaphorically in this poem? What does history have to do with this poem? What are the different ways mentioned in the poem that stories can be told? The poem illustrates photos of two different young men. Each has chosen to tell his story in different ways. Still, are there similarities in the stories each is telling? If you were to tell your story, in which way would you choose to tell it? Why? Why is it important for you to tell your story? How will the telling of your story affect you? Your family? Your community? The world? Is each of us responsible for telling the stories of our elders? Why or why not?

29. In the poem, "**My Creativity**," the poet speaks about creativity expressed through writing. How do you express your creativity? How do you feel when you express yourself in this way? Did you know that Creativity is one of the seven values in the *Black Value System (the Nguzo*

Saba) and the theme for the sixth day of *Kwanzaa*, an African American cultural celebration? What is the Kiswahili word for Creativity, which is celebrated during Kwanzaa?

30. The poem, "*I'll Take Laughter for Dessert*," takes an interesting view of laughter by relating it to a sweet dessert. When have you laughed so hard you actually felt full afterwards? How is laughter healing? Are you aware that there is research, which supports the theory that laughter is healing both physically and mentally? When in your life did you experience laughter as healing?

31. What is the main theme of the poem, '*What's the News*?" How do you stay abreast of news in your local community? In the nation? In the world? Is it important to stay aware of what's going on? Why or why not? The caption under the photo makes mention of a local San Diego newspaper called *The Voice & Viewpoint*, which chronicles news of particular interest to the African American community. If you live in San Diego how often do you read this newspaper? If you are not from San Diego, does your community have a similar publication? Why might it be important to support it?

32. In "*The Business of Building*," the poet speaks about building construction. How might a building contractor be compared to a politician? Or to an educator? Or a poet? How important is a building contractor to a community? Did you know that there was a Black Contractor's Association in San Diego? If you are not from San Diego is there a Black Contractor's Association in your city? If people are all the same, why do you think the Black Contractor's Association exists? Is such an association important in the community? Why or why not?

33. How do you think you would feel if you recited the statements in the poem *"Affirmations for Healing"* every morning out loud before you began your day? What affirmations do you currently say each day? Why? What relationship, if any, do you see between affirmations and the poem, *"The Marriage of Thought and Speech"* in the Savory section of this book? Explain.

34. The poem, *"The Importance of Health"* speaks about aging, among other things. How important is health to you? What are some of the things you are doing that are supportive of your health and wellbeing? How do you envision your life will be as you age? What are you doing now to take personal responsibility for your optimal health and wellbeing now and as you age?

35. The poem *"Moon"* speaks about appreciating godlike qualities in others. What have you seen in the actions or on the countenance of someone you know that inspires you to the point where you might say it is godlike? How has this affected you?

36. How do *The Spicy Poems* promote using our talents and creativity in socially responsible ways?

37. How do *The Spicy Poems* honor animals?

38. How do *The Spicy Poems* encourage us to support our communities in socially responsible ways?

39. What have you learned from *The Spicy Poems*? How will you use that learning in your life? How will you share what you have learned with others?

Study Questions: _____The SWEET Poems

1. Which was your favorite poem in this section? Why?

2. What thoughts came up for you as you read these poems?

3. What feelings came up for you as you read these poems?

4. If you were inspired to do one thing after reading the *Sweet Poems*, what would that be? Why?

5. What's one thing you learned either about yourself, others or the community by reading the poems in this section?

6. What's one thing you already knew or believed, but was affirmed for you by reading the poems in this section?

7. The *Sweet Poems* highlight life experiences having to do especially with idealized love, marriage, babies, children and family. Which poem reminds you of something you can relate to? Explain.

8. In your opinion, what is the most provocative issue that the *Sweet Poems* raise? Why?

9. In "***Putting Away Toys***" the poet uses a creative game to make putting away toys fun. How important is it for parents to be creative in their parenting? What other creative ideas might help teach children and make parenting a bit easier?

10. In "***Just Pretending***," the poet talks about a child pretending. How is pretending healthy for children? How might it be unhealthy? What did you like to pretend as a child? When did you begin to differentiate between fantasy and reality? How did you feel about that? As an adult do you believe that reality can be as much or more fun than fantasy? In what ways?

11. After reading the poem, "***Address to Happiness***," please explain how stable or elusive happiness seems to you in your life and why? In your opinion are you happy because of things external to you? Or, is your happiness based more on an internal state of being? Explain.

12. The poem "***Families***" is shown with photographs of two different families. One might be considered traditional and the other untraditional? Which photo represents which? How do you feel about traditional families? How do you feel about untraditional families? What is your definition of family? Was your family of origin *(i.e. the family where you spent the greater part of your formative years)* traditional or untraditional? Explain. Do you think society is accepting on the whole or unaccepting of untraditional families? Does the composition of a family really matter, or is the fact that a family is a unit, which cares about and supports each other more important? Some people grow up in more than one family. How have your experiences growing up in your family or families shaped your definition of families? How was your family responsive or unresponsive to your needs as you were growing up? If you have a new family or family of your own now, how is that family different or similar to your family of origin? What is one need you have that your family fulfills? What is one commitment you have made to your family?

13. What are some of the ways you can relate to the poem, "***Fashion Valley Mall***?" Regardless of where you live, do you believe malls have become social gathering places for individuals in a community? How so? What do you like or dislike about malls personally?

14. In the poem, "***Oh Life Before All Worlds***", to what is the poet referring when she says *"Oh Life before all worlds?"* How do you arrive at that conclusion?

543

15. After reading the poem, *"GBFG's Rap for Children,"* who do you believe yourself to be? Why?

16. In the poem, *"Love Tested*," the poet speaks about love. What are thoughts or feelings that came up for you as you read this poem? What might be a good quote from this poem, which you could use in your life? Why?

17. In the poem, *"Love Absolutely,"* the poet has a line that speaks about trading in fear for love. When in your life have you been able to do this? Or, when would you have liked to have traded fear for love?

18. In *"Soothing Coos*," who is being welcomed and spoken about? What language does the poet use in the poem, which speaks to the presence of a baby? Why do people coo and speak in silly syllables to a baby? How do you feel about that?

19. What are your thoughts after having read the poem, *"Every Woman – Not*?" Please explain. What women in your life are brought to mind after reading this poem. Why?

20. What can you relate to in the poem *"On Putting the Baby to Bed*?" Why? How is the person who is putting the baby to bed being smart? What other ways are there to put the baby to bed? What do you think is the best way? Why?

21. After reading the poem, *"Extended Family*," what is your definition of an extended family? If you have an extended family, what is your extended family like? Are they all related to you by blood? Or, have you expanded your extended family to include others? How? How do you contribute to the successful functioning of your extended family? What additional commitments could you make?

22. After reading the poem, "**Getting Married on Saturday**," what do you think the poet's opinion is about marriage? What do you think about marriage and the reasons why people get married? What are some things you believe people should know about themselves and their partners before they get married? What do you think is important for a marriage to be successful? Why?

23. What makes the ladies classy in the poem, **Classy Ladies**? What is your definition of a classy lady? Who are classy ladies in your life? What about them convinced you of this?

24. In the poem **"Your Own Self's Valentine"** what are ways you let yourself know how important you are to yourself?

25. What do you think the poem "**Mirror-Mirror**" is about? As you look at yourself critically in terms of the type of person you are and the character traits you have, how pleased are you with what you see? If you are not pleased, why aren't you? How is your view of yourself the same or different from what you believe other people see in you? What are you doing to make certain that what you are thinking, speaking and doing is consistent with the image you have of yourself? What are you doing to ensure that others treat you commensurately with how you see yourself?

26. What do you think the poem "**Extra Crispy – Extra Chunky**" is about? What traits do you have that you like about yourself that others may not like? What feeling does that bring up for you? How does this poem inspire you to think more positively about yourself or others?

27. In the poem, "**Love is Thicker than Blood**," the poet's premise is counter to the adage, "*Blood is Thicker Than Water*." How do you feel about this? Which of these attitudes is closer to what you believe or how you feel?

545

28. There is a supposition behind the poem, *"If I Call You,"* that we can empower ourselves to create our own families. How do you feel about that? In what ways have you already done this in your own life?

29. The poem *"Dating"* describes one view of a dating experience. How is this similar to or different from your own experiences in dating? If it is different, why do you believe it is different? What in your opinion would be an ideal dating experience? Why?

30. What thoughts or feelings did you have after reading the poem, *"Promise, Promised He*?" Where in the poem are the characters being serious? Where are they being humorous? How are these two attitudes and feeling states mixed during their conversation? What draws you into the characters world? How might you relate the poem to your own experience?

31. After reading *The Sweet Poems*, what have you learned about yourself or others? How are you planning to share what you have learned?

32. After reading *The Sweet Poems*, how important do you think idealized love, dating, families, children and parenting are to the wellbeing of a community? What do you think our greatest challenges are in these regards?

33. How have *The Sweet Poems* inspired you to think differently?

34. After reading *The Sweet Poems,* if you were to write a poem within this same scope of topics, what would the title be? Why?

Study Questions: _____The SOUR Poems

1. Which was your favorite poem in this section? Why?

2. What thoughts came up for you as you read these poems?

3. What feelings came up for you as you read these poems?

4. If you were inspired to do one thing after reading the *Sour Poems*, what would that be? Why?

5. What's one thing you learned either about yourself, others or the community by reading the poems in this section?

6. What's one thing you already knew or believed, but was affirmed for you by reading the poems in this section?

7. The *Sour Poems* highlight life experiences having to do especially with death, dying, grief, loss and fear. Which poem in this section speaks the most to something you can relate to? Why?

8. In your opinion, what is the most provocative issue that the *Sour Poems* raise? Why do you think that?

9. In the poem "**Sour**," the poet likens the taste of sour to death. What similarities or differences do you see as you compare the two?

10. In the poem, "**Grieving**," the poet speaks of looking to the comfort of today as a way to get through grieving. How do you feel this might be a viable option for someone who is going through a grief experience? How might it be difficult? What personal experience have you had with grief or loss where you have used this idea to assist you in getting through the experience?

11. The poem, *"Miss You,"* is about the loss of a dear friend. Have you had to deal with the loss of a friend to death? How did remembering that person's character or personality help you get through the loss? How did this remembering make the grieving process worse? If that person were able to give you once piece of advice today to help you in your grieving, what do you think it would it be?

12. The poem, *"Fear Factor"* takes the reader through a number of emotions, which for many people are connected to fear. Think of a time in your life when you may have experienced fear, even if you were worried about someone else's wellbeing. Which of the emotions revealed in the poem resonated most with you? In your opinion, how does fear hamper our progress? How can it be a motivator?

13. In the poem, *"In the Face of My Pain,"* the poet speaks of the audacity of the sun shining. Why did the author feel this way? Have you ever felt a bit upset when you were in pain, and others were feeling fantastic? Explain.

14. In the poem, *"There's a Peace,"* the poet speaks about a peace within. In your opinion, do you think it is possible for a person to find peace during a period in their life when they are grieving? And if so, how? What personal experience do you have that might shed light on this?

15. In the poem, *"Opportunity Knocking,"* the poet gives a reason for difficulties in life. What is that reason? What opportunities have come out of difficulties in your life?

16. *"For My Brother, Kelly,"* is a poem about the loss of a family member. The poet remembers things about her brother. Have you lost a family member or close friend before? If so, in what ways have you kept that person's memory alive? How has this helped with your grieving?

17. What is the theme that runs through the poem, "**A Melancholy Poem for All Seasons**?" What are feelings the poem brings up for you? Other than death, what are other common causes for sadness? Which of these have you experienced? How have you or how are you dealing with it?

18. In the poem, "**Journey**," what is the main mood expressed in the poem? What parts of the poem, if any, can you relate to? How?

19. In the poem, "**Mind Gumbo: Sorrow's Baby**," the poet writes about her great granddaughter. What type of sorrow is the poet speaking about in the poem? What parts of the poem, if any, can you relate to? Why?

20. In the poem, "**Still in Death**," the author mentions, *"the darkness lingering in the midst of the night never releases its hold from the earth completely."* What do you think the author meant by this statement? What are your thoughts or feelings about this?

21. What do you think the poet meant when she wrote *"and make of roses liars"* in the poem "**Mourning Clothes**?" What does this line have to do with grief?

22. In the poem, "**Killer Fear**," the poet speaks about the emotion of fear. Why do you suppose she calls fear a killer? What thoughts or feelings do you have about this?

23. How do you think the poet arrived at the name for the poem "**Black Psalm**?" Do you think by the author choosing to write the poem in dialect that it added to or detracted from the poem? What feelings or thoughts do you have about this poem?

24. What do you think is the theme of the poem, *"Pine Swept Moss?"* Have you ever lost a loved one, not due to death, but to a break-up? How did you feel? Do you think a break-up or a divorce is in some ways like a death? If so, in what ways?

25. Please discuss your thoughts about the poem *"Renewal."* In what ways have you shed your old behaviors or attitudes and experienced a sense of renewal? What precipitated this shift?

26. Please answer the questions raised in the poem, *"Have You."* What were the circumstances? How do you feel now, looking back at those times and situations?

27. In the poem, *"The Other Side,"* what is the poet speaking about? What are your thoughts and feelings about an afterlife? How did you come to arrive at this conclusion?

28. The poem, *"Maryam,"* is about a wonderful and enterprising immigrant woman who was selfless in her service to the community. Who do you know in your community who is committed to community service and tireless in their efforts to help others? How have you let that person know you appreciate him or her?

29. *"Treasure Chest"* is a poem about savoring the memories of a loved one who has passed. Do you have such a treasure chest of memories for someone who has transitioned? What did the poet mean by calling herself *"a wealthy pauper"* at the end of the poem?

30. After reading *The Sour Poems* what have you recognized about death, transition, fear, loss or grief? What if anything could you do to help others or ease your own grief by virtue of what you have learned?

Study Questions: _____The SAVORY Poems

1. Which was your favorite poem in this section? Why?

2. What thoughts came up for you as you read these poems?

3. What feelings came up for you as you read these poems?

4. If you were inspired to do one thing after reading the poems in this section, what would that be? Why?

5. What's one thing you learned either about yourself, others or the community by reading the poems in this section?

6. What's one thing you already knew or believed, but was affirmed for you by reading the poems in this section?

7. The *Savory Poems* highlight life experiences having to do especially with wisdom, philosophy, elders, friendships, values and the insightful lessons we often don't learn until our later years. Which poem in this section speaks the most to an experience you can relate to? Why?

8. In your opinion, what is the most provocative issue that the *Savory Poems* raise? Why do you think that?

9. In, "**Kwanzaa at the Butcher's Home**," the poet speaks of one family's Kwanzaa celebration. What is Kwanzaa? Have you ever celebrated it? Do you know of anyone who has? What do you think about how Kwanzaa is celebrated at the Butcher's home? What aspect of the celebration do you think would be most meaningful to you? Why?

10. In the poem, "**Since Second Grade**," the poet speaks about a long-term friendship. In reading about it, what about this friendship did you admire? What is the longest friendship you have had? What keeps your friendship alive?

551

11. In the poem, "*I am Up*," what is the poet speaking about? Is there more than one meaning to being "Up"? If so, what is it and what personal associations do you have to the poem's title?

12. In the poem, "*Courage*," the poet likens courage to that of the lion. What is your definition of courage? When if ever have you had to demonstrate courage in your life? The photo next to this poem identifies a man who teaches *Capoeira*. What do you know about this practice? How might it be related to courage?

13. After reading the poem, "*Unity*," how do you define unity? UMOJA is the Kiswahili word for unity. In what context have you heard this word before? What relationship does it have to the Black Value System or to the Kwanzaa cultural celebration? How important is unity to you?

14. In the poem, "*When the Going Gets Tough*," the poet speaks of what she does under pressure; what do you do when the going gets tough?

15. The poem, "*My Sistahs*," is one honoring the poet's relationship with her close women friends. What did you like about this poem? What could you relate to? What did you have difficulty relating to in the poem?

16. In the poem, "*Testing*," the poet asks the reader to put their thoughts, words and deeds to a test. What is this request designed to determine? Have you ever put your thoughts, words and deeds to this type of test? If you have, what was the result? If you have not, why not?

17. In the poem, "*To Educate*," the poet mentions two requisites in order for a teacher to be able to teach. What are they? What do you think about this? Think about the

552

best teachers you have had in your life, in what ways have they met these two criteria?

18. In the poem, "*I am a Recovering Hypocrite*," the poet speaks about *"finger-pointing"* and how we are often guilty of the same things for which we criticize others. Think about the last time you criticized or judged someone else; in what ways have you done something similar to what you had found fault in them? How will knowing this change your behavior?

19. In the poem, "*Purpose*," the poet likens finding ones purpose to painting a picture. In your opinion, what is the relationship between these two things? How did you go about finding your purpose in this life? If you have not yet discovered your purpose, how are you working on its discovery?

20. In the poem, "*A Thousand Tomorrows,*" the poet speaks about *"missed moments"* as being causative of *"tomorrow's woes."* What do you think about this?

21. What is the cautionary note the poet makes apparent in her poem, "*I Wish I Were You*?" Have you ever wished you were someone else? Why? What are some things you may not have considered you would have to deal with if you really *were* that person? Alternatively, what are some of the blessings you have realized you have because you are you?

22. What is the theme of the poem, "*The Marriage of Thought and Speech*?" How has the poet used personification in this poem? Describe how your last achievement came to be as a result of your own thoughts, your speech and your actions. How did you nurture your dreams or visions into reality? Do you think this really works? Or is this fantasy?

23. After reading the poem, "**Trust**," how many of the things mentioned in the poem do you trust in your life? What are things you trust the most in your life? Why is trust important to you?

24. What do you most relate to in the poem, "**The Internal House Voice Calls?**" How and why?

25. What is the poet speaking about in the poem, "**Which Original**?" Have you ever felt as if you needed to clone yourself to get done everything you need to get done? How do you think it might be possible to do this mentally?

26. In your opinion, what is the theme of the poem, "**Wise Enough**?" In what way can you relate any of the poem to your own life?

27. In the poem, "**Black Psychology**," the poet summarizes the origin of the Association of Black Psychologists. Do you feel there is a need for a separate association for Black psychologists? If so, why? If not, why not? What benefits if any, do you think might accrue to the African American community from such an association?

28. In the poem, "**America's Next Top**," what did you initially believe the author was writing about? Were you surprised at the end of the poem? How did you feel? What thoughts or feelings did you have after reading the poem? Generally speaking, do you think that models are demeaned and/or valued only for their looks? How realistic is it to expect that the people of the United States will elect a woman to the office of President of the United States? What is your personal opinion about how well a woman would function in that office? Do you think it is time for women to be on par with men in leadership positions both in government and private sector? Why or why not?

29. In the poem, *"Roll Call,"* the poet honors a number of individuals who are not mentioned elsewhere in this book for their community contributions. What was surprising about the listing? What was empowering about the listing? After reading *Roll Call*, who would you be interested in learning more about? Why? Who do you know of in the African American Community in San Diego who should have been listed, in your opinion? Why? If you are not from San Diego, what role models have been most influential in your area? What would you like to see written about you and your community contributions someday?

30. In *"Truth, Justice and Righteousness,"* the poet speaks about the principle of MAAT. What is the principle of MAAT? What are the origins of this principle? How might you relate this principle to your own life?

31. In the poem *"Ujamaa,"* what is the poet speaking about? Where does the term Ujamaa come from? How important do you think it is to your life? Do you think African Americans have a more difficult time operationalizing this principle than do others? If so, why? If not, why not? How important do you think it is to the success of a community?

32. After reading the poem, *"Respect,"* how would you define this concept? Who are those in your life for whom you have the most respect? Why? How do you demonstrate your respect for them? How important is it to show respect for people you don't know? How might you show respect for them? If you don't think it is important, why not?

33. What is the poet speaking about in the poem, *"Outdistanced by a Dream*?" The photo adjacent to this poem is the author in Cuba. What do you know about Cuba? What is an embargo? How did the U.S. come to place an embargo on interactions with Cuba? What do you

think about President Obama's efforts toward lifting the embargo that the U. S. currently has against Cuba? How would things change for Americans if the embargo was lifted? How would things change for Cubans?

34. The *"God and Allah"* poems are in five parts and chronicle different figurative interactions between God and Allah, if they were actually separate deities and actually walked the earth. What is your first impression of the God and Allah poems? What did you think? How did you feel? After reading all of the poems in the series, what were your thoughts and feelings? Do you think the poet used humor well in these poems or do you think the poet was inappropriate? Do you think the poems are insensitive to Muslims and/or Christians? If so, in what way do you feel they are insensitive? In your opinion, what do you think the poet's intention was in writing these poems? What if anything might a reader learn from reading the *"God and Allah"* poems? What did you learn from reading the photo captions, which are adjacent to the poems?

35. What is the realization the poet seems to come to at the end of the poem, *"When My Beauty Fades*?" What would you like your life to be like as you grow older?

36. In the poem, *"Gathering of the Women Who Write,"* what is the most appealing part of the poem to you? The most inspiring?

37. In the poem, *"Love Holds a Spot for You*," what is the poet's view of how love operates? What feelings do you have after reading this poem?

38. In the poem *"Close to Excellent,"* the poet describes her answer to the question of how she is doing. What is your pat answer to that question? What is the relationship, if

any, between how we feel and our service to others?

39. After reading the poem, *"Be Thankful,"* for what would you say you are most thankful?

40. In the poem, *"Do It Today,"* the poet compares the time or opportunities we have to take action to different forms of money. In what ways have you procrastinated in your life? If you were to take the advice given in the poem, what are some things you could do to overcome your procrastination?

41. After reading the poem, *"Life Issues,"* what thoughts might you have about your end of life issues? If you are not able to speak about it, why not? How were matters of this type dealt with in your family of origin?

42. After reading the poem, *"Sassy Old Lady,"* what women in your life might meet the description of the lady in the poem? In what way is the person you know similar to the poem's description? What do you like about the woman described in the poem?

43. The poem, *"Harvest What you Say,"* is about the power of speech to create our destiny. How have you seen this play out in your own life? How can you use this power to your advantage?

44. After reading the poem, *"The Magical Life,"* who do you know who seems to fit with the philosophy espoused in the poem? How similar or different do the descriptions in the poem fit with your own life? Discuss.

45. After reading, *"Erasing Isms,"* what are your thoughts and feelings? What kind of *"ism"* may have been omitted? What experiences have you had in your life, which may have underscored for you the importance of the message in this poem?

46. In the poem, *"Community: It takes a Crew,"* the poet speaks about a community. How do you define community? What do you consider to be your community? Why? How do you contribute to your community?

47. After reading the poem, *"Passage Rites,"* what thoughts or feelings do you have about the importance of rites of passage programs for children? What do you think are the main purposes of these programs?

48. The poem, *"There is a Place,"* was written about a figurative place within. What are your thoughts about whether or not there is a place within of calm and peace? What have been some experiences you may have had concerning such a place?

49. In the poem *"Grandmother Africa"* what part of this poem speaks most loudly to you? Why?

50. The poem *"Black Women: We Can Do Anything"* chronicles the life of Black women as a composite group over time. In what ways can you relate to this poem? In what ways is it difficult for you to connect to the poem?

51. The *"Our Elders"* poem, underscores the value of our elders. At the end of the poem, it mentions Black Lives Matter. How did this slogan get started? What meaning does this phrase have for you personally?

52. In the poem *"The Real Story"* the poet speaks about end of

life issues. Why do many people shy away from speaking about these matters? What would you want to have done for you when you transition? In other words, what would be your last requests?

53. The poem "**Maya Angelou: Wisdom Weaver"** was written in honor of the late, world-renowned poet, Maya Angelou. What have you learned about Maya Angelou after reading the poem? Which of her poems can you see referenced in this poem?

54. The poem "**Oprah, You Started Something Big"** was written to honor the famous talk show hostess and first African American woman billionaire, Oprah Winfrey. What was your favorite or most memorable episode of the Oprah Winfrey show? Why? Which part of the poem seemed most descriptive of who you know Oprah to be?

55. The poem, "**Mr. President Obama"** was written to honor President Barack Obama. What is one thing for which you would like to honor the president? Why?

56. After reading *The Savory Poems*, what have you learned about yourself or others? How are you planning to share what you have learned?

57. After reading *The Savory Poems*, how important do you think friendship, positive traits of character, wisdom and role models are to the wellbeing of a community? What do you think our greatest challenges are in these regards?

58. How have *The Savory Poems* been inspirational to you?

59. After reading *The Savory Poems,* if you were to write a poem within this same scope of topics, what would the title be? Why?

Study Questions _____Poems SPIRITUALLY SEASONED

1. Which was your favorite poem in this section? Why?

2. What thoughts came up for you as you read these poems?

3. What feelings came up for you as you read these poems?

4. If you were inspired to do one thing after reading the poems in this section, what would that be? Why?

5. What's one thing you learned either about yourself, others or the community by reading the poems in this section?

6. What's one thing you already knew or believed, but was affirmed for you by reading the poems in this section?

7. The *Poems Spiritually Seasoned* highlight life experiences having to do especially with the belief in or experience of God or a higher power and all that which we might refer to as spiritual or divine. Which poem in this section speaks the most to something you can relate to? Why?

8. In your opinion, what is the most provocative issue that the *Poems Spiritually Seasoned* raises? Why do you think that?

9. In the poem, "**Salvation**," the poet gives three steps to salvation. What is your definition? How important is this to you? Discuss from different religious perspectives.

10. In the poem, "***The Question,***" the poet chronicles questions a little girl has asked about her life, existence and God. What questions have you had about these things? What answers have you found? How did you find the answers?

11. In the poem, "**Wear your Crown**," the authors speak about qualities they believe we are all given. How do you feel about this? Do you feel as if you have been given qualities fit for a crown? If so, what are those qualities? How are you letting your best qualities shine in your life, regardless of what religion you might practice or even if you don't practice a religion at all?

12. The poem, "**Gratitude**," describes many things the poet has to be grateful for. What are you most grateful for in your life? Why? What are other thoughts and feelings you had after reading this poem?

13. In the poem, "**A Metronome of Grace**," the poet speaks about life as being a flowing, rhythmic and *grace-full* experience. When is your life most calm, flowing and peaceful? What do you do to ensure you are experiencing a graceful flow in your life?

14. In the poem, "**Evening Prayer**," the poet, speaks directly to a higher power. Have you ever created your own prayer? If so, was it a prayer asking for something, or for something to happen in your life or the life of someone else? Was it a prayer of gratitude? If you pray, what motivates your prayers most of the time? If you don't pray, what else do you do to feel a connection with a higher power, or even your own self?

15. In the poem, "**Don't Know What to Do**," the poet speaks about indecision and what to do about it. When have you had difficulty making a decision? What did you do to finally decide?

16. What is the poem "**Get Some for Yourself**" about? How can you relate this poem to your life?

17. The poem "**Bold Believers**," speaks about recognizing ones blessings and positioning one's self for receiving more. What are some of your beliefs about this? What if anything do you believe to be your blessings? How do you celebrate the blessings you have been given? What do you do to position yourself to receive greater abundance?

18. In the poem, "**My Earth; My Sky**," the poet uses an analogy of the earth and sky for her relationship with her creator. What parts of this poem can you relate to? Why?

19. What music is the poet speaking about in the poem, "**This Music**?" How do you know? Do you believe there is a music or harmony within? How do you come to that conclusion?

20. What is the poem, "**Holy Fire**," about? What experiences have you had that relate to something in this poem?

21. In your opinion, what is theme of the poem, "**Houseguest**?" When, if ever, have you felt like a guest in your own body? Explain.

22. In your opinion, what is the poem, "**It's Not Over**," about? Discuss a time in your life when you thought things were over or at a low point and then you were pleasantly surprised by something good.

23. What is the poem, "**The Beatific Vision**," about? How can you relate this poem to your life?

24. The poem, "**We Got the Power**," speaks about the power to change things. How powerful do you feel in your life? Why? If you don't feel powerful, what does the poem suggest might put you more in touch with your power? How willing are you to operationalize power in your own life?

563

25. What is the poem **"Bubbling Vessels"** about? How can you relate this poem to your life?

26. In your opinion, what is the poem, **"On Winning the Race,"** about? How is this poem relevant to your life?

27. After reading the poem **"Prayer, Patience and Persistence"** which of these practices have you found most useful in your life? Why?

28. Regardless of your religion, religious experience or belief system, what is the most inspirational thought or feeling that has been affirmed for you after reading the poems in this section?

If you are using this book in teaching a class, particularly a college or university course, there are several different ways that the study questions might be used. The following are a few examples as to how you might use the study questions to engage the students in your class:

➢ For an assignment, which might span several weeks, and depending on the topic of your class, you may wish to zero in on one particular section of the book, e.g. *the Salty Poems,* especially for classes involving youth or sexuality. Alternatively, have each individual student in your class select one poem from the *Bitter* section to serve as a foundation for a research paper. If there are study questions listed for the poem he or she selects, the student could be required to write a shorter opinion paper rather than a research paper. If there are no study questions provided for that poem, each student could be required to write his or her own question for that poem, which he or she would address in the paper.

➢ For an assignment of 2 - 3 weeks, you could select a particular section of the book, e.g., *the Bitter Poems,* especially for classes involving history, politics, sociology or philosophy. Divide the class into small groups and have each group select a poem about which to plan a group presentation.

➢ For an in-class assignment, you may wish to zero in on one particular section of the book, e.g., *the Spicy Poems,* especially for classes involving food, animals, nature, anthropology, literature, art, music, drama, history, psychology, or sociology. Divide the students in your class into groups of about 4 or 5 students each. Have each small group of students select one poem from that section for a discussion during that class session. Have students discuss that particular poem using the study questions that have been provided, their own questions or questions you develop yourself as a basis for their discussions. Have one person designated by each group as a spokesperson for that group to summarize their discussion once the larger group reconvenes.

➢ For another in-class assignment, have each student in your class turn to a pre-selected poem in a particular section of the book, e.g., *the Sweet Poems,* perhaps for classes involving psychology, sociology, child development, childcare, families and relationships. Have each student read the poem silently. Then, have each student jot down reactions to the poem, including thoughts, feelings, opinions, how they relate or do not relate to the poem and any question or controversial issue that they believe the poem raises. Discuss in small groups.

➢ Assign the reading of one of *the Sour Poems* as a prelude to discussion regarding loss, especially in classes having to do with psychology, counseling, gerontology, death and dying. Allow students time to write their thoughts in journals and/or discuss their feelings in small groups.

➢ Assign the reading of one of the poems from a particular section of the book, e.g., *the Savory Poems,* especially for classes in psychology, sociology, social work, literature, English, speech, history, political science, religion or philosophy. Award extra credit to an individual or a group for memorizing and reciting the poem for the class and sharing their reaction. For a group presentation, students may divide up stanzas of the poem, each taking one or two stanzas to memorize and recite. Alternatively, you may allow students to each choose his or her own poem to memorize, recite before the class and give their interpretation.

➢ Have students with contrasting opinions on one of the poems i.e., in *Poems Spiritually Seasoned* to debate a particular issue raised in the poem. Have students set their own ground rules for discussions concerning religion to ensure everyone's belief system is respected. Have student brainstorm ways in which mutual respect for religion might be achieved in our larger society.

➢ Award extra credit to students who visit and write a short paper on one of the local *(San Diego)* resources mentioned in this book, e.g., the *Casa Del Rey Moro Museum* in Old Town, the *World Beat Center* in Balboa Park or the *Malcolm X Library*. If in a different city, award extra credit to students who visit similar places in your city. If no similar resources exist, have students write a paper on why they think their city does *not* have a similar resource, what benefits might be gained if there was a resource of that type and what it would take to develop and implement such a resource in that city.

➢ Award extra credit to students who interview and write a short paper on one of the individuals mentioned in this book. If in a city other than San Diego, students may interview individuals who have made similar contributions to his or her own community.

➢ Instructors of English, creative writing, literature and/or speech may also review one or more of the poems in any of the sections of the book to illustrate a particular writing style or technique. The poems in the book may be compared or contrasted with one another, or with other works of literature the class is studying.

➢ Have students create their own poems reflecting their feelings or thoughts after reading a poem of a certain theme. Have students share their poems and discuss.

➢ Even for students who believe they cannot write they often surprise themselves by writing deeply and profoundly if given a time limit for an impromptu creative writing assignment. For example, using the *3-Minute Poem Technique*, set a timer and allow students 3 minutes only to write down their thoughts or feelings about whatever the theme is. Their writing can be a poem or just their thoughts. Amazingly, if students have 3 minutes to write down their thoughts and then 3 minutes to turn the writing into a poem, what results is masterful and deeply experienced.

➢ Have students select any poem and discuss why it is meaningful, either in large or small groups.

Seventh Course

Resources

BOOKS RECOMMENDED FOR GUMBO

❖ Chase, Leah, *The Dooky Chase Cookbook*, Pelican Publishing, Inc., Gretna, 2000

❖ Collins, Rima, and Richard Collins, *The New Orleans Cookbook,* Alfred A. Knopf, NY, 2005

❖ Curry, Dale, *Gumbo: A Savor the South Cookbook,* University of North Carolina Press, Chapel Hill, 2015

❖ Link, Donald, and Paula Disbrowe, *Real Cajun: Rustic Home Cooking from Donald Link's Louisiana*, Clarkson Potter Publishers/Crown Publishing Group, a division of Random House, Inc., NY, 2009

❖ McKee, Gwen, *The Little Gumbo Book*, Quail Ridge Press, Inc., Brandon, 1986

❖ Prudhomme, Paul, *Chef Paul Prudhomme's Louisiana Kitchen,* William Morrow & Company, NY, 1984

❖ Stewart, Richard, *Gumbo Shop: Traditional and Contemporary Creole Cuisine*, A New Orleans Restaurant Cookbook, Stewart Interests, LLC, New Orleans, 2008

WEBSITES RECOMMENDED FOR GUMBO

❖ www.allrecipes.com

❖ www.epicurious.com

❖ www.myrecipes.com

_____ BOOKS REFERENCED / RECOMMENDED

❖ Achebe, Chinua, *Things Fall Apart*, Anchor Books, NY, 1959

❖ Africa, Llaila, *African Holistic Health*, Adesegun, Johnson & Koram Publishers, 1983

❖ Africa, Llaila, *Melanin: What Makes Black People Black*, Seaburn Publishers, 2009

❖ Ahmed-Cawthorne, Francheska, *Sista, Girlfren' Breaks It Down . . . When Mom's Not Around*, Fireside Books, 1996

❖ Akbar, Na'im, *Natural Psychology and Human Transformation,* Mind Productions and Associates, Tallahassee, 1995

❖ Akbar, Na'im, and Asa Gl. Hilliard, III, *Know Thyself,* Mind Productions & Associates, Tallahassee, 1998

❖ Alexander, Michelle, *The New Jim Crow: Mass Incarceration in the Age of Colorblindness*, The New Press, 2010

❖ Allen, James and John Lewis, *Without Sanctuary: Lynching Photography in America*, Twain Palms Publishers, 2000

❖ Anderson, S.E. and Vanessa Holley, *The Black Holocaust for Beginners*, For Beginners Publishing, 2007

❖ Angelou, Maya, Ronda Buckley, Ed., *101 Quotes and Sayings from Maya Angelou: Inspirational Quotes from Phenomenal Woman*, Ronda Buckley Publisher, 2014

❖ Angelou, Maya, *And Still I Rise*, Random House, NY, 1978

❖ *Angelou, Maya, Gather Together* in My Name, Random House, NY, 1974

_____BOOKS REFERENCED / RECOMMENDED

❖ Angelou, Maya, *Great Food All Day Long: Cook Splendidly, Eat Smart,* Random House, NY, 2010

❖ Angelou, Maya, *Hallelujah! The Welcome Table: A Lifetime of Memories with Recipes*, Random House, NY, 2009

❖ Angelou, Maya, *I Know Why the Caged Bird Sings*, Random House/Ballantine Books, 2009

❖ Angelou, Maya, *Letter to My Daughter*, Random House, 2009

❖ Angelou, Maya, *Maya Angelou: Heart of a Woman,* Random House, NY, 2009

❖ Angelou, Maya, *Mom & Me & Mom*, Random House, NY, 2013

❖ Angelou, Maya, *Phenomenal Woman: 4 Poems Celebrating Women*, Random House, NY 1978

❖ Angelou, Maya, *The Complete Collected Poems of Maya Angelou*, Random House, NY 1994

❖ Angelou, Maya, *Rainbow in the Cloud: The Wisdom and Spirit of Maya Angelou*, Random House, NY, 2014

❖ Angelou, Maya, *Wouldn't Take Nothing for My Journey Now,* Random House, NY 1003

❖ Ani, Marimba, *Yurugu: An African-Centered Critique of European Cultural Thought and Behavior*, Africa World Press, Trenton, 1994

❖ Anuakan, R. Iset, *"We Real Cool" Beauty, Image, and Style in African American History: An Economic and Political History of Institutions*, Lambert Academic Publishing, 2010

572

BOOKS REFERENCED / RECOMMENDED

❖ Anuakan, R. Iset, *Soular System Resort: Poems for a Healing Nation,* R. Iset Anuakan, 2012

❖ Asante, M.K., Jr. *Buck*, Spiegel & Grau, N.Y., 2014

❖ Asante, Molefi Kete, Sr. & Ama Mazama, *Egypt Vs. Greece and the American Academy: The debate over the birth of civilization*, African American Images, Chicago, 2002

❖ Asim, Jabari, *The N Word: Who Can Say It, Who Shouldn't and Why*, Houghton Mifflin Books, New York, 2008

❖ Ausar, Anuk, *Metu Neter, Vol I: The Great Oracle of Tehuti & the Egyptian System of Spiritual Cultivation*, and *Vol. II: The Kamitic Initiation System*, Khamit Corp. Brooklyn, 1990 & 1994

❖ Baker, Thomas Jerome, *Black Lives Matter: From Holocaust to Lynching to Liberation*, Amazon Digital Services, 2015

❖ Baptist, Edward E., *The Half Has Never Been Told: Slavery & the Making of American Capitalism,* Basic Books, Philadelphia, 2014

❖ Ben-Jochannan, Yosef A.A., *Black Man of the Nile and His Family,* Black Classic Press, Baltimore, 1970

❖ Bilal, Rafiq and Thomas Goodwin, *Egyptian Sacred Science in Islam,* Bennu Publishers, San Francisco, 1987

❖ Blake, Jennifer, *Louisiana History Collection-Part 1,* Steel Magnolia Press, 2012

❖ Bloom, Lisa, *Suspicion Nation: The inside Story of the Trayvon Martin Injustice and Why We Continue to Repeat it,* Counterpoint Publishers, 2015

❖ Blue, Carroll Parrott, *The Dawn at My Back: Memoir of a Black Texas Upbringing,* University of Texas Press, 2003

❖ Browder, Anthony T. *Egypt on The Potomac: A Guide to Decoding Egyptian Architecture and Symbolism in Washington, D.C.,* IKG, Washington, D.C., 2004

❖ Cagan, Andrea, *Peace is Possible: The Life and Message of Prem Rawat,* Mighty River Press, Dresher, 2006

❖ Carruthers, Jacob, *Essays in Ancient Egyptian Studies,* University of Sankore Press, L.A. 1984

❖ Childs, Dennis, *Slaves of the State: Incarceration from the Chain Gang to the Penitentiary,* University of Minnesota Press, 2015

❖ Chomsky, Aviva, *A History of the Cuban Revolution,* Wiley-Blackwell, 2010

❖ Clark, Carl G., and Leilani Clark, *Children Crying in the Night,* Tarbaby Press, Poway, 1988

❖ Clarke, John Henrik, *Christopher Columbus and the Afrikan Holocaust: Slavery and the Rise of European Capitalism,* EWorld, Inc., 2011

❖ Cooper, J. California, *Family,* Anchor Books, NY, 1991

❖ Cornwell, JoAnne, *That Hair Thing - And the Sisterlocks Approach,* Sisterlocks Publishing, San Diego, 1997

❖ De Graaf, Lawrence B. (Ed.), Kevin Mulroy (Ed.) and Quintard Taylor (Ed.), *Seeking El Dorado: African Americans in California,* Autry Museum, Univ. of Washington Press, Seattle, 2001

574

❖ Dial, Kendrick, *Da Journey Not Withstanding: Life, Love, and Lessons Learnt*, Keytochange Pub. La Mesa, 2004

❖ Douglas, Frederick, *Narrative of the Life of Frederick Douglas,* Dover Publications, 1995

❖ Dowd, Maria, *Journey to a Blissful Life,* BET Publications, Washington, D.C. 2005

❖ Dowd, Maria, *Journey to Empowerment*, BET Publications, Washington, D.C. 2004

❖ Dray, Philip, *At the Hands of Persons Unknown: the Lynching of Black America*, Modern Library, 2003

❖ DuBois, W. E. B., *The Souls of Black Folk*, Dover Pub., 1994

❖ English, T.J., *Havana Nocturne: How the Mob Owned Cuba and Then Lost it to the Revolution*, William Morrow Paperbacks, 2009

❖ Equiano, Olaudah, *The Life of Olaudah Equiano*, Dover Pub., 1999

❖ Fanon, Frantz and Richard Philcox, *Black Skin, White Masks,* Grove Press, 2008

❖ Fanon, Frantz and Richard Philcox, *The Wretched of the Earth*, Grove Press, 2005

❖ Fikes, Robert Jr., *The Black in Crimson and Black: A History and Profiles of African Americans at SDSU,* 2015

❖ Garvey, Marcus, *Selected Writings and Speeches of Marcus Garvey,* Dover Publications, 2005

❖ Gates, Henry Louis, Jr., and Cornel West, *The Future of the Race*, Vintage Books, NY, 1996

❖ Gayton, Tomas' L., *Sojourn on the Bohemian Highway,* Poetic Matrix Press, 2013

❖ Gayton, Tomas' L. *Yazoo City Blues: Selected Poetry and Prose,* Drury Lane Press, 2005

❖ Gibbs, Jewelle Taylor, *Destiny's Child: Memoirs of a Preacher's Daughter,* Createspace Independent Publishing Platform, Charleston, 2014

❖ Greene, Ida, *Light the fire Within You,* PSI Publishers, San Diego, 1991

❖ Greenwald, Harold and Elizabeth Rich, *The Happy Person: A Seven-Step Plan,* Avon Books, 1985

❖ Grier, William H. and Price M. Cobbs, *Black Rage*, Bantam Doubleday @Dell books, 1968

❖ Gunn, Nneka, *Better Safe Than Dead: The Ultimate Guide to Surviving an Encounter with Law Enforcement*, Amazon Digital Services, 2015

❖ Gunter, Emily Diane, *Thirteen Golden Keys to Learning: A Spiritual Journey*, Urgent Press Publications, Miami, 2005

❖ Guthrie, Robert V., *Even the Rat Was White: A Historical View of Psychology*, Allyn & Bacon, Needham Hts., 1998

❖ Harley, Kasimu Richard, *For the Brothers Who Are Here*, Wind and Rock Press, Chula Vista 1995

❖ Harris, Emmanuel & Antonio D. Tillis, *The Trayvon Martin in US: An American Tragedy,* Peter Lang Publishing, 2015

❖ Hilliard, Asa G., Larry Williams and Nia Damali (Eds.) *The Teachings of Ptahhotep: The Oldest Book in the World,* Blackwood Press, Grand Forks, 1987

❖ Hilliard III, Asa G., and Wade W. Nobles, *SBA: The Reawakening of the African Mind,* Makare Publishing, Co, Gainesville, 1998

❖ Hollins, Ishe', *Sol, the Super Hairo,* Heart Love Pub., San Diego, 2013, solthesuperhairo@gmal.com

❖ Holmes, Leilani, *Ancestry of Experience: A Journey Into Hawaiian Ways of Knowing*, University of Hawaii Press, Honolulu, 2012

❖ Hudson, Beverly J., *From Bees to Baleens: The Rhyme & Rhythm of Living Things*, NETFA Educational Pub., National City, 2001

❖ Jackson, P. Tony, and Wade W. Nobles, *Black Male Violence in Perspective*, Lexington Books, Lanham, 2015

❖ Jacobs, Harriet Ann, *Incidents in the Life of a Slave Girl*, Dover Publications, 2001

❖ Jahn, Janheinz, *Muntu: African Culture and the Western World,* Grove Weidenfeld, NY, 1961

❖ James, George G. M., Stolen Legacy: *The Egyptian Origins of Western Philosophy,* Philosophical Library, 1954, African Publication Society, 1980

❖ Jean-Murat, Carolle, M.D., *Mind, Body, Soul & Money: Putting Your Life in Balance*, Mosley Pub., San Diego, 2002

❖ Jean-Murat, Carolle, M.D., *Voodoo in My Blood: A Healers Journey from Surgeon to Shaman*, Bettie Youngs, 2012

❖ Johnson, Umar, *Psycho-Academic Holocaust: The Special Education & ADHD Wars Against Black Boys,* Prince of Pan Africanism Publishing, 2013

❖ Johnson, Willis Fletcher, *The History of Cuba, Vol. 1,* Forgotten Books, 2015

❖ Jones, Steven, *Journey to Excellence*, Keytochange Publishing, 2003

❖ Kamboon, Kobi Kalongi, *Cultural Misorientation: The Greatest Threat to the Survival of the Black Race in the 21st Century,* Nubian Nation Publishers, Tallahassee, 2003

❖ Katznelson, Ira, *When Affirmative Action Was White: An Untold History of Racial Inequality in Twentieth-Century America*, W.W. Norton & Co., NY, 2005

❖ Kein, Sybil, *Creole: The History and Legacy of Louisiana' Free People of Color*, LSU Press, 2000

❖ Kennedy, Randall, *Nigger: The Strange Career of a Troublesome Word,* First Vintage Books, NY, 2003

❖ Kimmel, Allison Crotzer, *The Montgomery Bus Boycott: A Primary Source Exploration of the Protest for Equal Treatment*, Capstone Press, 2015

❖ Kunjufu, Jawanza, *Countering the Conspiracy to Destroy Black Boys*, African American Images, 1985

_____BOOKS REFERENCED / RECOMMENDED

❖ Leckie, William and Shirley A. Leckie, *The Buffalo Soldiers: A Narrative of the Black Calvary in the West,* Revised Edition, University of Oklahoma Press, 2012

❖ Leovy, Jill, *Ghettoside: A True Story of Murder in America,* Spiegel & Grau, NY, 2015

❖ Lewis, Starla, *Sunkisses*, Heart Love Publications, San Diego, 2008

❖ Llibagiza, Immaculee, *Left to Tell: Discovering God Amidst the Rwandan Holocaust*, Hay House, 2007

❖ MacCalla, Thomas, *Artistry in Word Music*, Xlibris US, 2014

❖ MacCalla, Thomas, *Rhythm & Muse: Shades of Thought in Cadence and Voices Within*, Kin Productions, La Jolla, 2007

❖ Madyum, Galil, Larry Malone, and Robert Fikes, *Black Pioneers in San Diego: 1880-1920*, San Diego Historical Society, San Diego, 1982

❖ Malcolm, Dave, *A Whole New Ball Game: A Close-Up Look at Diversity, Racism, Sexism, Affirmative Action, Cultural Pluralism & The Unfinished Business of Remaining in Twenty-first Century America*, Aslan Pub., Fairfield, 2005

❖ Malcolm X, *The Autobiography of Malcolm X: As Told to Alex Haley*, Ballantine Books, 1992

❖ Mandela, Nelson R., *Long Walk to Freedom: The Autobiography of Nelson Mandela,* Back Bay Books, 1995

❖ Marsh, Corinda, *Holocaust in the Homeland: Black Wall Street's Last Days,* Amazon Digital Services, 2014

_____BOOKS REFERENCED / RECOMMENDED

❖ Moore, Mafori, and Gwen Akua Gilford, Karen King, Nsenga Warfield-Coppock, *Transformation: A Rites of Passage Manual for African American Girls*, Stars Press, 1987

❖ Moore, Wes, *The Other Wes Moore: One Name, Two Faces,* Spiegel & Grau, 2010

❖ Moore, Wes, *The Work: My Search for a Life That Matters,* Spiegel & Grau, 2015

❖ Murray, Edward, L. III, *When Push Comes to Shove: A Tale of Three Goats,* Cricket Cottage Pub., LLC, Orlando, 2014

❖ Nelson, Kadir, *Change Has Come: An Artist Celebrates our American Spirit*, The drawings of Kadir Nelson with the words of Barack Obama, Simon and Schuster, NY, 2009

❖ Nelson, Kadir, *If You Plant a Seed*, Balzer and Bray/Harper Collins Publishers, NY, 2015

❖ Nieto, Clara and Gabriel Ponce de León, *Obama and the New Left in Latin America*, Createspace, 2015

❖ Nobles, Wade W., *African Psychology*, Institute for the Advanced Study of Black Family Life & Culture, Oakland, 1986

❖ Nobles, Wade W., *Africanity and the Black Family,* Institute for the Advanced Study of Black Family Life & Culture, Oakland, 1985

❖ Nobles, Wade W., *Seeking the Sakhu; Foundational Writings for an African Psychology*, Third World Press, Chicago, 2006

❖ Nobles, Wade W., *The Island of Memes: Haiti's Unfinished Revolution*, Black Classic Press, Baltimore, 2015

❖ Northrop, Solomon, *12 Years a Slave*, Canterbury Classics, 2014

❖ Obama, Barack, *Dreams from My Father: A Story of Race and Inheritance*, Broadway Books, 2004

❖ Obama, Barack, *The Audacity of Hope: Thoughts on Reclaiming the American Dream*, Vintage, 2008

❖ Obenga, Theéophile, *Ancient Egypt & Black Africa: A Student's Handbook for the Study of Ancient Egypt in Philosophy, Linguistics & Gender Relations*, Karnak House, Lawrenceville, 1992

❖ Parham, Thomas A., *Psychological Storms: The African American Struggle for Identity,* African American Images, Chicago, 1993

❖ Parham, Thomas A., *Counseling Persons of African Descent: Raising the Bar of Practitioner Competence,* Sage Publications, Thousand Oaks, 2002

❖ Parks, Rosa and Jim Haskins, *Rosa Parks: My Story,* Puffin Books, NY, 1992

❖ Pharaoh, *The Mystical Pleasures of Chocolate: Meditations,* Writers Club Press, San Jose, 2000

❖ Powell, Kevin, *The Black Male Handbook: A Blueprint for Life,* Atria Books, NY 2008

❖ Rashidi, Runoko, *African Star Over Asia: The Black Presence in the East*, Books of Africa, Ltd, London, 2012

❖ Rashidi, Runoko, *Black Star: The African Presence in Early Europe*, Books of Africa, Ltd, London, 2011

_____BOOKS REFERENCED / RECOMMENDED

❖ Reder, Alan, *In Pursuit of Principle and Profit: Business Success Through Social Responsibility*, Tarcher-Putnam Books, N.Y. 1994

❖ Riley, Dorothy Winb, *The Complete Kwanzaa: Celebrating Our Cultural Harvest*, Harper Perennial, 1996

❖ Robinson, Jo Ann and David J. Garrow, *Montgomery Bus Boycott and the Women Who Started It: the Memoir of Jo Ann Gibson Robinson*, University of Tennessee Press, Knoxville, 1987

❖ Roze', Sherehe Yamaisha, *Heart Love Messages of the Soul,* Night Star Publishing, San Diego, 2002

❖ Ryerson, Jim, *Swimming to Guantanamo: From Elian to Obama A Decade in Cuba Under the U.S. Embargo,* Amazon Digital Services, 2014

❖ Schubert, Frank N., *Voices of the Buffalo Soldier: Records, Reports and Recollections of Military Life and Service in the West*, University of New Mexico Press, 2003

❖ Sen, Amartya and Paul Farmer, *Pathologies of Power: Health, Human Rights, and the New War on the Poor,* University of California Press, 2004

❖ Smith, Dorothy, *My Face to the Rising Sun,* Grio Press, San Diego, 1999

❖ Some, Malidoma Patrice, *Of Water and the Spirit: Ritual, Magic and Initiation in the Life of an African Shaman*, Penguin Group, NY, 1995.

❖ St. Clair, Jeffrey, *Killing Trayvons: An Anthology of American Violence*, CounterPunch, Petrolia, 2014

582

_____BOOKS REFERENCED / RECOMMENDED

❖ Sublette, Ned, *The World That Made New Orleans: Spanish Silver to Congo Square*, Chicago Review, 2008

❖ Suttle, Earl and John Hubbard, *Enjoying Excellence: 30 Pearls of Wisdom*, Victory International Publishers, 2015

❖ Suttle, Earl and John Hubbard, *Preparing for and Managing High Risk Situations in the Lives of College Athletes,* Victory International Publishers, 2005

❖ Van Sertima, Ivan, *They Came Before Columbus: The African Presence in Ancient America*, 1976, Random House, Reprint Edition, NY, 2003

❖ Walker, Alice, *Anything We Love Can Be Saved: A Writer's Activism,* Random House, N.Y. 1997

❖ Warfield-Coppock, Nsenga, and Bertram Atiba Coppock, *Afrocentric Theory and Application: Advances in the Adolescent Rite of Passage*, Baobab Associates, Wash., D.C., 1992

❖ Warfield-Coppock, Nsenga, *The Forest and The Trees: The Balance and Connection of Manhood and Womanhood Rites of Passage*, AFDJ, 2009

❖ Waymon, Carrol W., *On Being Black in San Diego – Anytown U.S.A.*, WW. Publications, San Diego, 1994

❖ Wells-Barnett, Ida B., *Southern Horrors: Lynch Law in All its Phases,* Loki's Publishing, 2014, Createspace, 2015

❖ Wilburn, Gennene R., *Naked Journey: A Poetic Conversation of Transformation*, Ne-Ne's Collectibles Publishing, 2008

_____BOOKS REFERENCED / RECOMMENDED

❖ Wilburn, Gennene R., *Soulverse: Love, Pain & Bliss in Spoken Word,* Ne-Ne's Collectibles Publishing, 2008

❖ Williams, Chancellor, *Destruction of Black Civilization,* Third World Press, Chicago, 1987

❖ Williams, Robert L., *History of the Association of Black Psychologists: Profiles of Outstanding Black Psychologists,* AuthorHouse, Bloomington, 2008

❖ Winfrey, Oprah, *What I Know for Sure*, Hearst Communications, Inc., New York, 2014

❖ Wokocha, Eke F., and Kathleen O'Bannon, *Solving the World Crisis: A Blue Print for Action*, Health Alive, LLC, Lemon Grove, 2009

❖ Woodson, Carter G., *The Mis-Education of the Negro,* Tribeca Books, 2013

❖ Yetman, Norman R., (Ed.) *When I Was a Slave: Memoirs from the Slave Narrative Collection*, Dover Publications, 2002

African American Writers & Artists of San Diego
www.aawasd.org

African Holocaust, The
www.africanholocaust.net/html_ah/holocaustspecial.htm

African Museum Casa Del Rey Moro
www.africanmuseumsandiego.com

Alliance San Diego
http://www.alliancesd.org/our-story/

Association for the Advanced Study of Classical African Civilizations
www.ascac.squarespace.com

Association of African American Educators
www.aaaesandiego.org

Association of Black Psychologists
www.abpsi.org

Black American Political Association of California
San Diego Chapter
www.bapacsd.org

Black Business Network
http://www.blackbusinessnetwork.com/ccaesar

Black Chamber of Commerce, San Diego
http://www.csdbcc.com/index.php

Black Police Officer's Association
www.sandiegobpoa.org

Black Social Workers of San Diego
www.sdabsw.org

Black Storytellers of San Diego
www.bstsd.org

Can Muslims & Christians Work Together for Good?
http://whoonew.com/2014/02/interfaith-discussion-st-norbert/

Catfish Club, The
www.catfishclub.net/

Christian Answers about Islam
http://christiananswers.net/islam.html

Community Actor's Theatre
www.communityactorstheatre.com/

Consensus Organizing Center at SDSU
www.consensus.sdsu.edu/coc.html

Delta Sigma Theta Sorority, San Diego Alumnae Chapter
http://www.dstsandiego.org/

Dennard Clendenin
www.apbspeakers.com/speaker/dennard-clendenin

Earl B. Gilliam Bar Foundation
www.earlbgilliambar.org/

Elementary Institute of Science
www.eisca.org/

Golden Brown Fairy Godmother, The
http://alycesmithcooper.com/gbfg.html

Gennene Wilburn, Mpoweru
www.Mpoweru2.com

Dr. Ida Greene
www.idagreene.com

Harlem of the West
http://www.harlemofthewest.com/index.htm

Harmonious Solutions
www.harmoniouslifesolutions.org

Health Systems for Life
http://healthsystemsforlife.com/

Health Through Communications
www.healththroughcommunications.org

Honorable Dr. Shirley Weber
www.asmdc.org/members/a79

Institute for the Advanced Study of Black Family Life and Culture
(Oakland)
www.iasbflc.org

Ira Aldridge Repertory Players/Theatre
www.irapplayers.org/

Islamic Studies/Duke University
http://islamicstudies.duke.edu/disc-initiatives/transcultural-islam-project

Jack and Jill of America, Inc., San Diego Chapter
http://jjnorthcountysd.org/

Kadir Nelson
www.kadirnelson.com/

Links, The (San Diego Chapter)
http://sandiegolinks.org/

Lincoln High School Center for the Performing Arts
www.goldstar.com/venues/san-diego-ca/lincoln-high-school-center-for-the-performing-arts

Livin Out Loud *(Music Production/Performance Group)*
www.livinoutloud.co.uk/

Malcolm X Library *(Also see Valencia Park/Malcolm X Library)*
www.whatsnewinthevillage.com/2012/04/19/malcolm-x-library-free-events-calendar/

Martin Luther King, Jr. Recreation Center
www.sandiego.gov/park-and-recreation/centers/recctr/mlking.shtml

Mo'olelo Performing Arts Company/Theatre
www.moolelo.net/

Muslim Alliance with Christians and Jews
http://www.islamic-study.org/muslim_alliance_with_christians_and_jews.htm

Nakumbuka Day History
www.**nakumbuka**.org/history.html

National Association for the Advancement of Colored People/NAACP
www.sandiegonaacp.org/

National Black Child Development Institute
www.nbcdi.org/

National Council of Negro Women, San Diego
www.sandiegoncnw.org/

Pan African Association of America
http://www.panafricanassociation.org/

Pazzaz Educational Enrichment Centers
www.pazzaz.org

Parenting Service Station, GPS Productions
http://gpsproductions.net/

Runoko Rashidi, African Global Presence
www.runokorashidi.com

Self -Heal School for Herbal Studies
http://selfhealschool.com/

Sisterlocks
www.sisterlocks.com

San Diego Association of Black Social Workers
www.sdabsw.org/

San Diego Black Film Festival
http://www.sdbff.com/index.shtml

San Diego Black Health Associates
http://www.sdbha.org/

San Diego Black Nurses Association
www.sdblacknurses.org/

San Diego Black Police Officers Association
www.sandiegobpoa.org/

San Diego Voice & Viewpoint Newspaper
http://sdvoice.info/

So. California African American Museum of Fine Art
www.facebook.com/sdaamfa

Tribal Energy Cardio
www.facebook.com/pages/Tribal-Energy-Cardio/109820762409856

United African American Ministerial Alliance
http://www.uaamac.org/

Urban Collaborative Project
www.ucproject.org

Urban League, San Diego
www.ulsdc.org

Urgent, Inc. (Florida)
www.urgentinc.org

Valencia Park/Malcolm X Library
www.sandiego.gov/public-library/locations/

Water for Children, Africa
www.waterforchildrenafrica.org/

Women's Museum of California
http://womensmuseumca.org/

Words of Peace
www.wordsofpeace.org

World Council of Churches
http://www.oikoumene.org/en

Worldbeat Center, The
www.worldbeatcenter**.org**

Eighth Course: We'll Take Your Order!

The Poems in Alphabetical Order with Page Number

Ninth Course

Dessert: The Sweet Bios

James Gayles, Cover Artist Bio

Emmy Award winning artist James Gayles attended Pratt Institute in New York, where he studied under renowned painters Jacob Lawrence and Audrey Flack He simultaneously pursued careers in both fine and commercial art. As a commercial artist he established himself in New York as a Graphic Designer and Illustrator, becoming Assistant Director of Graphics at NewsCenter 4, NBC-TV. At NBC he won a television Emmy Award for design and illustration.

Also in New York he was also a two-time winner of Art Direction Magazine's Creativity Award, one for the NewsCenter 4 logo redesign, and the other for an editorial illustration for the New York Times. Here in the Bay Area he won the first place award for illustration at the California Newspaper Publishers' Awards.

In addition to NBC and the New York Times, James has illustrated for McGraw-Hill, Random House, Essence Magazine, Black Enterprise Magazine, as well as several advertising agencies on both the East and West coasts.

Galleries throughout the US have represented James' artwork. Most recently he won a public art commission from the City of Oakland Craft and Cultural Arts Department, in which he transferred his figurative painting technique to ceramic tile murals. In 2003 he was honored at the Art of Living Black by receiving the Jan Hart-Shuyers Award.

He has been selected twice to show at the California Biennial Watercolor exhibit at the Triton Museum in Santa Clara. The City of Richmond purchased one of his paintings for their Civic Center Public Art Project. He has received the City of Oakland's Individual Artist Grant in 2005 and 2007, and was recently commissioned by the Alameda County Art Commission and the City of Richmond to create a series of paintings.

Art critic and curator Adam Mikos had this to say about one of James' most recent exhibition BluesMasters: **"Gayles has focused his talents on fusing sight with sound, cajoling color and line to communicate like guitar strings and piano keys. Gayles clearly has a special touch with watercolors. Each portrait and image in the exhibition shows mastery over different styles of the medium. Dreamy realism, hard-edged contours, and abstraction push and pull on perspective. Gayles' use of color is stunning. These are not the grainy, black and white images many think of as representing the blues. Bright reds, oranges, and blues catch the eye immediately and allow the lyrical quality of the watercolors to lift off the wall."**

James Gayles has lived in Oakland, CA for over 25 years and currently works as an Illustrator for the Bay Area Newspapers Group.

To purchase artwork, please contact A. Kelly Paschal-Hunter at akpaschal@yahoo.com or at 925.785.7569 mobile.

The Authors' Bios

Alyce Smith Cooper, *also known as the* ***Golden Brown Fairy Godmother***, *is a mother, a grandmother and a great-grandmother. She is a seasoned ancestral storyteller, writer, poet, actor and T.V. host. In 2005, Alyce was inducted into the San Diego Women's Hall of Fame for her ability to celebrate diversity, transcend cultural differences, build bridges of hope and love between people, and generate healing through her stories, poems and presence. She currently works as a Registered Nurse and is an Associate Minister at Bethel A.M.E. Church in San Diego, California.*

Jaime Victoria Jones *was born in Coronado, California, and was raised in San Diego, one of four daughters. Jaime loves to write, and identifies as a scribe, a scholar and an educator. A fun-loving and life-affirming person, Jaime loves communicating ideas and empowering others. Her passion lies in GPS Productions (The Parenting Service Station) where she is invested in helping parents and troubled teens. She writes much like she cooks. Her main ingredient is always a large dose of love. She is convinced that love appeals to all of our senses.*

Judy Sundayo, Ph.D. *enjoys life and loves to cultivate a feeling of peace within. She is a mother, a grandmother and a sister-friend to many. As a licensed clinical psychologist and a college professor with decades of experience she enjoys reading and thinking critically. As a former recipient of the Outstanding Young Woman of America Award and the Bob Marley Peace Award, Judy is also dedicated to helping others. A writer since childhood, she shares her poetry to inspire, motivate and challenge our ordinary ways of thinking. Judy resides in La Jolla, California.*

601